First Steps in Research and Statistics

First Steps in Research and Statistics is a new, very accessible approach to learning about quantitative methods. No previous knowledge or experience is assumed and every stage of the research process is covered.

Key topics include:

- formulating your research questions
- how to choose the right statistical test for your research design
- important issues, such as questionnaire design, ethics, sampling, reliability and validity
- conducting simple statistics to describe and summarise your data
- using statistics to explore relationships and differences in your data
- writing up your research report and presenting statistics.

Simple and helpful worksheets and flow diagrams guide you through the research stages. Each chapter contains exercises with answers to check whether you've understood.

First Steps in Research and Statistics is essential reading for all psychology students who have to carry out practicals and projects in their course.

First Steps in Research and Statistics

A PRACTICAL WORKBOOK FOR PSYCHOLOGY STUDENTS

**DENNIS HOWITT
AND
DUNCAN CRAMER**

LONDON AND PHILADELPHIA

First published 2000
by Routledge
11 New Fetter Lane, London EC4P 4EE

Simultaneously published in the USA and Canada
by Taylor & Francis Inc
325 Chestnut Street, Philadelphia PA 19106

Routledge is an imprint of the Taylor & Francis Group

© 2000 Dennis Howitt and Duncan Cramer

Typeset in Plantin and Rockwell by Keystroke, Jacaranda Lodge, Wolverhampton
Printed and bound in Great Britain by TJ International Ltd, Padstow, Cornwall

British Library Cataloguing in Publication Data
A catalogue record for this book is available from the British Library

Library of Congress Cataloging in Publication Data
Howitt, Dennis.
    First steps in research and statistics : a practical workbook for
psychology students / Dennis Howitt and Duncan Cramer.
        p.   cm.
    Includes bibliographical references and index.
    1. Psychology—Research—Methodology. 2. Psychometrics.
I. Cramer, Duncan, 1948– . II. Title.
BF76.5.H69 2000
150′.7′2—dc21   99-38285
                                                        CIP

ISBN 0–415–20101–2

CONTENTS

List of boxes   vii

List of figures   ix

List of tables   xi

List of worksheets   xiv

Preface   xv

PART I
The basics of research   1

1   Asking research questions   3

2   Common research methods   11

3   Ethics in the conduct of research   21

4   Measuring variables   32

PART II
The statistical analysis of single variables and simple surveys   47

5   Two types of data analysis   49

6   Describing and summarising category data   53

7   Describing and summarising score data   63

8   Surveys and sampling   84

PART III
Exploring correlational relationships in
survey/non-experimental studies   99

  9 Examining relationships between two variables   101

 10 Numerical ways of describing relationships: correlation coefficients   110

 11 Statistical significance of the correlation coefficient   125

 12 Differences and associations among two sets of categories: chi-square   142

 13 Conducting survey/non-experimental studies   153

PART IV
Exploring differences between group means   159

 14 Testing for differences in means: more on significance testing   161

 15 Comparing the scores of two groups of people: Mann-Whitney *U*-test   177

 16 Comparing scores from the same group of people on two occasions:
     Wilcoxon matched-pairs test   190

PART V
The essentials of designing experiments   199

 17 Designing and running experiments   201

 18 Comparing the scores of a randomly assigned experimental and
     control group: unrelated *t*-test   218

 19 Comparing the scores of a counterbalanced related subjects experiment:
     related *t*-test   234

 20 Comparing three or more groups on a numerical score   248

PART VI
The report   267

 21 Writing a research report   269

References   280
Index   281

BOXES

3.1	Debriefing	25
3.2	Physiological research	28
3.3	Ethics questionnaire	29
4.1	Standard measures	33
4.2	Response formats for items on a questionnaire	40
7.1	Variance and standard deviation: estimates or not?	76
8.1	What is random sampling?	85
8.2	The sampling frame: the essential starting point of random sampling	90
8.3	Response rates	91
8.4	Random samples and statistics	97
10.1	The concept of the correlation coefficient	112
14.1	Random sampling with replacement	169
14.2	What actually happens in significance testing	172
15.1	Useful advice	179
15.2	Strengths and weaknesses of this design	179
15.3	What is the Mann-Whitney U-test?	183
15.4	The ideal dependent variable	184
16.1	Problems in assessing changes over time	193
16.2	When to use the Wilcoxon matched-pairs test	196
16.3	Matching	197
17.1	Some ways of randomly assigning participants to two conditions	202
17.2	Sample size	206
17.3	Experimenter bias	207

17.4   Participant bias and demand characteristics   208

18.1   Ideas on manipulating independent variables   223
18.2   More complex experiments   229

19.1   What is the related *t*-test?   242
19.2   Ideal analysis of counterbalanced related subjects experiment   243

FIGURES

1.1   Sources of ideas to test   8
1.2   Flow diagram showing major steps in planning research   9

2.1   Sexual passion as the cause of relationship satisfaction   15
2.2   Satisfaction as the cause of sexual passion   16
2.3   Satisfaction and sexual passion as both causes and effects of
       the other   16
2.4   The role of a third variable (length of couple's relationship)
       in the relationship between sexual passion and satisfaction   17

4.1   Hints about writing questions   42

5.1   Traditional approach to statistical measurement and measurement
       scales   51
5.2   Modern approaches to statistics and scales of measurement   52

6.1   Ways of summarising data   56
6.2   Pie-chart showing percentage of people in five employment
       categories   60
6.3   Bar chart showing percentage of people in five employment
       categories   60

7.1   Essential descriptive statistics for score variables   63
7.2   A distribution of scores which is symmetrical and peaked in the
       middle   68
7.3   A distribution of scores skewed to the left   69
7.4   A distribution of scores skewed to the right   69
7.5   A normal distribution of scores with percentages of cases falling
       within 1, 2 and 3 standard deviations on either side of the mean   78
7.6   A histogram of life satisfaction scores   79
7.7   The 22 scores written on separate pieces of paper   79

7.8	The 20 pieces of paper put in order and piled up	79
7.9	Histogram showing 20 scores grouped into intervals of 2	80
7.10	Histogram showing 20 scores grouped into intervals of 4	80
7.11	More conventional histogram	81
7.12	A polygon of life satisfaction scores	82
9.1	Possible relationships between intelligence and hard work	102
9.2	A scattergram showing a perfect positive relationship between intelligence and hard work	103
9.3	A scattergram showing a positive relationship between intelligence and hard work	104
9.4	A scattergram showing a negative relationship between intelligence and hard work	105
9.5	A scattergram showing a curvilinear relationship between intelligence and hard work	106
9.6	A scattergram showing no relationship between intelligence and hard work	107
9.7	Scattergram with outlier	108
10.1	Vital steps when calculating a correlation coefficient	123
11.1	Bell-shaped distribution of correlation values when there is no relationship between two variables in the population	130
11.2	Choosing between 1-tailed and 2-tailed tests of significance	132
12.1	When to use chi-square	146
13.1	Key aspects in planning a survey/non-experimental study	155
13.2	Major aspects of the statistical analysis of a survey/non-experimental study	157
18.1	Main characteristics of typical unrelated groups experiment	218
18.2	Choosing whether to use a Mann-Whitney U-test or an unrelated t-test	222
20.1	One possible interaction between working with music or no music and working in the morning or afternoon	258
20.2	Other possible interactions between treatment and time of testing	259
20.3	Possible non-interactions between treatment and time of testing	261
21.1	The sequential structure of a psychological report	270
21.2	Possible features of the introduction	273
21.3	Features of a discussion section	277

TABLES

2.1   Advantages of interviews and self-completion questionnaires
      compared   15
2.2   A comparison of the three research methods   19

4.1   The differences between reliability and validity   36
4.2   The structured–unstructured dimension in data collection
      methods   37
4.3   Some advantages and disadvantages of self-completion
      questionnaires   39

6.1   A table recording the sex, age, employment status and life
      satisfaction scores of 20 individuals   54
6.2   Frequency table for the category variable sex   56

7.1   Table showing the frequency of people grouped according to
      their age   64
7.2   Table showing the frequency of people grouped according to
      their life satisfaction score   64
7.3   Table ranking individuals according to age and life satisfaction
      scores   65
7.4   Table showing the ungrouped frequency data   77
7.5   Table showing the frequency of people grouped into four age
      categories   77
7.6   Means and standard deviations for age and life satisfaction in
      women and men   82

8.1   Comparison of major sampling methods   87
8.2   Statistical analyses for surveys   97

9.1   An example of a perfect positive linear relationship between
      intelligence and hard work   102

9.2	An example of a positive linear relationship between intelligence and hard work	103
9.3	An example of a negative linear relationship between intelligence and hard work	104
9.4	An example of a curvilinear relationship between intelligence and hard work	105
9.5	An example of no relationship between intelligence and hard work	106
9.6	An example of data with the influence of an outlier affecting the relationship between intelligence and hard work	108
10.1	Intelligence scores (X) and number of extra hours worked (Y)	115
10.2	Sex and employment status coded as two numerical values	119
10.3	A 2×2 contingency table showing the relationship between sex and employment status	119
11.1	The personality of 20 people described in terms of stability (S)/neuroticism (N) and introversion (I)/extraversion (E)	126
11.2	A 2×2 contingency table showing no relationship between neuroticism and introversion	126
11.3	A 2×2 contingency table showing a negative relationship between neuroticism and introversion	128
11.A1	Random number table	136
11.A2	One- and two-tailed 0.05 significance levels for Pearson's correlation	140
11.A3	One- and two-tailed 0.05 significance levels for Spearman's correlation	141
12.1	Sex differences in favourite leisure entertainment	142
12.2	Row and column totals of a 2×2 contingency table	144
12.3	Expected numbers or frequencies for a 2×2 contingency table	145
12.4	Observed numbers or frequencies in a 4×3 contingency table	147
12.5	The observed data and row, column and overall totals	147
12.6	The expected frequencies and row and column totals	148
12.7	The chi-square calculation for each cell	148
12.A1	Two-tailed 0.05 critical values for chi-square	152
13.1	Appropriate statistics according to the type of each variable	157
14.1	Criteria for 1- and 2-tailed tests	164
14.2	The scores for the ten women studied	165
14.3	The scores for the ten men studied	165
14.4	The male and female samples combined to give an estimate of the population characteristics	167
14.5	The estimated population adjusted to meet the requirements of the null hypothesis	167
14.6	Frequency table of the population of scores 'adjusted' to meet the requirements of the null hypothesis	168
14.7	A histogram giving the differences in the means of pairs of means taken from the null-hypothesis defined population in Tables 14.5 and 14.6	170

14.A1   Table of means of 'samples of men' and 'samples of women'
            selected at random from the estimated population under the
            null hypothesis (Table 14.5)   175

15.1   General research design for comparing two groups   178
15.2   Illustrating how the general research design in Table 15.1
            can be used for the women versus men drivers and the beaten
            versus non-beaten children investigations   178
15.3   Important statistical analyses to include in your report   183
15.A1   Data collection sheet   186
15.A2   5 per cent two-tailed significance table for the sum of ranks in
            the Mann-Whitney U-test   188

16.1   Some of the change over time studies illustrated in a general
            schematic form   190
16.2   Improvement in mental health following Gestalt psychotherapy   192
16.A1   One- and two-tailed 0.05 probability values for the Wilcoxon
            matched-pairs test   198

17.1   Data from drug experiment   204
17.2   Some advantages and disadvantages of controlled experiments   205
17.A1   Random allocation of experimental and control conditions   216
17.A2   Blocked random allocation table   217

18.1   Data from the poetry experiment   220
18.2   Statistics for the controlled experiment   221
18.A1   One- and two-tailed 0.05 probability values for the unrelated t-test 230
18.A2   Illustration of a data recording sheet for a controlled experiment 232

19.1   The weights experiment showing counterbalanced orders   236
19.2   The weights experiment rearranged into experimental and
            control condition columns   237
19.3   Statistical analysis of counterbalanced related experiment   241
19.4   Advantages and disadvantages of the counterbalanced related
            subjects design   244
19.A1   One- and two-tailed 0.05 probability values for the related t-test 245
19.A2   Random allocation of orders   246

20.1   The analysis of variance summary table   251
20.2   Mean depression scores for four marital groups   255
20.3   Means for mixed-design study of relaxation therapy   256
20.4   Mean scores of the work efficiency index for four groups   257
20.A1   5 per cent significant values of the F-ratio for ANOVA
            (two-tailed test)   263
20.A2   Two-tailed 0.05 critical values for 1 to 10 unplanned
            comparisons   265

WORKSHEETS

7.1	for the mean, mode and median	66
7.2	for variance	72
7.3	for standard deviation	74
8.1	for confidence intervals	94
10.1	for the Pearson correlation	113
10.2	for Spearman's rho	117
10.3	for phi (Pearson's correlation between two sets of dichotomous scores)	120
12.1	for chi-square	147
15.1	for the Mann-Whitney U-test	181
16.1	for the Wilcoxon matched-pairs test	194
17.1	step-by-step guide to the design and analysis of a controlled experiment using just one experimental and one control group	210
18.1	for the unrelated t-test	224
19.1	for the related t-test	238
20.1	for the unrelated one-way analysis of variance	250

PREFACE

- The aim of this book is to provide a clear and relatively short introduction to basic research ideas and statistics which students typically need when doing practical work in the early part of their courses. However, it is expected that the structured approach will also be useful at later stages of training in methods and research.

- Research issues covered include research methods and designs, questionnaire design, ethical principles, sampling, validity and reliability.

- Great emphasis is placed on the use of structured materials such as checklists, flow diagrams, etc. to help students with the practicalities of research and its analysis. Designing a good experiment, for example, is a skilled process and it is difficult to remember all of the aspects that need to be considered. Hence the importance of structured materials.

- An important objective of the book is to link basic research designs with the types of statistics normally used to analyse the data from those designs.

- Simple descriptive statistics covered include the mean, the standard deviation and correlation. The book stresses the need to examine data carefully prior to the use of inferential statistics.

- Inferential tests covered include non-parametric tests such as chi-square, the Mann-Whitney and the Wilcoxon matched-pairs test and parametric tests such as the related and unrelated t-test.

- Rather than merely providing computational formulae to calculate these statistics, their conceptual bases have been given. It is important to avoid leaving students with the impression that statistics is a thing of mystery. Careful thought is required which may be stifled by such an attitude on the part of students.

- Structured Worksheets have been provided to work out the statistics described. Many students who have difficulties with mathematics tend to be disordered in their approach to calculations. The use of worksheets makes their work more systematic.

- This workbook is designed throughout to provide both a model of the calculations and a structure for doing the calculations. Consequently our illustrative calculations are printed in grey which is easy to over-write in pencil or ball-point. Of course, some readers may wish to photocopy these Worksheets to protect the workbook.

- Detailed attention has been paid to how to write up the results of the different types of statistical analysis.

- Exercises have been incorporated in the text so that readers can check their understanding of the material with answers provided at the ends of chapters.

- Some useful significance tables have been supplied as appendix tables at the ends of relevant chapters.

- Above all, this workbook aims to provide the fastest possible practical introduction to research design, data collection and its subsequent statistical analysis.

Part I

The basics of research

1

Asking research questions

INTRODUCTION

We all have our own ideas of what determines people's thoughts and actions. Some of these ideas are seen as common sense. For example, it may seem obvious that similar people are likely to be attracted to each other. After all, 'birds of a feather flock together'. Confusingly, we believe that people who are very different from each other are likely to get involved in relationships – 'opposites attract'.

Testing the truth (validity) of such 'theories' is an important part of the work of many psychologists. Empirical research (collecting evidence by observation) is the main method by which this is achieved.

Try Exercise 1.1. This will get you thinking about possible psychological explanations of human behaviour.

Introductory textbooks in psychology contain numerous examples of the importance of research in psychological theory and knowledge. Research is an essential component of the discipline. Consequently students must know the broad principles of doing research. But, in addition, they must understand the more detailed practicalities of doing research. These are not the same activities. Reports of psychological research contain much detail but, nevertheless, lack many of the important details about the practicalities of doing research. This workbook is designed to help you to actually plan and do research.

In other words, we hope that you will learn how to do research to evaluate the explanations of human behaviour you listed in Exercise 1.1. Have you any ideas about how to do this now? As you work through this book you should begin to get more ideas.

A number of basic concepts such as variables and hypotheses need to be understood before you can get a clear idea about how psychologists answer questions through research.

EXERCISE 1.1   LIST EXPLANATIONS OF BEHAVIOUR

Write here three or more of your own or other people's favourite or most frequent explanatory principles of human behaviour. We have given suggestions in grey – you probably have better ones. You are welcome to write over our humble efforts.

1   Blood is thicker than water.

_____

2   Men with big powerful cars are disguising their sexual inadequacies.

_____

3   Children of lone-parent families are at risk of delinquency.

_____

VARIABLES

The concept of *variable* is basic to psychological research. A variable is anything that varies and can be measured.

Put another way, a variable is any characteristic that varies in the sense of having more than one *value*. For example, the variable of attraction (as in opposites attract) consists of two values at the very least. An individual is either 'attracted' to the other person or 'not attracted'. 'Attracted' and 'not attracted' are the two different values of the variable when we measure it in this way.

Of course, the variable of attraction may have a whole range of different values – from 'strongly attracted' through 'neither attracted nor unattracted' to 'strongly unattracted'. The number of different values a variable has depends on just how the psychologist decides to measure that variable. A common way of measuring psychological variables is to use a simple five-point measuring scale such as:

1 Very attracted
2 Attracted
3 Neither attracted nor unattracted
4 Unattracted
5 Very unattracted.

As you can see, this scale has five different possible answers or values.

THE HYPOTHESIS

Very simple research may be concerned with counting how common a particular form of behaviour is among people. For example, we could research the number of people who have ever fallen in love at first sight. The answer to this question may be of great interest. For example, if research shows that 75 per cent of people had fallen in love at first sight then we would know that this is a very common human experience.

However, relatively little psychological research aims *only* to count the frequency of occurrence of things. More often, psychologists want to find the reasons *why* things occur, that is to *explain* their occurrence. Consequently most research tests a specific idea or *hypothesis*. The hypothesis is sometimes called the alternate hypothesis. An example of a hypothesis might be based on the suggestion that we are likely to fall in love at first sight with physically attractive people. Thus the hypothesis might be written: 'The physical attractiveness of the other person affects the likelihood of falling in love with them at first sight.'

A research hypothesis has *two* essential features: 1) it contains a minimum of two variables; and 2) it suggests that there is a relationship between these two variables.

Another feature is not essential but nevertheless desirable. The hypothesis *may* describe what the researcher expects the relationship between the variables to be. We expect that people will be more likely to fall in love with someone generally thought to be physically attractive. This is the same as saying that they will be less likely to fall in love with someone generally considered physically unattractive. A *directional hypothesis* is one in which we specify what we expect the relationship between the variables to be.

The alternative to the directional hypothesis is, not surprisingly, called a non-directional hypothesis. A *non-directional hypothesis* is employed when we expect that there is a relationship between the variables but cannot specify its nature with any certainty. For example, we might think that there is a relationship between falling in love at first sight and physical attractiveness but feel uncertain quite what the relationship is. It is possible that we fall in love at first sight because the physical attractiveness of the other person makes them super-sexy to us. However, the fact that they are physically attractive may give us the impression that they are attractive to many people. This may warn us that they are likely to reject our advances and chat-up lines. Consequently we protect ourselves by *not* falling in love with them. Both of these alternatives may appear equally feasible to us. In these circumstances, because we are not sure which relationship is likely to be correct, we may prefer a non-directional hypothesis.

Directional hypotheses are more exacting than non-directional hypotheses. The convention is that in order to test a directional hypothesis in a statistical analysis, the researcher *must* be able to strongly justify its use on sound theoretical grounds or on the grounds of expectations generated by previous research. Obviously students must develop a degree of familiarity with the theoretical and empirical research literature before they can convincingly use directional hypotheses. Nevertheless, it is relatively easy to rephrase a non-directional hypothesis as a directional hypothesis. Exercise 1.2 gives you practice in using the appropriate phrases, though not the theoretical and research justification for your prediction.

EXERCISE 1.2 MAKING NON-DIRECTIONAL HYPOTHESES

Reword the following directional hypotheses to make them non-directional.

1 People with higher self-esteem will feel more accepted by their parents.

_____

(e.g. Self-esteem is related to parental acceptance.)

2 Boys brought up without fathers will be less masculine than boys brought up with fathers.

_____

3 Unemployment leads to increased stealing.

_____

Note

Suggested answers are found at the end of the chapters for this and most of the remaining exercises in the book.

EXERCISE 1.3 CHANGING NON-DIRECTIONAL INTO DIRECTIONAL HYPOTHESES

Reword the following non-directional hypothesis so that they become directional hypotheses.

1 The number of children in a family will be related to children's co-operativeness with others.

_____

(e.g. Children from large families are more co-operative with others.)

2 Emotional stability will be related to satisfaction with close relationships.

_____

3 Pet ownership is related to stress.

_____

It is also useful to be able to turn non-directional hypotheses into directional ones. Exercise 1.3 gives you some practice in doing this.

Note that each of the hypotheses in Exercises 1.2 and 1.3 consist of *two* variables. So in Exercise 1.2 the pairs of variables are self-esteem and feeling accepted, father absence and masculinity, and employment status and theft. What are the pairs of variables in Exercise 1.3?

There is a big difference between psychological language and ordinary language. Psychologists when they put forward a research hypothesis, such as 'Unemployment leads to increased stealing', do not assume that *all* unemployed people steal and all employed people are honest. In psychology, the assumption is merely that the likelihood (or probability) of unemployed people stealing is higher than that for employed people. In other words, we anticipate that the percentage or proportion of unemployed people stealing will be greater than the percentage or proportion of employed people stealing.

THE NULL HYPOTHESIS

For every hypothesis in research, there is a *null* hypothesis. This is virtually the same as the hypothesis but states that there is *no* relationship between the two variables.

So the statement, 'There is no relationship between self-esteem and parental acceptance', is an example of a null hypothesis.

The job of the researcher is to decide whether the hypothesis (sometimes called the alternative hypothesis) is more likely to be true than the null hypothesis. As they are essentially opposites, only one can be true.

The null hypothesis is particularly important in statistics as we shall see in Chapter 11.

RESEARCH IDEAS

Students are often encouraged to think of their own ideas to test. The more familiar you are with psychological research and theory the easier this will be. Figure 1.1 gives a few suggestions of obvious sources of ideas.

There are no shortcuts to the generation of research ideas; it is quite a creative process. However, generally speaking the more practice you have in thinking up research ideas the easier it becomes.

MAJOR STEPS IN TESTING A RESEARCH HYPOTHESIS

Beginning researchers often fail to appreciate the number of essential stages in planning research. The stages may sometimes be relatively simple in themselves but the number involved can be confusing. Figure 1.2 is a flow diagram schematically representing the major stages in conducting any research study to test a research hypothesis. Some of the steps may not be clear until you have read further through this workbook.

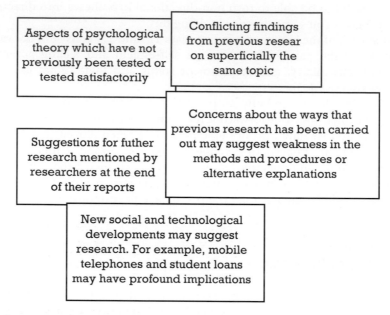

Figure 1.1 Sources of ideas to test

SUMMARY

- Much psychological research involves testing hypotheses.
- A research hypothesis predicts a relationship between two variables (or sometimes more).
- A non-directional hypothesis simply asserts that there is a degree of relationship between the variables. Directional hypotheses specify whether one variable increases or decreases as the second variable increases or whether one group is higher than another on some variable.
- A hypothesis just says what the general trend of the data is. Not all participants in the research would have to demonstrate this trend.

ANSWERS TO SELECTED EXERCISES

Answers to Exercise 1.2

1 Self-esteem will be related to parental acceptance.
2 Masculinity in boys will be related to paternal presence during childhood.
3 Unemployment will be related to stealing.

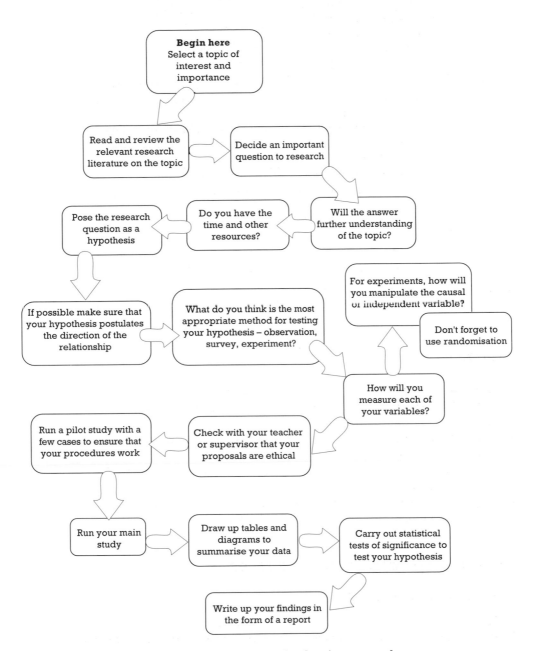

Figure 1.2 Flow diagram showing major steps in planning research

Answers to Exercise 1.3

A non-directional hypothesis can be converted into at least two directional hypotheses, examples of which are given below.

1a Children from larger families will be more co-operative than those from smaller families.
1b Children from larger families will be less co-operative than those from smaller families.

2a Emotionally stable individuals will be more satisfied with their close relationships.
2b Emotionally stable individuals will be less satisfied with their close relationships.

3a People owning pets are less stressed than those not owning pets.
3b People owning pets are more stressed than those not owning pets.

2

Common research methods

INTRODUCTION

Of course, there are many different ways of testing the research hypotheses we discussed in Chapter 1. No book could do full justice to all of them.

Although this is an oversimplification, the following three general research methods may be distinguished:

- experiments;
- surveys/non-experiments; and
- observation.

This is *not* a complete list by any means. However, it does include most of the research methods likely to be used by beginning researchers.

EXPERIMENTS

It is difficult to imagine psychology without experiments. The experimental method is so common in psychological research that it is almost a defining characteristic of the discipline. The use of experiments in psychology reflects the intellectual origins of psychology in disciplines such as physics and biology in which experiments were commonplace.

Experiments involve intervening in a situation in order to see whether this intervention changes things. There is a great deal more about experiments in Chapter 17. The following should provide enough information for immediate purposes.

- Experiments in psychology are almost always controlled experiments. This means that at a minimum they involve an experimental group and a control group which are treated differently. Differences in the way in which the two or more groups are treated may influence differentially measurements of a particular variable.

- No other research method in psychology is able to explore *causal* relationships between two variables as effectively as the best experiments can. A causal relationship is merely one in which a particular variable influences another variable. In the real world outside the psychological experiment it is often very difficult to say whether a relationship between two variables is causal or not. For example, if parents treat their daughters differently from their sons we cannot say whether this difference is because of the behaviour of the parents or the behaviour of the children. Boys may differ from girls and it may be this difference which influences the behaviour of their parents rather than the behaviour of the parents causing the differences between the boys and girls. Daughters and sons may behave differently which causes their parents to behave differently towards them.
- *A cause-and-effect relationship* is another way of saying causal relationship. It merely means that one variable is causing an effect on the another variable. The variable doing the causing is called the *independent* variable and the variable being affected is called the *dependent* variable.
- Many psychologists believe that the most appropriate method for determining causality is the experiment. On the other hand, many others suggest that for some kinds of research experiments result in trivial and confusing findings.
- *Randomisation* is crucial in experiments. The term refers to an unbiased way of allocating individuals to the experimental and control conditions. Tossing a coin is one possible random procedure for allocating participants into the experimental and control conditions. If the coin lands heads then we would allocate the next participant to the experimental group, if tails to the control group. Without random allocation one cannot be certain that the people in the experimental group are similar to those in the control group on some pre-existing basis.
- Because it is essential to standardise procedures, experiments sometimes appear more contrived than other forms of research. However, every research method has its limitation and different methods have different limitations as will be seen.
- An example of an experiment may involve testing the hypothesis that sexual arousal increases feelings of love for one's partner. We could randomly assign people with partners to one of two conditions. In one condition, people would read a sexually exciting passage from a magazine before rating how much they loved their partner while in the other condition they would read a passage which was not sexually exciting. A sufficiently large difference in the average rating in the two different conditions would reflect the causal influence of sexual arousal on feelings of love.

Essential characteristics of experiments

As indicated already, experiments have three defining characteristics.

- Manipulation: a variable is manipulated to assess whether this affects a second variable.
- Control: great care is taken to ensure that apart from this manipulation, everything is the same for the research participants in all other possible respects.
- Random assignment: participants in the research are allocated to the different variants of the procedure (i.e. the manipulation) by a random method so that no systematic biases occur in the characteristics of people in the different conditions.

The manipulation of variables   Rather than examining the effects of naturally occurring variations, experimenters deliberately set up conditions which they vary in certain ways. For example, the hypothesis that increased exercise leads to greater self-reported health implies that exercise is the cause of good health. So if we vary the amount of exercise people take, we would expect that their physical health would improve according to the amount of exercise we asked them to take. For the simplest experimental design, there would have to be two *levels* or *conditions* of exercise. In other words, the people in one condition take more exercise than those in the other condition. The bigger the difference between the two conditions is in terms of the extent to which the variable is manipulated, the bigger the difference should be in terms of the size of the effect, all other things being equal, of course.

Psychologists speak of independent and dependent variables. The *independent* variable is merely the variable that *may* have an effect on the *dependent* variable. In other words, the dependent variable is dependent on the level of the independent variable. Obviously the researcher is in a position to manipulate or vary the level of the independent variable. A somewhat confusing variety of terms are used to describe the different variations of the independent variable (e.g. greater versus lesser exercise) – the levels of the treatment, the treatments, the conditions, the experimental versus control conditions and the experimental manipulation. These all mean more or less the same thing.

Precise procedural controls There is little point in deliberately manipulating a key variable while at the same time allowing other sources of variation to creep into an experiment. Consequently, an ideal in experimental work is that the only difference between the conditions is the deliberately imposed variation reflecting the independent variable. In all other respects, the experiences of people in the different conditions should be exactly the same. This is difficult to achieve perfectly for a number of reasons. Factors such as the time of the day that the research is conducted or the day of the week in question may at first seem irrelevant. However, they may have profound influences on how the participants in the research behave. For example, research conducted after lunch may well find the participants rather sleepy and inattentive which could influence the outcome.

The people taking part in experiments vary enormously. Their characteristics can influence how they behave in the different conditions just as much as variations in the independent variable can. The obvious way of controlling for this variation is to use the same people in all of the conditions of the experiment. Since the same people are in all conditions, differences cannot be due to different people being in different conditions. However, this may not be practicable when exposure to one condition affects how one behaves in another condition.

Random assignment of participants The final crucial feature of a controlled experiment is the use of random procedures to allocate participants to the different conditions. If people are assigned to the experimental and control conditions at random, in the long run the people in the experimental and control conditions will be the same in all important respects.

This is because randomisation is the unbiased allocation to the different conditions. By unbiased we simply mean that each participant has as much chance as any other participant of being chosen for the experimental condition. Randomisation also means that they have an equal chance of being chosen for the control condition.

Through the use of randomisation and careful standardisation of procedures, we ensure that the different conditions of an experiment are likely to be the same in every respect other than the independent variable. As a consequence, any differences between the experimental conditions must be something due to the effects of the experimental manipulation (i.e. the independent variable).

SURVEYS/NON-EXPERIMENTS

You should find the following helpful in getting an impression of how surveys/ non-experimental studies are different from experiments. The distinction between these two broad types of research is one of the most important aspects of research methodology in psychology.

In some ways, non-experimental studies are the simplest form of research. It might merely involve asking people about their behaviour and/or that of others. This can be done face-to-face as in an interview or, alternatively, people may complete a questionnaire (self-completion questionnaire) which they return to the researcher.

Be careful, though. Do not assume that non-experimental studies have to involve people answering questions. Other aspects of their behaviour could be assessed. Similarly, experiments may involve the use of questionnaires. Nevertheless, questioning of some sort is probably the commonest non-experimental research carried out by students.

Interviews are obviously time-consuming for the researcher since usually only one person can be interviewed at a time by any one interviewer. Questionnaires may involve relatively little time on the part of the researcher since these can be distributed and collected later.

The choice of interviews or self-completion questionnaires is a complex matter. There are costs and benefits to each. The final choice has to depend on the exact purposes of the research. Table 2.1 compares the advantages of interviews and self-completion questionnaires.

Both interviews and questionnaires share a potential major weakness. Often it is assumed that people are able and want to report accurately aspects about themselves such as their thoughts and behaviours. This assumption may be well founded in many cases. However, in some circumstances it may be a risky assumption. For example, asking very young or elderly people apparently simple things such as their age may cause difficulties.

Of course, many researchers are interested in what people *say* about their behaviour and thoughts as a research topic in its own right. They are not interested in what they see as an easy way of collecting information about actual thoughts and behaviours.

Compared with other research methods, surveys/non-experimental studies enable researchers to gather information or data easily even on aspects which are difficult to observe (such as people's sexual behaviour). Furthermore, information can be gathered on a wide variety of variables at the same time. Neither of these is always desirable.

Table 2.1 Advantages of interviews and self-completion questionnaires compared

Interview	Self-completion questionnaire
Reading and writing not needed by participant	Anonymous and potentially less embarrassing
Possible for interviewer to probe participant's answers for more detail, clarification, etc.	Less subject to the influence of the person carrying out the research
Participant is not so constrained to answer from a range of alternatives supplied by the researcher	Multiple-choice questionnaires are relatively easy to process and analyse
Participant can ask for more information or clarification easily	
May motivate participants more because of the greater involvement of time and effort by the interviewer	

Cause and effect in survey/non-experimental research

Suppose, for example, we are interested in establishing whether sexual passion influences how satisfied we are with our partner. Put this way, the idea implies that sexual passion is the cause of the effect of partner satisfaction. In other words, sexual passion is the cause and satisfaction with the relationship is the effect. If sexual passion is the cause of satisfaction then people with the greater amount of sexual passion for their partner should feel more satisfied with the relationship as shown in Figure 2.1.

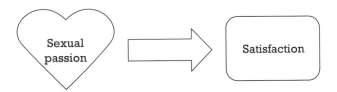

Figure 2.1 Sexual passion as the cause of relationship satisfaction

With a little nerve and imagination we could easily determine whether sexual passion was related to relationship satisfaction using a survey. All we would need to do is to ask people about their sexual passion for their partner and how satisfied they are with their partners.

However, what if we found that people who had a greater sexual passion for their partner were also more likely to indicate that they were satisfied with their partner? Would this conclusively show that sexual passion was the *cause* of relationship satisfaction? The answer is no because both of these variables (passion and satisfaction) were measured at the same time and there is another sequence possible. People who are satisfied with their partner may become sexually more passionate about them. In this case, satisfaction is the cause and passion the effect as shown in Figure 2.2.

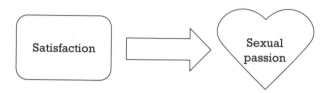

Figure 2.2 Satisfaction as the cause of sexual passion

Both of these cause-and-effect patterns make sense. Of course we are likely to be satisfied with a partner who turns us on but we are likely to be turned on by partners with whom we are generally satisfied. We are hardly likely to be aroused by someone who insults us, who smells, and who has affairs with other people.

There is yet another possibility. The relationship between sexual passion and satisfaction could be a two-way process so that both the above causal relationships are in fact true as shown in Figure 2.3.

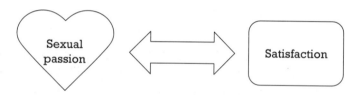

Figure 2.3 Satisfaction and sexual passion as both causes and effects of the other

There is a final possibility. That is, despite the relationship found in the survey between sexual passion and satisfaction with the relationship, neither is actually the cause of the other. In other words, there is no cause-and-effect relationship in either direction. How can this be? The answer is that there may be a third variable which actually creates the apparent relationship between satisfaction and sexual passion. Sometimes it is difficult to say what this third variable is. In our example it could be that the length of the couple's relationship is related to both sexual passion and satisfaction with the relationship as shown in Figure 2.4. As the relationship gets older sexual passion declines together with satisfaction because the relationship is getting stale in both respects. Because of this common feature there appears to be a relationship between sexual passion and satisfaction with the relationship when there is none in reality.

A relationship which is really the consequence of other variables acting on both variables at the same time is known as a *spurious* relationship. The factor or factors that are responsible for the spurious relationship are often referred to as *confounding* variables.

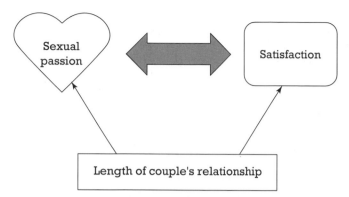

Figure 2.4 The role of a third variable (length of couple's relationship) in the relationship between sexual passion and satisfaction

Some psychologists would argue that as a consequence of this it is important to use an experimental design to determine whether sexual passion does increase satisfaction in a relationship. That is to say, the researcher should try to think of ways of manipulating one of the variables to see if this had an effect on the other variable. Could we, for example, manipulate sexual passion experimentally to see whether this had an effect on satisfaction with one's partner? One possibility (though perhaps not ethical) would be to give some participants in the study a pill known to increase the sex drive while the other participants receive an inactive pill. If satisfaction with one's partner increased with the active pill this would be evidence of a cause and effect relationship.

Unfortunately, the precision of experiments also has a cost. Relationships are not formed and do not normally develop under the influence of pills, so the experiment might have little to do with real sexual passion and real relationship satisfaction in the real world. This lack of relevance to the real world is termed a lack of *ecological validity* by researchers. It merely means that the environment of the laboratory experiment is nothing like the environment in which relationships normally occur.

OBSERVATION

Some aspects of human thought and behaviour may not be suitable for studying by survey techniques or experiments. For example, we might wish to *avoid* using surveys/non-experimental studies in the following circumstances:

- where people lack insight into their own thoughts and actions;
- where people might be motivated to lie about their beliefs and actions (e.g. questions about their honesty);
- where the behaviours and thoughts are so complex that they are difficult to summarise;
- where the behaviours are so simple that they can readily be observed;
- where we want to relate what they say about their thoughts and behaviour with what they can be observed as doing;

- where we know so little about a particular topic that it is difficult to begin to write a questionnaire or plan a survey; and
- where we want to place their actions in the context of the physical and social environment of people's lives.

In any of these circumstances we may prefer to observe their activities. For example, if we wished to establish whether parents treat daughters differently from sons then we might doubt whether parents would be willing to admit that they buy their daughters dolls and their sons toy guns. If we wished to know whether babies smile less at strangers than their parents we could not interview babies. Furthermore, we might suspect that parents are proud to believe that they have a special relationship with their child and consequently believe that they can get their child to smile at them as a result of this.

On the other hand, simple practicalities may encourage us to prefer survey methods to observation. So, for example, we might not use observation to find out whether exercise was related to mental health since some people go jogging at six o'clock in the morning whereas others go to the gym at midnight! Observation may be simply beyond the available financial and time resources of the researcher. Furthermore, it may be difficult to assess mental health just by observation at a few points in time.

One of the disadvantages of observation is that it can be more difficult to collect the data. The problem is that the observed behaviours have to be coded (or classified) into categories or ratings generated by the researcher. For example, when measuring smiling in babies we need to decide what is a smile and what is not. In addition, one should ideally use at least two observers to determine the extent of agreement on how they coded the behaviour. Disagreements between observers of the same behaviour may reflect the inadequacy of our definition of what is and what is not a smile. In this case the definition would need improvement. Alternatively, the disagreement may mean that the observers did not understand the definition of smiling clearly enough. In these circumstances we might have to train our observers better in the use of our definition.

Of course, observation is eased by the use of modern technology such as video and audio recordings which allow replay and rechecking, though some participants may find them obtrusive. However, the problem of classifying the contents of the recordings remains.

COMPARING RESEARCH METHODS

The three research methods described above are not merely alternatives. Their use has different costs and benefits for the researcher. Understanding the advantages and disadvantages of the different methods is an important component of your research skills and their development. Table 2.2 lists some advantages and disadvantages of the different methods. Careful examination of the table may convince you that one particular method is the most appropriate for the particular research you want to do.

Many researchers stick to preferred research methods. On the other hand, you may decide that no single research method is appropriate in all circumstances. For now the important issue is that you try to understand the methods and realise that choices have to be made among them.

Table 2.2 A comparison of the three research methods

	Experiments	Surveys/ non-experimental studies	Observation
Advantages	Enable cause and effect to be determined	Can collect information on variables which are not readily observable	Does not rely on participants' ability to report their own behaviour accurately
	Findings can be relatively easy to interpret	Are superficially relatively easy to carry out	
		Can gather information on many variables at the same time	
Disadvantages	Can be time consuming to carry out	Assume that people can and do report their thoughts and actions accurately	Can be time consuming to collect and classify observation data
	Trying to control the independent variable and procedures can make for very artificial situations	Do not allow cause and effect to be determined	Can mainly be used for readily observable data
	Relatively few variables can be investigated at any one time		Generally does not allow cause and effect to be determined

The advantages and disadvantages of methods lead to rather partisan preferences for some researchers. This is part of the challenge of psychology – to understand that the method is both a liberating and constraining aspect of the discipline.

SUMMARY

- The three main methods for testing hypotheses are surveys/non-experiments, observation and experiments.
- A causal hypothesis says that the variation in one variable *causes* the variation in the other variable.
- Experiments can be used to test causal hypotheses with more certainty than other research methods because the researcher actually manipulates the causal variable in order to see whether it has an effect.
- Surveys/non-experimental studies and observation are not so good at testing causal relationships because they involve greater uncertainty as to which variable is influencing the other.
- In an experiment the variable thought to be the cause is manipulated. It is known as the independent variable. The dependent variable is the variable which may be affected by the independent variable.
- The three major defining characteristics of an experiment are: (a) the manipulation of the independent variable; (b) strict standardisation to keep as many factors as possible as constant as possible; and (c) random assignment of participants.

3
—

Ethics in the conduct of research

INTRODUCTION

Frequently we see on television examples of conduct that would be unethical for psychologists carrying out research. These activities include:

*   hidden cameras taking pictures of illegal activities without the consent of those involved;
*   reporters misinforming individuals about the purpose of interviews;
*   chat shows in which the private lives of people not present in the studio are discussed; and
*   people being made to look foolish in candid camera situations.

Each of these practices would probably be unacceptable as part of psychological research. Psychological researchers must uphold the dignity of people if the discipline is to have any public credibility.

WHAT ARE RESEARCH ETHICS?

> Research using animals is not discussed in this chapter. It is a complex area on which legislation applies in many countries. Few psychologists nowadays conduct practical research with animals.

Research ethics are the broad moral principles and rules of conduct that guide psychologists when doing their research. The following points should be noted:

*   Ethics are not legal matters as such although researchers should not do anything illegal or encourage others to do anything illegal during the course of research.

- Research ethics are in addition to the other ethical standards which psychologists are expected to uphold. So, for example, although sexual harassment is not discussed below, the psychologist would be expected to adhere to the profession's standards in this regard.
- Violation of ethics may result in disciplinary action by psychologists' professional bodies such as the American Psychological Association and the British Psychological Society.
- Organisations (especially universities and hospitals) that employ researchers often have research committees. These committees vet research proposals. This is not entirely a concern with ethics for their own sake. There can be major repercussions if problems arise as a result of research. Organisations risk being sued in court by individuals feeling harmed by unethical research.
- Ethical research protects participants from serious risk of unpleasant experiences such as being deceived, stressed, or having confidential information about themselves spread around.
- Unethical research is bad for psychology as a whole in that it creates a bad reputation for the profession. This in its turn may deter people from taking part in psychological research. Furthermore, unethical research may lead to public condemnation and embarrassment for the profession that may lead to legal or other controls on the profession. Most professions prefer to control the activities of their members themselves rather than to be subject to legislation.
- Psychology's professional bodies in various countries have published guidelines for ethical conduct. These should be consulted for details of policies:

  - American Psychological Association (1992) Ethical principles of psychologists and code of conduct, *American Psychologist* 47: 1597–1611.
  - British Psychological Society (1993) Ethical principles for conducting research with human participants, *The Psychologist* 6(1): 33–35.

RESEARCH WITH ETHICAL PROBLEMS

Relatively little psychological research has severe ethical problems. This is partly the result of the considerable efforts of the discipline to develop and publicise ethical standards for research in psychology.

One of the most famous studies in psychology was also the one that has received the greatest amount of ethical debate. Milgram's (1963, 1974) classic research on obedience is familiar to most students. Most introductory textbooks describe it in detail. Basically this involved the participant in the research being instructed by the researcher to administer increasingly greater and apparently increasingly dangerous levels of electric shock to another individual. It was found that a significant proportion of participants would give up to the greatest levels of shock although the proportions varied according to the precise circumstances. The procedures involved in these studies were stressful to those participating. Although the apparatus was rigged so that in actual fact no shock was delivered, the participants were not to know this as the individual receiving the shock playacted severe distress at times. The ethical questions about this are numerous (e.g. Baumrind 1964; Milgram 1964). They include questions of whether it can be right to pressure people to do things that appear to be so harmful to another individual. But, as is sometimes the case, the ethical debate surrounding this study is not one-sided. Milgram's (1964, 1974) own defence of his research included its relevance to the holocaust of the Second World War when many soldiers and civilians were involved in the genocide of Jewish, Gypsy, and other peoples. Milgram wished to understand how this could happen and he conceived his research as being relevant to this understanding.

Another example of research which raises ethical questions is the study by Howitt and Owusu-Bempah (1990) on institutional racism in charitable organisations which had subscribed to an anti-racism alliance. This follows the style of previous research on racism and organisations. The researchers sent letters to each of these organisations asking if there was any voluntary work available with that organisation at that time. Some of the letters had 'foreign' names for the signature while others had traditional English names. The researchers wanted to know whether the organisations responded to the letters differentially along racial lines. The short answer is that they did. But, the letters were not what they appeared to be and essentially the researchers were not disclosing the purpose of the research. It is also the case that the organisations were not allowed to decide whether to participate in the research. Furthermore, in a sense, the researchers were also using the time and resources of the organisations that replied to the letters. However, since the research was investigating racism in organisations opposed to racism, it can be argued that this research is justified in its lack of openness since these organisations are unlikely to admit to racial discrimination or to be aware of their racism.

BASIC PRINCIPLES OF ETHICAL RESEARCH

The main aspects of ethical research are as follows:

a   the consent of participants in research;
b   protecting participants from psychological or physical harm; and
c   consultation with colleagues and more experienced researchers.

Consent

- Consent: People must participate in research freely and should not feel under pressure to take part. This is consent.
- Informed consent: The basis of consenting to take part in research is a reasonable understanding of to what one is committing oneself. Simply agreeing to take part in a study with no idea of what it entails is *not* informed consent.
- Participants in research must be aware that they can withdraw from the research at any stage.
- People who are unaware that they are taking part in a research study (e.g. because they are being secretly observed) cannot give informed consent by definition.
- People who have been actively deceived about what is involved in the research cannot give informed consent.
- If they so wish, participants in research who decide to withdraw from the research at any stage should be able to withdraw any data they have supplied up to that point.

Thus their questionnaires, interview tapes, videos, and even computer-recorded data should be destroyed, wiped-clean, deleted or given to the participant to take away if they so choose. Any promises to destroy the data should be fulfilled.

- Some individuals because of, for example, their youth or mental state, cannot give consent. In these circumstance, the permission of responsible adults should be sought, especially parents. Furthermore, knowledgeable and independent individuals should be consulted about the use of such participants.
- Researchers should protect the dignity of participants in their research.

Protection of participants

- Research involves an element of trust between researcher and participant. The researcher is the only person fully aware of the nature of the research. Consequently the research participant should not be subject to risk of physical or psychological harm by the researcher.
- All equipment, furnishing and other apparatus used by the researcher should be physically sound and safe. Electrical and mechanical apparatus should be regularly checked for safety.
- Research participants should not be subjected to procedures involving a tangible physical risk. Exercise, sudden surprises, stress, strobe lights, deprivation of food and water and similar factors may have serious effects in some circumstances.
- Psychological harm may be caused by some procedures. For example, the effects of research procedures that leave the participant feeling stupid or inadequate may not be reversible by the debriefing procedures employed (see Box 3.1).
- In some cases people may have an unrealistic understanding of the ability of psychologists to gain insight into their mind, personality, thinking and so forth. Thus psychological measures may sometimes appear to be more threatening to the participant than to the researcher.

Consultation

- No one can be the sole authority on whether or not her or his research is ethical.
- It is the responsibility of all researchers to consult with colleagues and other peers about the ethics of their research and to encourage their active comments and to consider this advice carefully and act on it appropriately.
- Beginning researchers, especially, need to consult with their superiors on ethical issues and to take their advice seriously. This may be a teacher or lecturer or others more experienced in psychological research.
- Research should only be carried out in institutional settings with the formal approval of that organisation.
- Some organisations have research or ethics committees to consider applications from inside researchers to do research. These must be consulted.
- Some organisations have research or ethics committees that vet applications from outside researchers to do research in that organisation. These must be approached. All research data are confidential in that they should not name individuals or provide sufficient information that individuals may be identified.
- In short, ethically you are not a lone psychologist planning and executing research in grand isolation. You are part of a community of researchers and contacts with the

community should be used to encourage a free discussion of the ethics of any research you are planning.

• Of course, for much research consultation is likely to reveal no problems.

BOX 3.1 DEBRIEFING

Debriefing should be a feature of most research. It allows you to give complete information about the nature and purpose of your research. At its simplest level it involves giving the participants in your research more detailed information about the purposes and aims of the research than you had been able to do earlier. In addition, debriefing allows you to find out more about how the research participants experienced the research. You might find it useful to know what the participants believed the research to be about or why they responded in the way they did in the study. It is an opportunity for the researcher to thank the participants in the research and spend time explaining features of the study which the participants would like to discuss such as its purpose, to what purposes the findings will be put, and whether the research will be submitted for publication. All of these functions of debriefing are positive contributions to the researcher's work.

• Debriefing is both an informative and courteous part of research that is *not* intended to free researchers from obligations to make their research ethical.
• Debriefing may provide a reason for reconsidering the degree to which the research is ethical. This should not be ignored.
• In the exceptional circumstances that debriefing is used to inform participants of deceit in the research procedures, the adequacy of the debriefing as a tool for doing so should be monitored and assessed.
• Information from debriefing should be systematically gathered.

Debriefing can include the following and more:

• The impressions that the participant had about the study or experiment – what they thought the study was about.
• Whether they had any problems understanding the procedures and questionnaires.
• What they saw their behaviours and answers to be affected by in the study.
• Any specific areas of concern that the researcher has with the study.
• A general exchange of information between researcher and participant.

RESEARCH ETHICS AT THE PROFESSIONAL LEVEL

• Research by professionally qualified psychologists may sometimes stray into ethical areas that would be inappropriate for the training of novice psychologists.
• Ethics are not really rules but complex matters sometimes involving fine judgement.

Research on demonstrably socially important topics may justify procedures which would be ethically dubious in trivial research.

- The methodological soundness of a study may be a factor in evaluating whether marginally ethically acceptable studies should be carried out.
- The more that a study touches the margins of ethical acceptability the more consultation with other psychologists is required.
- Psychologists should monitor the activities of colleagues and feel free to raise any ethical issues with them and others.

'RULES' FOR ETHICAL RESEARCH FOR BEGINNING RESEARCHERS

> The following 'rules' are designed to help beginning researchers to avoid obvious ethical difficulties. In themselves, they are not intended to deal with all possible ethical dilemmas. In some circumstances, they would prevent important and ethical research from being conducted. The 'rules' are intended for students doing training in research and do not necessarily apply to qualified psychologists in every instance.

- Only conduct research on people capable of fully anticipating and understanding what might be involved in your research. Only do research on those under 16 years old with the express permission of their parents or another adult responsible for that person.
- Do not place any pressure on potential participants to take part in your research other than a polite request that they do so. Financial or other tangible inducements can be problematic and should *not* be offered by student researchers.
- If you are a student, tell the participants in your research that you are a student and that the research is being conducted as part of your work as a student.
- As part of the process of recruiting participants, you need to inform them as fully as possible about what they are being asked to do. If they are to be questioned on their attitudes or on other matters some indication should be given about the range of issues to be covered. If they are to be given some other task (such as memorising a list of words) then this task should be briefly described.
- There is no need to reveal details of the research hypothesis or what tasks participants in another experimental condition (e.g. the control group) will be asked to do. However, given that your participants have given their time freely, it is good manners and good ethics to 'debrief' them afterwards about the purpose of the research and to answer any questions they may have.
- Explain to each participant when they are recruited and at the start of data collection that their participation is entirely voluntary. They are entitled to withdraw from the study at any stage and have their data destroyed if they so wish. Ensure that there can be no repercussions for them for having withdrawn.
- If possible, get your participants to sign that they understand the voluntary basis of their participation in your research and include a brief description of what they are to be asked to do.
- Do not tell lies or deliberately deceive your research participants in other ways.

~ Do not subject your research participants to deliberately unpleasant or stressful experiences. Causing them stress, giving them false information about their personality or abilities, frightening them, angering them, and other manipulations are difficult to justify. As such, they should have no part in research designed to train students in research methods.

~ Record the data using a code number (instead of the person's real name). If it is essential to be able to identify the research participant (e.g. because you may wish to obtain further data from them at a later stage) keep a list of code numbers and names separate from the code numbered data.

~ Never discuss an identified or identifiable participant with anyone except for the possible exception of others working with you on the research and even then only in exceptional circumstances.

~ Take special care if your research involves two or more interacting participants. Avoid any procedures likely to cause serious conflict or ill-feeling.

~ Never make observations of people in private settings without their awareness. This includes videos, one-way mirror screens, tape recordings and the like. It is usually reasonable to study people in clearly public settings but only if special care is taken to protect their identity.

~ Any apparatus that you use should be safe electrically, mechanically and structurally. As a student, check with teachers, lecturers and laboratory technicians that apparatus conforms to high standards.

~ Always discuss the ethical implications of research with friends and teachers. Make the effort to discuss the ethical implications of your research with people similar to the participants in your research whenever possible.

~ Never, ever, under any circumstances give counselling or psychological advice to participants in your research. Student researchers generally lack sufficient training to do this so it is best avoided entirely. It is appropriate for student researchers to supply contact information about counselling services and self-help groups if asked. This information should be prepared, if possible, in advance of the study. It is inappropriate for a student researcher to suggest to a participant that they need psychological advice or treatment. (Qualified psychologists doing research should consult the Ethical Principles for Conducting Research issued by their professional body since the above advice is intended for unqualified, student researchers.)

~ Never, as a student researcher, be tempted to ignore ethical requirements because, for example, you are researching others in your class or your friends. You need to practise your research ethics as much as any other aspect of your research.

Comments on physiological research are given in Box 3.2.

RESEARCH ON SENSITIVE TOPICS: ADVICE FOR MORE ADVANCED STUDENT RESEARCHERS

~ There is nothing intrinsically unethical about conducting research on sensitive or personal matters.

~ Some matters may be stressful for participants to discuss. For example, topics such as child abuse, depression and abortion may involve painful recollections.

↬ However, such research is not unethical for that reason. Participants may be more than willing to discuss such aspects even through tear-filled eyes. Obviously to treat such interviews in a trivial or condemnatory manner would be unethical.

↬ Research on sensitive matters needs to proceed sensitively and the researcher should be aware of the possible risks of premature and intrusive interviewing.

It is important to distinguish between the feelings of the participants and the anxieties and concerns of the researcher which may underlie reluctance to do research on sensitive topics.

↬ It would be inappropriate for novice researchers to study such sensitive topics simply as a way of learning basic research skills. However, students in their final year of a degree course, for example, may be ready for such research and it may contribute to their professional development.

↬ Measuring intelligence, aptitudes and abilities may be a sensitive matter given the belief in the general public that psychologists can make accurate assessments of individuals. Do nothing to suggest to people that your measures reflect the general abilities of individuals with any degree of precision.

↬ Carrying out research on sensitive topics using friends and acquaintances can be a risky business. Sometimes a professional distance is essential to avoid future demands. This is not easily achieved with friends and acquaintances. It is difficult to maintain confidentiality of information in the long term.

↬ Of course, the more sensitive the material the even greater the need to ensure that your research and procedures meet ethical standards.

BOX 3.2 PHYSIOLOGICAL RESEARCH

The following comments are designed for student researchers. They may not all apply to experienced researchers trained in physiological methods.

- Some psychological research is physiological in nature. This sort of research is often strictly controlled by institutional research ethics committees.
- Never do research involving the taking of physiological samples without prior approval of the appropriate research ethics committee. If no such committee is available simply do not do the research.
- Never do research which involves giving drugs of any sort without prior approval of an institutional ethics committee. Even such seemingly innocuous substances as aspirin or alcohol should not be used.
- Never do research using procedures which may cause extreme physiological reactions without the approval of an institutional research ethics committee and without appropriate medical precautions. Flashing lights (because they might lead to epileptic responses), extremes of heat and cold even though in natural circumstances, extremely loud noises, extremely bright lights and a range of other stimuli can be dangerous in some circumstances for some individuals.
- The agreement of the participant to this sort of treatment does not in itself make it ethical.

CONSENT FORMS

Some researchers specifically request that participants sign a consent form which indicates their consent to taking part in the research. This form will include an indication of what is involved in the research as well as a brief statement of the voluntary nature of taking part in the research and that the participant may withdraw from the study at any stage. This is especially important when, say, parents give their agreement to their child taking part in research.

The difficulty with release forms is that they do not free researchers from the requirements of ethical research. Researchers remain responsible for their research. On the other hand, release forms do help ensure that participants in the research understand their rights.

A simple consent form might be along the following lines:

I agree to taking part in the research study into attitudes to sex offenders being carried out by Fred Smith of Winchester University. I understand that my participation is voluntary and that I have the right to ccase participation at any stage and to request the return or destruction of any information or data provided.

Obviously the wording will have to be modified according to circumstances.

BOX 3.3 ETHICS QUESTIONNAIRE

The following brief questionnaire will help you identify many of the ethical difficulties to which student research may succumb.

✎ Will participants be told that they are free to withdraw from the experiment at any stage and to request that any data collected be destroyed?   Yes   No

If your answer is NO justify your position below and consult a teacher, lecturer or an experienced psychologist about whether to proceed.

_____

_____

✎ Will participants in your research be assured of the confidentiality of the information they supply you with?   Yes   No

If YES explain how you intend to protect their identities?

_____

_____

If NO then consult your teacher or lecturer.

✎ Will participants in the research be put through any unpleasant, stressful or dangerous procedures or experience the use of physiological measures which may hurt the participant?   Yes   No

If your answer is YES write down your justification for this procedure and consult your teacher or lecturer. *You are advised that such procedures are likely to be unethical without express permission of a knowledgeable and qualified psychologist. Do not carry them out unless this can be obtained.*

_____

_____

✎ Will participants be deceived about the purpose of the experiment?
                                                                          Yes   No

(*This does NOT mean that you have to tell participants everything about your research down to the last detail of your hypothesis. It means that you should not lie to them and tell them things about the experiment or themselves or anyone else which are not true.*)

If YES then justify this deception.

_____

_____

You are advised that the use of deception may be unethical. You should obtain the express permission of a knowledgeable and qualified psychologist before using deception. Do not carry on with your research without consultation.

SUMMARY

- Ethical research involves a number of major considerations including: (a) the consent of participants to taking part in the research; (b) the requirement to protect participants in research from psychological or physical harm; and (c) consultation with colleagues and more experienced researchers.
- Students doing research, especially at the early stages, should *always* check their planned research against the basic 'rules'. Completion of the questionnaire in Box 3.3 is probably the easiest way of doing this although this is no substitute for being aware of the detail of this chapter. If the rules raise any doubts they should be discussed with an experienced psychologist such as a teacher or lecturer.

- Animal and physiological research are complex areas needing special help and expertise in their ethical planning.
- Students at the later stages of their research training may soon be occupying responsible positions as psychologists. At this time, therefore, they may be appropriately considering research on sensitive topics.

4

Measuring variables

INTRODUCTION

The basic requirement of all research in psychology is that you are able to measure the variables of interest to you. Some psychological variables may be measured in many different ways, perhaps none of which are entirely satisfactory. There may be no perfect way of assessing them. Their measurement is approximate. Nevertheless even these imperfect measurements allow important research to be carried out. Take the variable 'relationship satisfaction' which is difficult to specify accurately. Some researchers may choose to measure this by asking directly 'How satisfied are you with your partner?' while others might decide that the percentage of time partners spend in very close physical proximity might be a better measure. Measures such as these may agree poorly – they are merely different facets of something difficult to define. There is a fundamental difference between a psychological concept such as 'relationship satisfaction' and the means we employ to measure it. The problem is that psychological concepts are often hard to define precisely and consequently it is difficult to know precisely what we are measuring and how to measure it.

Standard measures, widely adopted by researchers studying a particular topic, may be used. This allows easy comparison between studies using that measure. The disadvantage is that much rests on one way of measuring the psychological concept. For example, the standard measure may not assess important aspects of the variable being measured (see Box 4.1).

Decisions about how to measure a particular psychological concept often depend on a multitude of factors. If we have evidence that questionnaires will assess a variable reasonably well we might be content to use questionnaires. However, we might have reason to think that other approaches should be considered. Do we think that men will accurately report their sexual activities on a questionnaire? Or do we think that their answers will reflect more accurately the image of themselves that they are keen to portray? We may have to concede that certain aspects of people's lives are difficult to assess and that no particularly strong case can be made for any of the alternative methods. A frequent and often satisfactory compromise is to use a variety of different measures of the same psychological concept or variable. If they all suggest similar relationships then there is little problem. If they fail to agree, there are obviously difficulties of interpretation.

All of this may appear to be something of a nuisance. However, psychological research is not like measuring pieces of wood at the DIY store. Measurements in psychology are frequently matters of controversy and dispute as much as psychological theories are. The problems are part of the intellectual fascination of psychology.

BOX 4.1   STANDARD MEASURES

In many fields of psychology there exist well-established measuring techniques. These have been studied extensively and found to be generally effective ways of measuring particular variables. Variables such as intelligence, personality and job aptitude are typical examples.

As a great deal of time and money has been invested in developing such measures, they are obviously attractive to researchers and their use can avoid much time and effort devoted to creating new measures.

Some of the best of these measures are available commercially to qualified individuals and institutions. Such measures are often listed in catalogues provided by the publishers and distributors. Students generally cannot buy these materials but many universities and colleges will keep a stock of some of them or may be willing to obtain them.

Other measures may not be available commercially. However, it is common practice for researchers to publish details of their tests and measures in books and journal articles. So when doing a thorough search for published research in a particular field you are very likely to come across them.

There is a trend for non-commercial measures to be less thoroughly researched than commercially available materials. However, despite their possible inadequacies often these measures are useful enough for research purposes.

The advantage of using standard measures is that they make comparisons with previous research findings easier.

The main disadvantage is that if everyone uses the same measure it becomes harder to spot difficulties with a particular measure. Often it is better to use a variety of measures.

Another disadvantage of standard measures is that they may not be tailored for the particular group of participants you are studying.

Irrespective of all of this, it is important to find evidence of the reliability and validity of any measures you are using.

Sometimes students will learn more by trying to develop their own measures than by using ones 'off the shelf'.

DISCRETE AND CONTINUOUS VARIABLES

Variables having only a small number of values are described as *discrete* variables. Sex and gender normally consist of two values – a person is either female or male.

Other variables, such as age, which potentially have an infinite number of values if measured sufficiently accurately are called *continuous* variables. For example, if we gave a person's age in *days* there would be 36,500 different age values for people up to a hundred years old. (Yes we have forgotten to include leap years so a more accurate figure might be 36,525 or so.) For most purposes expressing age in years is sufficient. If our participants were very young children though, we might wish to record their ages in months as young children develop psychologically very rapidly and a month may make a considerable difference. There are no absolute rules about these matters; you need to consider *all* aspects of your measurements very carefully.

The one really important issue, though, is that your measurements should be precise enough so that there is some discrimination between people. It would be stupid to ask people their age with the question, 'Are you under 150 years of age?' Everyone would say 'yes' which means that you are not discriminating between them in terms of age. Once again, there are no hard-and-fast rules about how discriminating your measure should be. But it is an important matter to consider for your particular research.

RELIABILITY AND VALIDITY

Most forms of measurement in psychology need to be as reliable and as valid as possible. Reliability is the extent to which the measure will give the same response under similar circumstances. Take, for example, the simple case of measuring someone's weight. If we measure a person's weight twice within a minute on the same weighing scale, we expect the two readings to be identical within a very small margin of error. If the readings differ widely, we would conclude that the weighing scale was unreliable. We expect people's weight to be relatively stable and unchanging in the short term so variations on different scales are seen as a problem of the scales.

Reliability

Reliability actually refers to a variety of concepts that have little in common at first sight. There are two major types of reliability which need to be mentioned at this point. One is called *test–retest* reliability. It involves measuring something at two different points in time. The interval between the measures may have a substantial influence on the reliability of the measure. An interval of 20 years may produce relatively low test–retest reliability for a variable like weight whereas an interval of a day would yield relatively high test–retest reliability. It all depends on the stability of the variable being measured over time. This sort of reliability is essentially about *stability* over time.

Another form of reliability is really about *consistency* in response to slightly different measures of the same thing made at the same time. Various names are given to it depending on precise details of to what it is being applied. We shall call it *inter-item* reliability when speaking of a set of questions supposedly measuring the same thing. If a questionnaire has 30 items measuring a concept such as sexual attraction, we would expect that these items would tend to be related as they supposedly are measuring the same thing.

Inter-item reliability is known as *inter-rater* or *inter-judge* reliability when two or more observers, judges or raters are asked to measure the presence of a characteristic in other people for example.

Validity

Validity refers to whether a measure actually measures what it is supposed to measure. There is no fixed link between reliability and validity. For example, we might invent an electronic instrument to measure, say, heart rate. If we attach the instrument to a marathon runner for a week we would expect that her heart rate would not be consistent over time. When sitting down watching a video her heart rate may be low whereas at the end of a half-marathon we would expect it to be high. We do not expect heart-rate to be stable irrespective of what exercise the individual is engaged in. Only dead people have a stable heart rate and that is zero. Indeed, if heart beat was constant throughout the period we might suspect that there was something wrong with the measuring instrument – the indicator needle had got stuck or something like that.

Various types of validity are discussed by psychologists:

- *Face* validity is merely based on the researcher's impression that the measure appears to be measuring what it is supposed to be measuring. So, for example, the face validity of a questionnaire measuring love would be assessed simply by looking through the questionnaire to see whether the questions seem to be measuring aspects of love.
- *Convergent* validity indicates the extent to which a measure is strongly related to other measures expected or known to measure the same thing.
- *Discriminant* validity indicates the extent that a measure *does not* measure the things it is not supposed to measure. For example, we would expect a measure of intelligence to be strongly related to other measures of intelligence (convergent validity) but not to be related to measures of other variables such as anxiety and aggression (discriminant validity).
- *Construct* validity represents the degree to which a measure responds in the way it is supposed to respond theoretically. For example, we would expect students to show greater anxiety prior to taking an exam than prior to listening to a lecture. If our measure did not discriminate between those two situations, we may question its construct validity.

Although good reliability is not a requirement of a valid measure of an *unstable* variable, it is important if the variable in question should be stable. In order for a *stable* measure to be valid, it has to be reliable. A weighing scale that gives different readings when the same bag of sugar is weighed several times cannot be a valid measure.

Furthermore, a measure valid or reliable for one purpose may be useless in other circumstances. A tape measure may give a reliable and valid measure of length but is invalid as a measure of weight. Table 4.1 summarises some of the major differences between reliability and validity.

Reliability and validity are often reported in terms of variants of the correlation coefficient discussed in Chapter 10.

Table 4.1 The differences between reliability and validity

Reliability	Validity
Indicates how consistent measurements are over time or using different measures of the same thing	Indicates the extent to which a measurement measures what it is supposed to measure
A reliable measure does not have to be valid. A broken watch gives consistently the same time but not the right time	A valid measure does not have to be consistent over time unless it is measuring something which ought to be stable over time such as intelligence
The main forms of reliability are test–retest and inter-item reliability	The main forms of validity are face, convergent, discriminant and construct validity

A measure of a psychological characteristic which can be expected to be
fairly stable over time should show good reliability and good validity

OBJECTIVE AND SUBJECTIVE MEASURES

It is traditional in psychology to differentiate between objective and subjective measures. The distinction is essentially between observations that all observers will agree about (objective measures) and those observations which are idiosyncratic to a particular observer and which are not shared by all observers (subjective measures). Research psychologists traditionally avoid subjective measurements though the subjectivity of variables may be their important characteristic.

Objective measures are those measures which detached observers of events will agree on. The most objective measures tend to be those which are the most easily measured or quantified. Examples include speed of reaction time to a signal which can be measured precisely by the use of electronic circuits, the number of words correctly recalled from a list to be memorised, the quantity of alcohol in a urine sample, the number of days a person spends in hospital and so on. They generally refer to the number, size or duration of specific units that can be recorded without too much disagreement.

Subjective measures tend to be measures of concepts rather difficult to define and on which it is difficult to get much agreement. A good example of this would be psychologists' assessments of the dangerousness of a sex offender. What is the risk that they will re-offend? Measurements or assessments of this sort of risk are likely to differ considerably from psychologist to psychologist.

Rarely in psychology is a measure completely objective or completely subjective. Completely objective measures tend to be of relatively simple things. There is often a trade-off between the degree of objectivity of measurements and the complexity of the psychological variables the researcher wishes to investigate. Sometimes objectivity merely refers to the accuracy with which data can be transcribed. It is hardly surprising that multiple-choice questions are described as objective questionnaires. The term objective in this context merely means that most psychologists will be able to record accurately the answers chosen by different participants.

STRUCTURED VERSUS UNSTRUCTURED MEASURES

Research methods in psychology vary greatly in the degree of structuring involved. Highly structured methods are employed when there is a degree of clarity about the nature of the variables being measured and the likely range of different answers. They are not particularly good at allowing participants to express themselves in detail. Unstructured methods are employed more when the psychologist is exploring issues that have not been widely researched before. They allow the respondent to give a richness of detail in ways that are not possible with structured measures.

There are advantages and disadvantages of each type of approach.

- Highly structured materials are easy to analyse because they can be pre-coded.
- Highly structured materials may not be very motivating to respondents who feel that they wish to express themselves precisely about an issue and are not given the opportunity to do so.
- Unstructured materials may provide richer data but the researcher needs to be able to take advantage of this richness, otherwise the effort is wasted.
- Unstructured materials are particularly suited to exploratory and pilot studies.

The structured–unstructured distinction is not a characteristic of a particular research method but a dimension along which data collection procedures can vary. This is illustrated in Table 4.2. In fact all of the combinations are possible and each is used by at least some researchers. It is recommended that newcomers to psychological research concentrate on the structured methods because these tend to be the easiest to analyse.

The major difference in practice between structured and unstructured methods lies in when structure is imposed. Structured materials are structured *before* the data are collected whereas unstructured materials are structured *after* the data are collected.

Table 4.2 The structured–unstructured dimension in data collection methods

	Structured	*Unstructured*
Observation	✔	✔
Interview	✔	✔
Questionnaire	✔	✔

WAYS OF MEASURING IN PSYCHOLOGY

A wide range of different measures are used in psychological research. This is hardly surprising given the immense variety of activities that go under the name of psychology. These range from investigations virtually indistinguishable, for example, from the activities of biologists to introspective accounts of the experience of illness and beyond. It would be impossible and largely fruitless to try to catalogue all of the different approaches to measurement employed in psychological research. However, a few important points ought to be highlighted by way of illustration:

- The use of scientific instrumentation is commonplace in certain areas of psychology. Over the years numerous different forms of instrumentation have been employed. Among the obvious examples are the use of EEG machines in clinical and sleep research, the use of brain scanners in psychophysiological (or neuropsychological) applications and the use of plethysmography to measure the erections of sexual offenders to pictures of women and children. Computers are commonplace in a wide range of applications. Most of these instruments are not generally available for student research. They also may not be particularly useful in other branches of psychology for a range of reasons. For example, it would probably not be very practical to study children's playground interactions using brain scanners!

- Researchers in certain branches of psychology are more inclined to use observations of behaviour. Again certain topics are more suited than others to this approach. Researchers investigating the development of babies would find it more profitable to try to observe their activities directly or via video recordings than to interview them or give the babies a questionnaire to complete!

- Interviews are a common way of collecting data in psychology. They vary a great deal in terms of their style. Some interviews are highly structured and demand precise answers to precise questions. Other interviews tend to be much more open ended and unstructured – that is the interview attempts to encourage the participant to give discursive, rich and full replies. The style of the interview is dependent on a range of factors such as the extent to which the subject matter has been clearly defined by the researcher and the extent that the purpose of the research is to explore issues.

- Possibly the most typical method of measurement in psychology is the self-completion questionnaire. Much of the early expansion of psychology at the start of the twentieth century is associated with their introduction. They have a number of advantages. These are listed in Table 4.3. There is one sort of questionnaire, which is known as a *scale*, which tries to measure complex psychological variables using a variety of questions. Other questionnaires merely measure a whole variety of different variables at the same time without attempting to measure a single complex psychological variable.

SELF-COMPLETION SCALES

Self-completion questionnaires are extremely common in many areas of psychological research. Indeed they are so common that many newcomers to psychological research might be tempted to regard them as the ideal data collection method in psychology. However, the value of a measurement technique lies in the evidence of its reliability and validity.

Their overriding advantage is that they measure aspects that are otherwise difficult or impossible to measure. Most psychological variables are difficult to define and, consequently, there is no obvious single way of measuring them. Intelligence, for example, is one of the most common and controversial variables in psychology. The question is just what is it? The answer is that it is a psychological concept that reflects people's abilities in a wide range of different circumstances. As it is an abstract rather than physical characteristic, there is a case for measuring a variety of its aspects.

Table 4.3 Some advantages and disadvantages of self-completion questionnaires

Advantages	Disadvantages
1 Enable variables to be measured which are otherwise difficult or impossible to measure	These variables are studied solely through the words of individuals who may be unable to report accurately on their beliefs and behaviour
2 Can measure fairly complex thoughts, feelings and beliefs which can only be measured otherwise with interviews	Without other ways of collecting information on the same topic, there is no check on the accuracy of individual's claims
3 Are efficient ways of collecting data in terms of costs and time involved	Some aspects of human life need lengthy and detailed study and may need great care to elicit information from participants
4 Substantial amounts of information can be collected at any one time	The researcher may collect data just in case it can be used rather than because it is a key part of the study
5 The use of multiple choice/fixed answer formats means that answers do not have to be classified by the researcher	The imposition of answer formats gives participants little opportunity to clarify or expand their answers
6	Unless very skilfully done they may alienate people because of their superficiality or difficulty of answering

Questionnaires are well suited to collect a range of different pieces of information at the same time.

A questionnaire that aims to ask a variety of questions about essentially the same variable is often described as a *scale*. Such questionnaire scales are used to measure social attitudes (such as attitudes towards abortion), personality traits (such as extraversion), moods and emotions.

Major advantages of using scales

A single question may be a very poor measure of what it is supposed to be measuring. By combining several items in these circumstances we may produce a better estimate of what we are trying to measure. Generally speaking, the reliability of a measure increases the more items there are.

Having more than one item allows us to measure the inter-item reliability of the scale. This gives us an idea of how consistent the items are as measures of the same characteristic.

The use of several items allows us to assess the variable in different circumstances. For example, a measure of honesty might not be much use if it simply samples a single domain of experience. A good measure of honesty might include honesty in relation to one's mother, one's partner, the tax inspector, the boss, and so forth. A much poorer measure may result if we simply restrict questions about honesty to one's partner.

Finally, the greater number of items may increase our ability to discriminate between people. A single item which allows either yes or no as the answer can only allocate people to one of these two answer categories. However, if we have two items, both of which allow yes or no answers, then we have four possible different combinations.

Response formats for answers

A variety of formats exist for the respondent's replies as shown in Box 4.2. Although in many cases these are interchangeable they are not completely so and care needs to be taken in choosing one.

BOX 4.2   RESPONSE FORMATS FOR ITEMS ON A QUESTIONNAIRE

Careful consideration needs to be given to the response format for any question-naire. They are not all equivalent in their implications. A few examples of different types are given below.

Binary answers:
1 Life is the pits.   Agree   Disagree

Binary answers with Don't Know:
2 Life is the pits.   Agree   ?   Disagree

Ratings by numbers:
3 Life is the pits.   1   2   3   4   5
                              (1 = Strongly agree, 5 = Strongly disagree)

Verbal scale:
4 Life is the pits.   Agree   Agree   Neither   Disagree   Disagree
                              strongly   strongly

Bipolar rating scale:
5 Life is great   1   2   3   4   5   6   7 Life is the pits

Frequency scale
6 I feel that life is the pits
   All of the time   Often   Fairly often   Occasionally   Never

Open ended:
7 Write down a few sentences to describe how you feel about life at the moment.

Open-ended formats should be used with caution since the respondent's reply will have to be processed further to be compared with the answers of other participants. This is because virtually every one of the replies will be expressed in different words from the others. These different replies will have to be classified or coded into different categories by the researcher if any numerical analysis of the data is to be carried out. These categories will have to be developed by the researcher. This classification and coding procedure may be time consuming.

Dichotomous formats (where participants have the choice between two alternatives such as agree–disagree or yes–no) are simple but may not discriminate very well between people in all circumstance. Thus there may be few people who would agree with an extreme statement that life is the pits even though they are to a degree depressed or unhappy with life. Similarly, few people might say that they have never told a lie. This question might classify virtually all participants as liars despite the fact that some people may lie much more frequently than other people.

Ratings by numerical and verbal scales allow people to be a little more precise as to where they fall on an issue. The commonest scales have just 5 different points although 7 and 9 are also common scale lengths. There are no rules about this. Verbal scales are more common than numerical scales for the simple reason that they require less explanation at the start of the questionnaire and do not require the participant to remember what each number means.

The discriminating power of the different answer formats only increases with the number of different response alternatives if people use more response alternatives if they are made available. Items to which virtually everyone gives the same reply have poor discriminating power no matter how many different response alternatives there are. So care needs to be taken to ensure that questionnaire items actually do produce a variety of answer. Figure 4.1 should be helpful in this context.

SCORING QUESTIONNAIRE SCALES

Psychologists have fairly conventional ways of turning the sorts of verbal responses made in answer to questionnaires into numerical values or scores. A score is merely a number that indicates the extent to which an individual shows a particular characteristic. Height is a score in that a person's height is described numerically. Answers to questions are turned into scores that numerically indicate the extent of their agreement with a question or statement.

- The conventional scoring of a binary response format is to allocate the numbers 1 and 2 to the alternatives. Thus yes = 1 and no = 2 or agree = 1 and disagree = 2.
- A five-point response format can be scored as follows: agree very much = 5, agree = 4, neither agree nor disagree = 3, disagree = 2, disagree very much = 1.
- Obviously more points on the scale means that more numbers can be given. A nine-point scale can be scored from 1 to 9.
- Although this is uncommon, answers can be weighted to give more emphasis to certain replies. So the Yes ? No format might be scored: Yes = 2, and ? or No = 0.

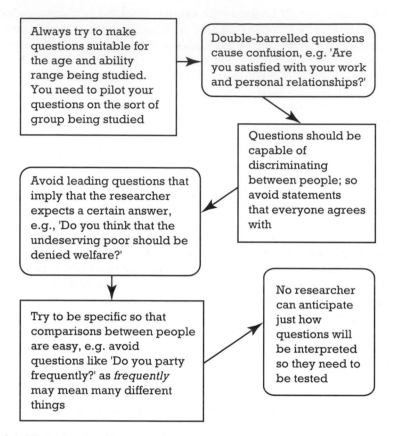

Figure 4.1 Hints about writing questions

Scoring a short scale of four items

Imagine, for instance, that we came up with the following four statements to assess life satisfaction which are to be answered with either a 'Yes' or 'No'.

1 Life is interesting	Yes	No
2 I enjoy life	Yes	No
3 I look forward to each new day	Yes	No
4 I'm generally content	Yes	No

To score such a scale of four items, we could assign 2 to 'Yes' and 1 to 'No'. We would then add the number of 2s or 'Yes's and the number of 1s or 'No's. Thus the biggest score anyone could have on life satisfaction is 8 and the smallest score is 4. To get 8 they would have to reply yes to each of the statements above and to get 4 they would have to answer no to each of the statements. Higher scores on this scale would indicate greater life satisfaction and lower scores would indicate lower life satisfaction.

We would follow a similar procedure for scoring this set of four items if, instead of having Yes/No answers, we used the following 5-point response scale.

1 Life is interesting	Strongly disagree	Disagree	Neither agree nor disagree	Agree	Strongly agree
2 I enjoy life	Strongly disagree	Disagree	Neither agree nor disagree	Agree	Strongly agree
3 I look forward to each new day	Strongly disagree	Disagree	Neither agree nor disagree	Agree	Strongly agree
4 I'm generally content	Strongly disagree	Disagree	Neither agree nor disagree	Agree	Strongly agree

The response scale could be assigned a numerical score. For example, 'Strongly disagree' = 1, 'Disagree' = 2 and so on until 'Strongly agree' = 5. We would then add up the numbers that corresponded to each person's pattern of answers to the four items. The minimum score for this scale would be 4 (for answering 'Strongly disagree' to all four items) and the maximum score would be 20 (for answering 'Strongly agree' to all four items). Thus the higher the score on the scale the greater the individual's satisfaction with life.

Now complete Exercise 4.1.

EXERCISE 4.1 SCORING A FOUR-ITEM SCALE

A person has answered these four items by <u>underlining</u> the appropriate response. Work out their total score for life satisfaction if Strongly disagree = 1, Disagree = 2, etc.

1 Life is interesting	Strongly disagree	Disagree	Neither agree nor disagree	Agree	<u>Strongly agree</u>
2 I enjoy life	Strongly disagree	Disagree	Neither agree nor disagree	<u>Agree</u>	Strongly agree
3 I look forward to each new day	Strongly disagree	Disagree	<u>Neither agree nor disagree</u>	Agree	Strongly agree
4 I'm generally content	Strongly disagree	Disagree	Neither agree nor disagree	<u>Agree</u>	Strongly agree

Response sets

There is a very obvious problem with our little scale measuring satisfaction with life. Agreement always indicates satisfaction and disagreement always indicates dissatisfaction. The problem with this is that it is known from research that some people have a tendency to agree with items irrespective of their content. These individuals would tend to agree with a statement like 'I'm generally content' and with the statement 'I'm generally discontent with life'. This tendency is an example of what is known as a response set or a response style – in this case it is called *acquiescence* or *yea-saying*. These yea-sayers will appear to be content with life on our short scale. Other individuals may have a tendency to disagree with items, a response set known as *nay-saying*, irrespective of their content.

The usual way of reducing the effect of response sets is to word half of the items in a positive direction and the other half in a negative direction. Thus half of the items would be worded so that agreement with them indicates a high level of satisfaction with life. The other half of the items would be worded such that agreement with them would indicate a low level of satisfaction with life. Balancing the items in this way means that yea- and nay-sayers will tend to end up with scores in the mid-range of the scale.

To control for response set in our four-item life satisfaction scale, we would change the wording of two of the items so that agreement with them would indicate low rather

---

EXERCISE 4.2   SCORING A FOUR-ITEM SCALE WHERE THE CONTENT OF TWO ITEMS EXPRESSES DISSATISFACTION RATHER THAN SATISFACTION

A person has answered these four items by <u>underlining</u> the appropriate response. Work out their total score for life satisfaction. The higher the score, the greater the life satisfaction.

1 Life is dull	Strongly disagree	<u>Disagree</u>	Neither agree nor disagree	Agree	Strongly agree
2 I enjoy life	Strongly disagree	Disagree	<u>Neither agree nor disagree</u>	Agree agree	Strongly
3 I look forward to each new day	Strongly disagree	Disagree	Neither agree nor disagree	<u>Agree</u>	Strongly agree
4 I'm seldom content	Strongly disagree	<u>Disagree</u>	Neither agree nor disagree	Agree	Strongly agree

than high life satisfaction. For example, we could rewrite the first item ('Life is interesting') as 'Life is dull'. Similarly, we could reword the fourth item ('I'm generally content') as 'I'm seldom content'. When we do this, it is important to remember that the scoring for these items is reversed so that 'Strongly agree' is now coded as 1, 'Agree' as 2 and so on.

Now carry out Exercise 4.2.

SUMMARY

- All empirical research requires the measurement of one or more variables.
- Measurement consists of assigning numbers to categories of units such as responses and events.
- Where categories can be arranged in order of increasing quantity, higher numbers should be assigned to categories of greater quantity.
- To enable comparisons with previous research, well-established measures should be used to assess variables.
- Measures should be both reliable and valid.
- Test–retest reliability indicates the extent to which similar scores are obtained on two occasions within a relatively short period of each other and under similar circumstances.
- Inter-item reliability reflects the extent to which items measuring the same variable are answered in the same way.
- Inter-rater reliability shows the extent to which raters make similar judgements.
- Convergent validity indicates the extent to which a measure is related to measures assessing the same variable.
- Discriminant validity is the extent to which a measure is unrelated to measures assessing different variables.
- Construct validity indicates the extent to which a measure behaves in theoretically expected ways.
- Reliability, discriminability and representativeness can be increased by increasing the number of elements that make up the measure for assessing that particular variable.
- Questionnaire scales comprise a number of items developed to assess the same variable.
- To score a questionnaire scale, the numbers that correspond to the answers chosen are added together for all the items.
- To control for response set, half the items are worded to express a high level of the variable while the other half are worded to express a low level.

ANSWERS TO EXERCISES

Answer to Exercise 4.1

The numerical values for the four items are 5, 4, 3 and 4 respectively. Adding these up gives a total score of 16.

Answer to Exercise 4.2

The numerical values for the four items are 4 (when reversed), 3, 4 and 4 (when reversed), giving a total score of 15.

Part II

The statistical analysis of single variables and simple surveys

Part II

5

Two types of data analysis

INTRODUCTION

There is a crucial step in all research – moving from the measures the researcher takes to the statistical analysis of these measures. In other words, how does one statistically analyse data? Generally speaking, the statistical analysis of data is dependent on one crucial decision about the nature of the measurement of each of the variables:

- The choice is largely between variables which are measured in terms of numerical scores and variables which are measured in terms of their belonging to non-numerical categories.

A numerical score is a measure of a variable using numbers which indicate different degrees of that variable. A person's height or weight is a numerical score since the number indicates an increasing amount of height or weight. This is the case with the majority of psychological measurements.

Other measurements are simply the allocation of individuals to named (or sometimes numbered) categories. People's jobs would be an example of named categories. With category measurement of this sort it is impossible to say that people possess different *quantities* of the variable; it is merely that the *qualities* of the categories vary.

This is an area that has caused some controversy in psychological research. It has also been made unnecessarily complicated. We will try to explain the issues and then offer the simplest solution we know.

DIFFERENT TYPES OF MEASUREMENT

One difficulty is that the best ways of explaining the issues have nothing to do with psychology and much more to do with physical measurement.

Imagine that you are a lumberjack. Wandering through vast rain forests you are able to categorise each of the different trees. That tree is mahogany, the next tree is teak, the next tree is ebony and so forth. That is to say, you are naming the different types of tree or, in other words, putting them into different categories of tree. This sort of measurement is known as *nominal* or *category* measurement. It is a common enough form of measurement. It is essentially *classification*. The only numbers that can be assigned to this form of measurement are known as *frequencies*. Frequencies are merely counts or tallies of the objects of a particular type or category. For example, there may be 49 mahogany trees, 23 teak trees, 12 ebony trees and so forth. These numbers are the frequency of occurrence of each type of tree. The different types are known as different *values* of the variable.

But what if you wanted to assess more than the number of each type of tree? What if you wanted to estimate the height of each tree? Just how long is each tree trunk? Remember that we are in a tropical rain forest and we simply do not have a tape measure available. One solution to the problem of measuring the length of the tree trunks would be to get Tarzan to find the longest vine that he can and tie knots in the vine at intervals along its length. Because vine varies in thickness and flexibility along its length, the knots are at varying distances apart despite Tarzan's best efforts. Nevertheless, the knotted vine is still useful. If we count the number of knots from the bottom to the top of the tree trunks, the number of knots gives us an indication of which trees are the tallest and which are the smallest.

We can put them in order from smallest to largest by using the number of knots. This is an example of what is known as an *ordinal* measure. All this means is that we can order the trees from largest to smallest. Ordinal, then, equals the order. Because we can rank this order (i.e. this tree is the 1st tallest in height, that tree is the 2nd tallest in height, that one over there is the 3rd tallest in height and so forth) we can also call these data rank data although data are normally not collected in the form of ranks. This form of measurement has the obvious weakness of the rough-and-ready nature of the knotted vine as a measure.

Fortunately, you are able to send for properly made and calibrated tapes which have the lengths clearly marked in metres and centimetres. This may sound very obvious but markings are accurate so that the distance between 4 and 5 metres on the tape is exactly the same as the distance between 12 and 13 metres on the tape and this is exactly the same as the distance between 37 and 38 metres on the tape. These differences are all one metre after all and we would expect them to be identical. Such a measure as this is said to be *equal interval* or *interval* measurement. It means literally what it says: the size of the interval between two adjacent points is the same as that between any other two adjacent points.

You make a fortune exporting logs but you begin to find that there are some problems. The main one is that you sell the trees before they are cut and because you sell on the basis of the estimated length of the trunk you begin to think you could make even more money. The trees are not sawn down but dragged out by powerful machinery. This means that there is a short extra length of underground trunk pulled out and in a sense this is given to your customers for nothing. This short extra length is always about a metre for the types of trees you are selling. By using a measuring scale set on the ground at one end and reaching up to the top of the trunk means that you are selling more tree for the money. Properly, then, the measurement should always start 1 metre underground. In order to start at zero, we should measure from a metre underground. If we have the absolute zero of a measure and its steps are equal interval, we call this *ratio* measurement. It is called this because you can accurately talk about a measure being twice as much as another measure or a third of another measure. This can only be done when the proper zero point is reached – the point at which a variable cannot get smaller.

TYPES OF MEASUREMENT AND PSYCHOLOGY

To repeat, this is an analogy that comes from physical measurement. What are the parallels in psychology? The answer is that it is very difficult to make the parallel. Most psychological measures are based on concepts that are difficult to quantify. We have seen that questionnaires are very common. So how do we know that we have equal intervals or even ratio measurement?

The short answer is that you cannot know for certain with anything so abstract as most psychological concepts. They are measured, at best, only approximately. This in the past led psychologists to believe that apart from nominal measurement involving putting people into categories, all other psychological measurements are ordinal data. There is a specialised branch of statistics that deals with data that can be analysed in the form of ranks. We will see examples of this later.

However, it is current practice to view the debate with some suspicion. Current statistical practice works on the assumption that it is the numerical properties of the scores themselves which are important and not the unanswerable question of whether the underlying psychological variable has ordinal, interval or ratio characteristics. This is not universally accepted as adequate but it does have the major advantage of opening up a wide variety of convenient statistical techniques for use.

Figures 5.1 and 5.2 illustrate the issue. Nominal (or category) data consisting of frequencies in categories are always analysed as a distinct form of data. They have their own statistical techniques – for example, chi-square is used to analyse frequency data (Chapter 12).

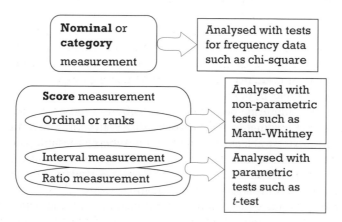

Figure 5.1 Traditional approach to statistical measurement and measurement scales

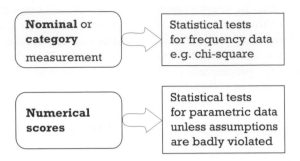

Figure 5.2 Modern approaches to statistics and scales of measurement

However, ordinal, interval and ratio data may be treated in different ways by different analysts. The traditional pattern is:

* Tests usually called *non-parametric* tests are used when the data are numerical and only an ordinal level of measurement can be assumed.
* Virtually the same tests are used for interval and ratio data in psychological research. These tests are known as *parametric* tests and are among the commonest statistics in psychology.

The major trouble with this traditional pattern is the obvious one that it is hard to know whether any psychological measures are interval or ratio in nature.

The alternative 'modern' approach is to equate ordinal, interval and ratio measures with numerical scores and apply parametric tests to virtually any data which take the form of numerical scores.

Although the traditional approach is most commonly adopted in statistics textbooks, a period of time devoted to studying psychological journals will reveal that virtually any score data are almost invariably analysed using parametric tests.

SUMMARY

* Nominal (or category) data are data in which objects are merely classified.
* Score data are data in which a number is assigned to the object being measured which indicates the extent to which a particular individual possesses the characteristic being measured.
* Conventionally, psychologists recognise four different types of measurement: nominal (or category), ordinal (or ranks), equal interval, and ratio. Three different types of statistical analysis are used. There is one type of statistics for nominal or category data (largely chi-square); there is another type of statistics for ordinal or ranked data (non-parametric statistics); and there is a third type of statistics for equal interval or ratio data (parametric statistics).
* However, modern practice is largely to regard data as either nominal (category) or score.

6

—

Describing and summarising category data

INTRODUCTION

The important point to have learnt from Chapter 5 is that different sorts of statistical analysis apply to different sorts of data. In this chapter we will look at how nominal or category data can be summarised statistically. Remember that this form of data merely involves classifying cases into different categories.

In this chapter, we will confine ourselves to describing and summarising statistically data on individual category variables. Chapter 7 explains how score data may be described and summarised. Category and score data differ a great deal statistically and it is important to understand these differences.

Irrespective of the sort of data you have, it is essential to keep a clear, well-labelled record of your data. Data on scraps of paper are likely to get lost or forgotten. Simple data tables are usually effective enough for keeping a record of your data when you begin research. Table 6.1 shows one way of effectively recording data. Each row represents an individual (or case) and each column represents a variable. The data in Table 6.1 consist of four variables obtained in a small survey of 20 individuals:

> the person's biological sex;
> their age in years;
> their employment status (full-time, part-time, homework, student and seeking
> work); and
> their life satisfaction score ranging from 4 to 20.

The names of the categories, of course, could be abbreviated. For example, 'Female' could be abbreviated to 'F', 'Male' to 'M', 'Full-time' to 'F' or 'FT' and so on. Only use abbreviations of this sort if space constraints force it.

The exact way in which the data are arranged depends on the particular analysis and the nature of your research design. Other examples are provided later in the book. At first it may appear to be something of a nuisance to record your data in this way but the

Table 6.1 A table recording the sex, age, employment status and life satisfaction scores of 20 individuals

Individual	Sex	Age (years)	Employment status	Life satisfaction
1	Female	18	Student	16
2	Female	21	Student	17
3	Female	25	Student	15
4	Female	20	Seeking work	12
5	Female	35	Seeking work	14
6	Female	27	Full-time	18
7	Female	43	Full-time	17
8	Female	55	Part-time	19
9	Female	28	Homework	17
10	Female	41	Homework	18
11	Male	19	Student	17
12	Male	24	Student	16
13	Male	21	Student	18
14	Male	37	Seeking work	13
15	Male	53	Seeking work	11
16	Male	31	Full-time	17
17	Male	49	Full-time	18
18	Male	26	Full-time	16
19	Male	34	Full-time	17
20	Male	44	Part-time	16

EXERCISE 6.1   DISTINGUISHING CATEGORY AND SCORE DATA IN TABLE 6.1

List the category variables in Table 6.1:

_____

List the score variables in Table 6.1:

_____

---

benefits in the long run are well worth the effort. Clearly presented data are far easier to understand.

With category data (such as a person's sex or their employment status) each person is assigned to one category. For score data (such as a person's age or their life satisfaction) a person is assigned a number which indicates the extent to which he or she is characterised by that variable.

Score data consist of numbers which indicate the amount or quantity of a particular characteristic the individual possesses. Thus age is score data because the numbers tell you the relative ages of individuals. Similarly, life satisfaction is score data because the bigger the number the greater the life satisfaction.

A variable consisting of only two categories such as sex is called a *dichotomous* variable. Dichotomous is derived from Greek meaning a cut (toma) in two (dicha). Such variables hold a special place because they are the only sort of nominal or category variable that can also be treated as if it were a score. The reason for this is that for dichotomous variables such as sex or gender (male or female) one category actually indicates a greater quantity of something – so the category female indicates a greater quantity of femininity than the category male. For this reason it is common to score the two categories of a binomial variable such as sex as 1 and 2 (perhaps male = 1, female = 2). If this is done, sex can be treated exactly as a score variable. It must be stressed that this is *only* possible with binary variables. It does not and cannot work with nominal or category variables with three or more different values.

Generally speaking, if you have nominal categories such as occupation type (employment status in Table 6.1) then frequency counts are the main way in which you can summarise the data. Frequency counts are simply the number of individuals that fall into each category.

Score data can be summarised in a greater variety of ways. The average or mean score is just one example of a statistical summary of score data. To summarise the data in Table 6.1 for the two category variables of sex and employment, we could simply count the number of people that fell into the two categories of sex and the five categories of employment status. There are 10 females and 10 males. Of the 20 people, 6 are students, 4 are seeking work, 6 are in full-time employment, 2 are in part-time employment and 2 are employed in the home.

Now carry out Exercise 6.1.

WAYS OF SUMMARISING DATA: CATEGORY VERSUS SCORE DATA

Statistical analysis has the overriding aim of organising, clarifying and, it is to be hoped, simplifying the original data. This generally involves the researcher considering carefully the best ways for effectively communicating the trends in the data.

Common methods of summarising data are familiar to anyone who has ever read a newspaper, watched the television or taken elementary mathematics. These tend to be graphs and charts such as bar charts, pie-diagrams and histograms because of their instant visual impact. These are all important in psychological statistics but many mathematical ways of summarising the main characteristics are perhaps much more commonly used. Figure 6.1 gives examples of ways of summarising data. The different approaches for score data and category data are very evident.

Not all of the terms in Figure 6.1 will be familiar. An understanding of these terms will be gradually built up in this and later chapters.

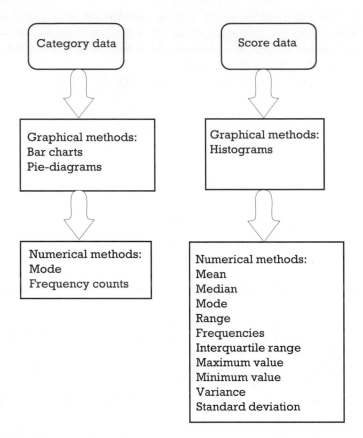

Figure 6.1 Ways of summarising data

FREQUENCIES, PERCENTAGES AND PROPORTIONS

Percentages

Table 6.2 Frequency table for the category variable sex

	Frequency	Percentage frequency
Male	10	50
Female	10	50

Frequencies are simply the numbers of cases falling into each of the values of a variable. For example, the frequency of females in our example is 10 and the frequency of males is also 10. This is easily entered into a simple frequency table such as Table 6.2. Frequencies are sometimes abbreviated as f so you might read f = 10 meaning that the frequency is 10.

It can be useful to convert frequencies such as these into *percentages* of the total sample. This is especially useful when comparing frequencies of a particular category from different samples. This has been done in Table 6.2 which contains both frequencies and percentage frequencies.

A percentage is the number of cases out of (per) a hundred (cent) that fall in a particular category. To calculate percentage frequencies we need the frequencies in each category and the total of these frequencies for all of the categories of that variable.

$$\text{Percentage frequency of females} \ = \ \frac{\text{frequency of category}}{\text{frequency of all categories}} \times 100$$

$$= \ \frac{\text{frequency of females}}{\text{frequency of males and females}} \times 100$$

$$= \ \frac{10}{20} \times 100$$

$$= \ 0.5 \times 100$$

$$= \ 50.00\%$$

The advantage of expressing the number of people that fall into a particular category as a percentage (or a proportion) is that it gives us a quick indication of the relative number of people in that group. This is particularly useful if you are comparing more than two categories in more than one group where the groups contain differing numbers of people.

Suppose, for example, that 7 out of 27 people in one sample and 23 out of 65 people in another sample are in part-time employment. It would be difficult to estimate whether the two samples were similar in terms of frequency of part-time workers. Percentages can clarify this greatly.

The percentage of people in part-time work in the first sample is about 26

$$\frac{7}{27} \times 100 \ = \ 25.93\%$$

and in the second sample is about 35

$$\frac{23}{65} \times 100 \ = \ 35.38\%$$

From these percentages, we can quickly see that the percentage of people in part-time work in the second sample (35.38%) is greater than that in the first sample (25.93%).

Now carry out Exercise 6.2.

EXERCISE 6.2 CALCULATING PERCENTAGES

1 Calculate the percentage of people in the data shown in Table 6.1 who are students.

2 Calculate the percentage of people who are seeking work.

3 Calculate the percentage of people who are in part-time employment.

Proportions

Proportions are similar to percentages but they are expressed out of 1 rather than out of 100. They are most commonly used in statistics when describing probabilities. The calculation of the proportion of females in our data is as follows:

$$\text{Proportion of females} \ = \ \frac{\text{frequency of category}}{\text{frequency of all categories}}$$

$$= \ \frac{10}{20}$$

$$= \ 0.50$$

Rounding decimals in calculations

Notice that we have expressed the above calculations to two decimal places. That is, there are two numbers after the decimal point or full stop. This is generally sufficiently accurate for most psychological data. However, in the steps leading to our final calculation we would work to 3 decimal places or use a calculator. You will find it easier to work out these figures and other calculations in this book with an electronic calculator as we have done.

Dividing one number by another will often result in a figure which will have a number of decimal places. For example, when our calculator divides 7 by 27 it gives a figure of 0.2592592 which is difficult to take in and which is far more accurate than we need. To shorten or round this figure to two decimal places we look at the number in the third decimal place which is 9. If this number is larger than 4 we increase the number in the second decimal place by 1. Because in this case the figure in the third decimal place is 9, we round up the figure in the second place (which is 5) by 1, making it 6. In other words, 0.2592592 rounded to two decimal places is 0.26.

If the number in the third decimal place is less than 5, the number in the second decimal place remains the same. Suppose, for example, the number we had to round to two decimal places had been 0.2542592. Because the 4 in the third decimal place is less than 5, the 5 in the second decimal place remains as 5. In other words, 0.2542592 rounded to two decimal places is 0.25.

Now carry out Exercise 6.3.

EXERCISE 6.3   ROUNDING NUMBERS TO TWO DECIMAL PLACES

Round the following numbers to two decimal places:

1 7.352
2 18.7459
3 134.89519
4 29.410556
5 6.6666667
6 3.3333333

VISUAL REPRESENTATIONS OF DATA

Pie-charts

Some people find it easier to visualise data in terms of pictures. When presenting data to a live audience it is often better to present your data as a chart or diagram than verbally. A very familiar way of pictorially presenting category data that are simply the frequencies in each category is to use the pie-chart or pie-diagram. The pie-chart consists of a circle (representing a pie) as shown in Figure 6.2.

This circle is divided into portions or slices which reflect the proportion of people or cases in each category. Bigger slices denote more people. Because a circle consists of 360 degrees, the number of degrees in a slice is calculated by multiplying the proportion of people in that category by 360.

The formula for deciding the angle of the slice is:

$$\text{Degrees of slice} = \frac{\text{Number of people in a category}}{\text{Total number of people in the sample}} \times 360$$

So, the degrees of a pie-chart slice representing the proportion of females in our sample would be:

$$\text{Degrees of female slice} = \frac{10}{20} \times 360 = 180 \text{ degrees}$$

We could draw the circle with a compass and mark off the angle representing the appropriate number of degrees with a protractor. In this case, we would simply divide our circle into two halves through its centre. We could shade or colour the two slices differently to distinguish them more easily and label them with the category and the percentage of people in that category.

Now carry out Exercise 6.4.

EXERCISE 6.4   CALCULATING THE NUMBER OF DEGREES FOR A PIE-CHART

Calculate the number of degrees that are needed to represent the proportion of people in Table 6.1 who fall into the five employment categories of full-time, part-time, homework, student and seeking work.

Your results from Exercise 6.4 are displayed in the pie-chart of Figure 6.2 on the next page.

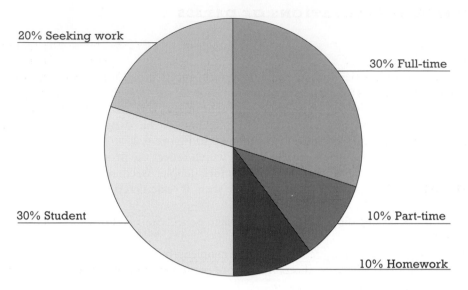

Figure 6.2 Pie-chart showing percentage of people in five employment categories

Bar charts

Another way of presenting category data pictorially is the bar chart as shown in Figure 6.3. Each category is represented by a separate bar which is physically separated from the bar beside it. The height of the bar corresponds to the number of people in that category which may be alternatively expressed as a percentage or proportion of the total sample.

Without the gap between the bars the bar chart looks like a histogram (see Figure 7.6). Consequently it is easy to get a bar chart confused with a histogram. Make sure that the gap always occurs between the bars in a bar chart.

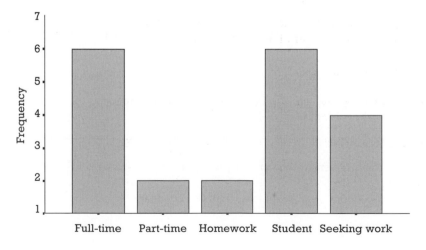

Figure 6.3 Bar chart showing percentage of people in five employment categories

REPORTING DESCRIPTIVE STATISTICS

With data which only consist of categories, all that can be reported is the number (and/or percentage) of cases that fall within each category. If you go back to Figure 6.1, you can see that these are the only important methods of presenting data on individual variables involving category measurement. So it should be clear that a basic analysis of category data is simply to present in either table or graph form the number of cases (frequency) in each category. Chapter 10 explains how to show relationships between pairs of category variables.

SUMMARY

- When summarising data, category variables should be distinguished from score variables.
- Data should be arranged into tables to ease the analysis.
- Category data can only be summarised by describing the number or frequency of cases that fall within each category.
- These frequencies can be re-expressed as a proportion or percentage of the total number to indicate their relative size.
- They can also be displayed as a pie-chart, a bar chart or a table.
- For any category (or nominal) variable, an effective way of presenting the data is merely to present one of the following: a frequency table, a bar chart or a pie-chart. If these are presented as percentages it is also necessary to give the value of N – the number of cases or people involved.

ANSWERS TO EXERCISES

Answers to Exercise 6.1

The category variables are sex and employment status.
The score variables are age and life satisfaction.

Answers to Exercise 6.2

1 Percentage of students $= \dfrac{6}{20} \times 100 = \dfrac{600}{20} = 30\%.$

2 Percentage seeking work $= \dfrac{4}{20} \times 100 = \dfrac{400}{20} = 20\%.$

3 Percentage part-time $= \dfrac{2}{20} \times 100 = \dfrac{200}{20} = 10\%.$

Answers to Exercise 6.3

1	7.352	=	7.35
2	18.7459	=	18.75
3	134.89519	=	134.90
4	29.410556	=	29.41
5	6.6666667	=	6.67
6	3.3333333	=	3.33

Answers to Exercise 6.4

1 Full-time $= \dfrac{6}{20} \times 360 = \dfrac{2160}{20} = 108°$

2 Part-time $= \dfrac{2}{20} \times 360 = \dfrac{720}{20} = 36°$

3 Homework $= \dfrac{2}{20} \times 360 = \dfrac{720}{20} = 36°$

4 Student $= \dfrac{6}{20} \times 360 = \dfrac{2160}{20} = 108°$

5 Seeking work $= \dfrac{4}{20} \times 360 = \dfrac{1440}{20} = 72°$

7

Describing and summarising score data

INTRODUCTION

In Chapter 6 we explained how to describe and summarise category data. This chapter concentrates on the ways of describing and summarising numerical score data. Refer again to Table 6.1, p. 54. It contains data on a number of variables. Some of the data are in the form of numerical scores.

Because scores contain much more information than category data, there are many more appropriate ways of describing and summarising score data. Summarising a score variable such as age or scores on a life satisfaction scale can involve tables and diagrams but may involve numerical indexes. Figure 7.1 shows some of the many ways of summarising score data.

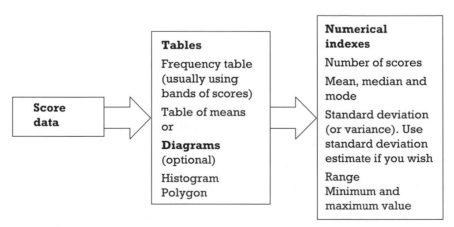

Figure 7.1 Essential descriptive statistics for score variables

Table 7.1 Table showing the frequency of people grouped according to their age

Age	Frequency
18	1
19	1
20	1
21	2
24	1
25	1
26	1
27	1
28	1
31	1
34	1
35	1
37	1
41	1
43	1
44	1
49	1
53	1
55	1

Table 7.2 Table showing the frequency of people grouped according to their life satisfaction score

Score	Frequency
11	1
12	1
13	1
14	1
15	1
16	4
17	6
18	4
19	1

FREQUENCY TABLES

As a first step in presenting score data for a variable, it is useful to draw up a frequency table like those shown in Tables 7.1 and 7.2 for age and life satisfaction score respectively. On the left side of the tables are the numbers (or categories) of the variable ordered in increasing size while on the right side are the frequency of cases that have received that number. For example, in Table 7.1 we can see that two people are aged 21 while there is only one person for each of the other ages listed.

Table 7.1 illustrates that although something is to be gained by constructing frequency tables, they do not always result in vastly improved clarification of the data. The individual ages of 18 of the 20 people are still being shown. It can take quite a lot of effort to create a useful histogram for some data. We will demonstrate later on in this chapter how scores can be grouped to improve the effectiveness of a frequency table.

In contrast, Table 7.2 shows a frequency table that indicates clearer trends without any adjustment. This table is quite useful as it stands without any further adjustment. This is partly because of the smaller number of different scores (values) for this variable. However, the fact that most of the scores are between 16 and 18 also helps because it shows a clear trend in the data.

HOW TO DESCRIBE A SET OF SCORES

When summarising a distribution of scores like these, three main features need to be described.

- The first is what value characterises the central score of the distribution.
- The second is what value or values characterise the spread or dispersion of scores.
- The third is what shape characterises the distribution of scores.

We shall outline the most common measures for describing these features in the following sections.

MEASURES OF CENTRAL TENDENCY

There are three main measures for describing the central position of a distribution called the *mode*, the *median* and the *arithmetic mean* (or just mean for short as it is the mean most commonly used).

We have included Worksheet 7.1 to help you with calculating these different measures of central tendency. Although these measures are easily calculated without the worksheet, it is useful to familiarise yourself with this style of working as there are many other calculation worksheets in this book.

Mode

The mode is simply the most commonly occurring value (i.e. score, but it can also be applied to categories in category data). It can be quickly obtained from a frequency table. For example, the mode for age in Table 7.1 is 21 and is 17 for the life satisfaction score in Table 7.2. There can be more than one mode if the highest frequency is shared by several values. For example, if two people in Table 7.1 were aged 18 and two were aged 19, there would be three modes which would be 18, 19 and 21.

Median

The median is the score that divides the sample of scores into two equal groups where half the sample has scores at and above the median while the other half has scores at and below the median. We can work out the median from the frequency table although it is a little easier to do this if one rank orders the scores for all the individuals as shown in Table 7.3.

When the number of cases is an odd number (e.g. 1, 3, 5, etc.), the median is the score of the individual at the midpoint. This is the easiest circumstance as one just has to find the middle score and this is the median. Only when there is an odd number of cases do you find an exact midpoint.

When the number of cases is even (e.g. 2, 4, 6, etc.), there is a slight degree of estimation involved. To work out the median age for all 20 individuals in Table 7.3, we need to find the age of the 10th individual and that of the 11th individual and take the average. The age of the 10th individual is 28 and the age of the 11th individual is 31, so the median lies midway between 28 and 31. By adding these two ages together (28 + 31 = 59) and dividing this sum by 2 (59/2 = 29.50) we find the value of the median to be 29.5. In other words, half the people in the sample are aged 29.5 or above, while half are aged 29.5 or below. For the life satisfaction variable, the 10th and 11th individuals both have scores of 17, so the median is 17.

The median is harder to explain than to calculate.

Table 7.3 Table ranking individuals according to age and life satisfaction scores

Rank order	Age	Life satisfaction	Rank order	Age	Life satisfaction
1	18	11	11	31	17
2	19	12	12	34	17
3	20	13	13	35	17
4	21	14	14	37	17
5	21	15	15	41	17
6	24	16	16	43	18
7	25	16	17	44	18
8	26	16	18	49	18
9	27	16	19	53	18
10	28	17	20	55	19

Worksheet 7.1 for the mean, mode and median

Calculating mean Enter each of your scores on selected variable below	*Calculating mode* List below all the DIFFERENT values in your data. Then count the frequency of each of these values and insert it below	*Calculating median* Enter your scores from lowest to highest below
Score 1 = 18	Value = 18 : Frequency = 1	Lowest = 18
Score 2 = 21	Value = 19 : Frequency = 1	2nd = 19
Score 3 = 25	Value = 20 : Frequency = 1	3rd = 20
Score 4 = 20	Value = 21 : Frequency = 2	4th = 21
Score 5 = 35	Value = 24 : Frequency = 1	5th = 21
Score 6 = 27	Value = 25 : Frequency = 1	6th = 24
Score 7 = 43	Value = 26 : Frequency = 1	7th = 25
Score 8 = 55	Value = 27 : Frequency = 1	8th = 26
Score 9 = 28	Value = 28 : Frequency = 1	9th = 27
Score 10 = 41	Value = 31 : Frequency = 1	10th = 28
Score 11 = 19	Value = 34 : Frequency = 1	11th = 31
Score 12 = 24	Value = 35 : Frequency = 1	12th = 34
Score 13 = 21	Value = 37 : Frequency = 1	13th = 35
Score 14 = 37	Value = 41 : Frequency = 1	14th = 37
Score 15 = 53	Value = 43 : Frequency = 1	15th = 41
Score 16 = 31	Value = 44 : Frequency = 1	16th = 43
Score 17 = 49	Value = 49 : Frequency = 1	17th = 44
Score 18 = 26	Value = 53 : Frequency = 1	18th = 49
Score 19 = 34	Value = 55 : Frequency = 1	19th = 53
Score 20 = 44	Value = : Frequency =	20th = 55

$\sum X$ = add above scores = 651

N = number of scores = 20

N = number of scores = 20

If N is an odd number, the median is $\frac{(N + 1)}{2}$ score =

Mean = $\frac{\sum X}{N}$ =

The mode is the most frequent value in above column = 21 years

If N is an even number, the median is the *average* of the $\frac{N}{2}$ score and the $\frac{(N + 2)}{2}$ score =

$\frac{651}{20}$ = 32.55 years

$\frac{20}{2} + \frac{22}{2}$ = 10th + 11th score

Median = $\frac{28}{2} + \frac{31}{2} = \frac{59}{2}$

= 29.50 years

Reporting your findings

Probably the best way of reporting the mean, median and mode is as part of a table which gives the names of each of the score variables in your study and important descriptive statistics such as the mean, median, mode and standard deviation under separate columns. Alternatively, if there are just one or two variables, the values of the descriptive statistics can be put in your report when you mention the variable. You might write something like 'The mean age was 32.6 years (mode = 21 years, median = 29.5 years).'

Mean

The mean is the sum of the scores for all the individuals in the sample divided by the number of such scores. It is what most people would mean by the average.

$$\text{Mean} \quad = \quad \frac{\text{Sum of scores}}{\text{Number of scores}} \quad = \quad \frac{\sum X}{N}$$

$\sum$ (called sigma) is the statistical symbol for sum. X stands for scores and N stands for the number of scores. Sometimes the mean is given the symbol M and sometimes $\bar{X}$.

To work out the mean age of the sample of 20 individuals in Table 7.3, we first add up their individual ages which gives a sum of 651.

18 + 21 + 25 + 20 + 35 + 27 + 43 + 55 + 28 + 41 + 19 + 24 + 21 + 37 + 53 + 31 + 49 + 26 + 34 + 44 = 651

That is, $\sum X = 651$.

As the number of individual ages is 20, we divide this sum by 20 which gives us a mean age of 32.55 years.

$$\text{Mean age} \quad = \quad \frac{\text{Sum of ages}}{\text{Number of ages}} \quad = \quad \frac{\sum X}{N} \quad = \quad \frac{651}{20}$$
$$= \quad 32.55 \text{ years}$$

In reports, the mean would often be reported in the form $M = 32.55$ years.

Comparison of the mean, median and mode

*   The mean, median and mode provide different types of information and it is not possible to say that one is better than another.
*   Differences between the mean, median and mode can be quite revealing about the distribution of the scores on a variable.
*   When the distribution of scores is symmetrical and peaked in the middle like that shown in Figure 7.2, all three measures give the same result.

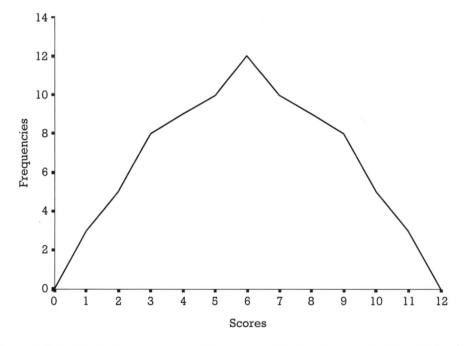

Figure 7.2 A distribution of scores which is symmetrical and peaked in the middle

*   When the distribution is not shaped like this, the measures give different results.
*   If the scores are skewed to the left as shown in Figure 7.3, the mode is to the left, the mean is to the right and the median is in-between.
*   If the scores are skewed to the right as shown in Figure 7.4, the mode is to the right, the mean is to the left and the median is in-between.
*   For most purposes the mean is the most frequently used of the three measures.

    We suggest you now carry out Exercise 7.1.

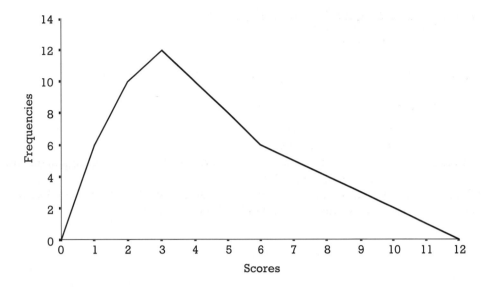

Figure 7.3 A distribution of scores skewed to the left

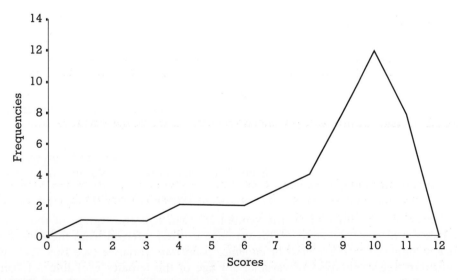

Figure 7.4 A distribution of scores skewed to the right

EXERCISE 7.1   CALCULATING MEASURES OF CENTRAL TENDENCY

Calculate the mode, median and mean life satisfaction of the 10 females in Table 6.1. You may like to use Worksheet 7.1 to work these out.

MEASURES OF DISPERSION

There are three main measures for describing the dispersion of a distribution called the *range*, the *variance* and the *standard deviation*. Of these, the standard deviation is probably the most commonly used.

Range

The range is simply the difference between the lowest and the highest score in a distribution. For example, the lowest score for age in Table 6.1 is 18 and the highest score is 55, therefore the range of ages is 37 years (55 – 18 = 37). The range is easy – just remember that it is a single value in statistics.

Variance

Variance is a measure of the amount of variation in *all* of the scores on a variable. This is distinct from range which only involves the extremes of the values.

Variance is essentially the average of the squared deviations of scores from the mean of the scores on a variable. The formula for variance is as follows:

$$\text{Variance} = \frac{\text{Sum of squared differences of each score from its mean}}{\text{Number of scores}}$$

$$= \frac{\sum (X - \bar{X})^2}{N}$$

This formula says exactly what variance is. It is the averaged squared deviation. The trouble with this formula is that it is slightly laborious to calculate since it involves a lot of subtracting. It is more useful to apply the following computational formula which is quicker to calculate as it involves fewer steps:

$$\text{(Computational formula) Variance} = \frac{\text{Sum of squared scores} - \dfrac{\text{Squared sum of scores}}{\text{Number of scores}}}{\text{Number of scores}}$$

The variance is sometimes given the symbol σ^2 (which is the square of the Greek symbol sigma, or sigma squared). This variance is often referred to as the *population* variance as opposed to the *sample* or *estimated population* variance (see Box 7.1). We shall illustrate the calculation of variance for age of the females in Table 6.1 using Worksheet 7.2.

The interpretation of variance is not easy because its value depends on the measurement taken. Measurements which have a big range will have a greater variance than measurements with a smaller range of scores. In other words, the value of variance is describing features of your data. Of course, it is possible to compare the variance of the scores of one group of participants with the variance of another group of participants. For example, you can compare the scores of males and females on age because they are being compared on something which is similar.

Standard deviation

The standard deviation may be thought of as the average difference of the scores from the mean of the distribution. It is a little more complicated than that in that the deviations or differences are initially squared and then averaged to form what is called the *variance*. Taking the square root of the variance converts the mean squared deviations into units similar to the original ones (i.e. units which are unsquared).

The usual way of trying to summarise such a series of calculations is to present them in terms of a formula. The standard deviation has the following formula:

$$\text{Standard deviation} = \sqrt{\frac{\text{Sum of squared difference of each score from its mean}}{\text{Number of scores}}}$$

$$= \sqrt{\frac{\sum\left(X - \overline{X}\right)^2}{N}}$$

We can calculate the standard deviation using this formula. However, unless we do not round the decimal places when working out the mean, in many cases it will give a slightly less accurate standard deviation than that calculated with what is called the computational formula. The computational formula is simply another way of working out the standard deviation which involves later and less dividing. The computational formula of the standard deviation is:

$$\text{Standard deviation} = \sqrt{\frac{\text{Sum of squared scores} - \dfrac{\text{Squared sum of scores}}{\text{Number of scores}}}{\text{Number of scores}}}$$

The calculation of standard deviation simply involves taking the square root of the variance. The square root of the variance of age (128.61) for females in Table 6.1 gives a standard deviation of 11.34 ($\sqrt{128.61} = 11.34$).

- The population standard deviation is sometimes given the symbol σ (which is the Greek symbol sigma).
- In reports the standard deviation is often abbreviated as SD.

We recommend that at this point you do Exercise 7.2.

Worksheet 7.2 for variance

Step 1: Copy the following table and insert your scores. Carry out the calculations as instructed.

Insert scores below for *variable* Age X	Square each score X^2
18	324
21	441
25	625
20	400
35	1225
27	729
43	1849
55	3025
28	784
41	1681
$\sum X$ = total of above scores = 313	$\sum X^2$ = total of above squares = 11083
$\left(\sum X\right)^2$ = above total squared = 97969	N = number of scores = 10

Step 2: Substitute the above calculated values in the computational formula:

$$\text{Variance}_{\text{computational formula}} = \frac{\sum X^2 - \frac{\left(\sum X\right)^2}{N}}{N}$$

$$= \frac{11083 - \frac{97969}{10}}{10}$$

$$= \frac{11083 - 9796.90}{10}$$

$$= \frac{1286.10}{10}$$

$$= 128.61$$

Reporting your findings

There is not a great deal that needs to be reported about your variance calculation and it is more usual to give the standard deviation as calculated in Worksheet 7.3 anyway. Probably the best way of reporting the variance is as part of a table which gives the names of each of the score variables in your study and important descriptive statistics such as the mean, median, mode and variance under separate columns. Alternatively, if there are just one or two variables, the values of the descriptive statistics can be put in your report when you mention the variable. You might write something like 'The mean age was 32.6 years ($\sigma^2 = 128.61$, mode = 21 years).'

EXERCISE 7.2 CALCULATING MEASURES OF DISPERSION

Calculate the range, variance and standard deviation of life satisfaction of the 10 females in Table 6.1. You may like to use Worksheet 7.3 to work out the standard deviation which involves calculating the variance.

Worksheet 7.3 for standard deviation

Step 1: Copy the following table and insert your scores. Carry out the calculations as instructed.

Insert scores below for *variable* Age X	Square each score X^2
18	324
21	441
25	625
20	400
35	1225
27	729
43	1849
55	3025
28	784
41	1681
$\sum X$ = total of above scores = 313	$\sum X^2$ = total of above squares = 11083
$\left(\sum X\right)^2$ = above total squared = 97969	N = number of scores = 10

Step 2: Substitute the above calculated values in the computational formula:

$$\text{Standard deviation}_{\text{(computational formula)}} = \sqrt{\dfrac{\sum X^2 - \dfrac{\left(\sum X\right)^2}{N}}{N}}$$

$$= \sqrt{\dfrac{11083 - \dfrac{97969}{10}}{10}}$$

$$= \sqrt{\dfrac{11083 - 97969.90}{10}}$$

$$= \sqrt{\dfrac{128.61}{10}}$$

$$= \sqrt{128.61}$$

$$= 11.34$$

Reporting your findings

As with the other descriptive statistics discussed in this chapter, if you have several variables then probably the easiest way of reporting your findings is to draw up a table listing the separate variables as the rows and the different descriptive statistics as the columns. If you have only one or two variables then you can write things such as 'The mean age was 32.6 years (s.d. = 11.34, mode = 21 years).'

BOX 7.1   VARIANCE AND STANDARD DEVIATION: ESTIMATES OR NOT?

- In this chapter we have discussed the variance and standard deviation of a set of scores. Their computation has been shown.
- However, it is fairly common practice in psychology to use slightly different formulae for these calculations. The difference is the lower part of the formulae where we have told you to divide by the sample size (or N). These alternative formulae tell you to divide instead by $N–1$.
- Why the difference? The answer is that when you divide by $N–1$ you are actually calculating the variance estimate or the standard deviation estimate.

$$\text{Variance estimate} = \frac{\text{Sum of squared scores} - \dfrac{\text{Squared sum of scores}}{\text{Number of scores}}}{\text{Number of scores} - 1}$$

$$\text{Standard deviation estimate} = \sqrt{\frac{\text{Sum of squared scores} - \dfrac{\text{Squared sum of scores}}{\text{Number of scores}}}{\text{Number of scores} - 1}}$$

- What are these estimates of? Well they are estimates of the population variance and the population standard deviation based on the data from a sample. As you can see, they give higher values than division by N would.
- Some researchers always use the above formulae on the grounds that in research we are always trying to use samples to estimate the characteristics of the population. Unfortunately, when learning statistics these formulae do nothing to clarify the concepts.
- We would suggest that you identify when you are using the variance estimate or the standard deviation estimate by adding the term 'estimate'.
- The concepts of sample and population are discussed in detail in Chapter 8.

SHAPE OF DISTRIBUTIONS

Although there are statistical measures for doing this, it is often useful to plot the distribution of scores to gain a diagrammatic impression of their shape.

Where there is a large range of scores and many of the scores in that range have low frequencies or are not represented, it may be helpful to group the scores together into larger units of equal range. An example of such a case is age in Table 7.4 which has a range of 37 years and where only 19 of these are represented, with 18 of them only containing one individual. We could group these 19 ages into larger units containing a range of 10 years each, starting at age 16. Thus the first group would contain ages 16 to 25, the second group ages 26 to 35, the third group ages 36 to 45 and the fourth

Table 7.4 Table showing the ungrouped frequency data

Age	Frequency
18	1
19	1
20	1
21	2
24	1
25	1
26	1
27	1
28	1
31	1
34	1
35	1
37	1
41	1
43	1
44	1
49	1
53	1
55	1

Table 7.5 Table showing the frequency of people grouped into four age categories

Age range (years)	Grouped frequency
16–25	7
26–35	6
36–45	4
46–56	3

group ages 46 to 55. If we did this, the frequencies of cases in these larger age groups would be respectively as shown in Table 7.5. Re-arranged in this way, we can more readily see that the distribution is skewed to the left with more people in the younger age range.

The normal curve

One advantage of the standard deviation as a measure of dispersion is that when the distribution of scores is what is called *normal* and is bell-shaped as shown in Figure 7.5, the percentages of cases that fall within any two values of the variable can be obtained from tables.

This involves using the following formula first of all:

$$z = \frac{\text{a score} - \text{the mean of the set of scores}}{\text{the standard deviation of the set of scores}}$$

So, z is merely the number of standard deviations the particular score is from the mean of the set of scores.

If the distribution is normal in shape (normally distributed), then a score which is one standard deviation from the mean (i.e. its z-score = 1 or –1) will be among the 68.26 per cent of scores closest to the mean. This is one standard deviation above or below the mean. In other words, over two-thirds of scores are within one standard deviation of the mean if the distribution is normally distributed.

A score which is two standard deviations or less from the mean (either above or below it) is in the middle 95.44 per cent of scores. In other words, over 95 per cent of scores are within two standard deviations of the mean. Fewer than 5 per cent are more than two standard deviations from the mean.

Finally, 99.70 per cent of scores are within three standard deviations of the mean. In other words, very few scores are more than three standard deviations from the mean.

It should be apparent that if the scores are normally distributed, the standard deviation contains a great deal of information about the distribution of the scores.

DIAGRAMS

There are two main ways we can represent distributions of scores diagrammatically, called *histograms* and *polygons*, which are relatively easy to draw on graph paper.

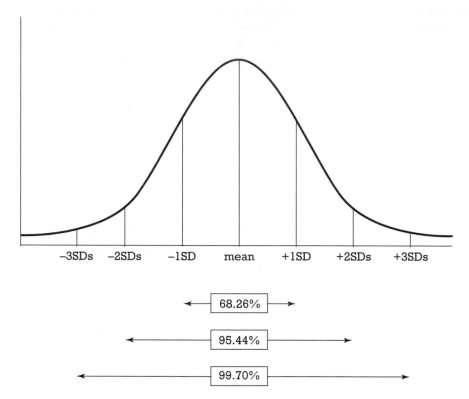

Figure 7.5 A normal distribution of scores with percentages of cases falling within 1, 2 and 3 standard deviations on either side of the mean

Histograms

In a histogram the frequency of each score in a range of scores is represented by a rectangle whose height reflects its frequency. Taller rectangles signify larger frequencies. A histogram of the life satisfaction scores for the 20 individuals in Table 6.1 is presented in Figure 7.6. The midpoint of the base of the rectangle corresponds to the score itself while the upward lines on either side correspond to the lower and upper limits of that score respectively. So, for example, the lower and upper *limits* of the life satisfaction score of 11 are 10.50 and 11.49 respectively, and of 12 the limits are 11.50 and 12.49 respectively. Note that the life satisfaction scores are not normally distributed but skewed to the right.

Getting histograms right

The basics of drawing a histogram are not too difficult. The problem is that your first efforts may not be very impressive. One common reason for this is that if you have relatively little data then you normally need to express scores in *bands* rather than as individual scores. Much of the research done by students tends to involve relatively few cases.

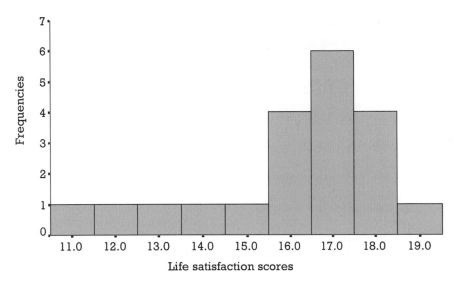

Figure 7.6 A histogram of life satisfaction scores

Take, for example, the following data. There are in total 22 scores:

13, 15, 10, 7, 16, 5, 12, 8, 7, 11, 12, 9, 8, 6, 3, 1, 6, 10, 11, 6, 5, 9

Obviously it is difficult to see any trends here since the data are not in numerical order. You might find it useful to put each of these 22 scores on separate pieces of paper since then they can be moved around and piled up as necessary (Figure 7.7)

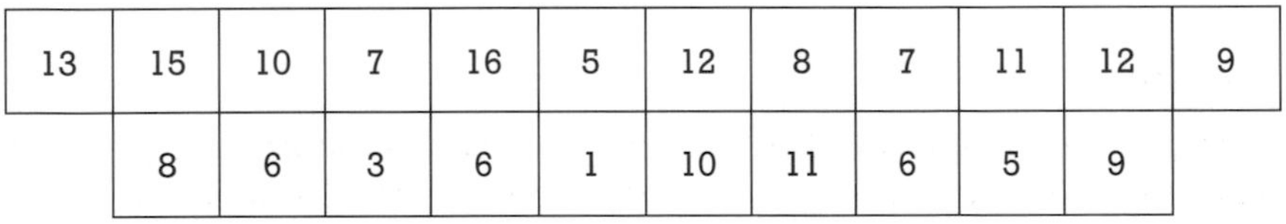

13	15	10	7	16	5	12	8	7	11	12	9
	8	6	3	6	1	10	11	6	5	9	

Figure 7.7 The 22 scores written on separate pieces of paper

These slips of paper can be arranged in numerical order and piled up to indicate how many there are with a particular score on them (Figure 7.8).

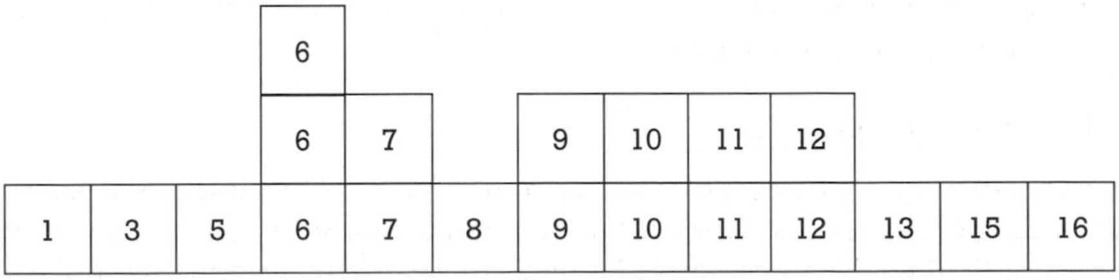

			6									
			6	7		9	10	11	12			
1	3	5	6	7	8	9	10	11	12	13	15	16

Figure 7.8 The 20 pieces of paper put in order and piled up

While this is a direct representation of the data, there are problems with it. The first is that it fails to indicate the absence of scores like 2, 4 and 14. This would be easily dealt with by simply leaving gaps for the missing scores. The second problem is that although it is accurate it is a rather flat distribution. It is possible to sort this problem out too.

Figure 7.9 takes the data and organises them so that all possible scores are included and combines adjacent categories so as to do something about the flatness of the bars which makes trends in the data difficult to recognise.

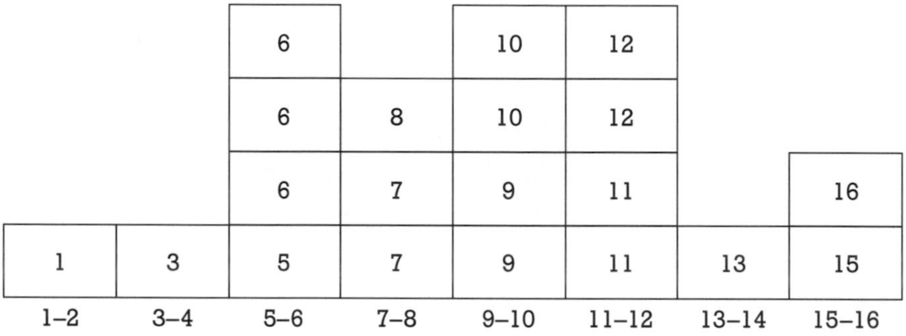

1-2	3-4	5-6	7-8	9-10	11-12	13-14	15-16
		6		10	12		
		6	8	10	12		
		6	7	9	11		16
1	3	5	7	9	11	13	15

Figure 7.9 Histogram showing 20 scores grouped into intervals of 2

This rearrangement makes it more instantly clear that the majority of scores tend to be in the range 5 to 12 and that the distribution is reasonably symmetrical. But there is no reason to leave things like this since it may be worthwhile combining a greater range of scores. Instead of taking intervals of 2, the data in Figure 7.10 are based on intervals of 4.

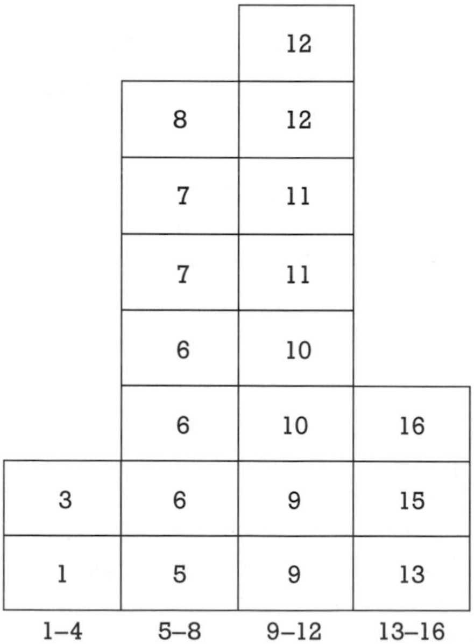

1-4	5-8	9-12	13-16
		12	
	8	12	
	7	11	
	7	11	
	6	10	
	6	10	16
3	6	9	15
1	5	9	13

Figure 7.10 Histogram showing 20 scores grouped into intervals of 4

This seems to be an improvement since it is possible to see the trends instantly. We could combine more scores together but this may not be an improvement – try it.

We can re-draw this histogram in a more conventional form as in Figure 7.11 and include an indication of the frequency of scores.

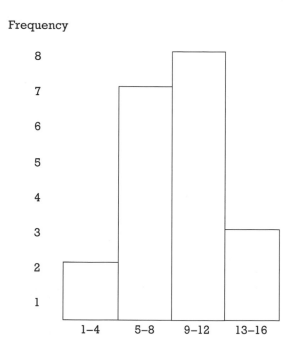

Figure 7.11 More conventional histogram

Although there are no firm rules about the construction of histograms, we would recommend that you combine categories in order to make the data diagram as simple and direct as possible. Diagrams needing a great deal of effort to understand are of little use.

Polygons

In a polygon the frequency of each score in a range of scores is represented by a point whose height reflects its frequency. Higher points indicate higher frequencies. A polygon of the life satisfaction scores for the 20 individuals in Table 6.1 is presented in Figure 7.12. The points are connected by straight lines. The lines are extended to the horizontal axis to the score (10) just below the lowest score (11) and to the score (20) just above the highest score (19) so that the area on either side of the polygon is bounded.

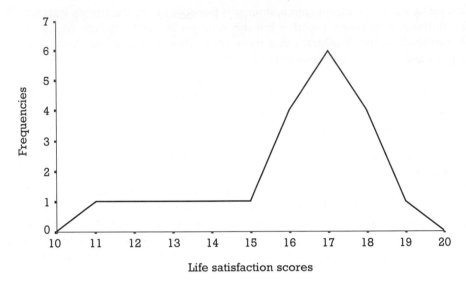

Figure 7.12 A polygon of life satisfaction scores

REPORTING DESCRIPTIVE STATISTICS

At first sight, we have covered much in this chapter and you may be confused as to which of these statistics to include in your reports. They are all descriptive statistics because they merely describe the characteristics of your data.

The short answer is that you should include a complete set of the numerically based indexes and consider carefully whether you would be better using a frequency table or a chart/diagram to give information about the distribution of your data.

With data which consist of scores of the sort this chapter deals with, it is customary to simply report the mean and the standard deviation for the relevant samples. For example, one way of writing up the data in Table 6.1 would be to state that 'The mean age was 31.30 years (SD = 11.95) for women and 33.80 years (SD = 11.84) for men. The mean life satisfaction score was 16.30 (SD = 2.11) for women and 15.90 (SD = 2.23) for men.' Note that figures are given to two decimal places which is sufficiently accurate for most purposes, and the values for the standard deviation are placed in parentheses.

If we had to report the means and standard deviations for a large number of groups or variables, it may be more appropriate to present these in the form of a table such as Table 7.6.

Table 7.6 Means and standard deviations for age and life satisfaction in women and men

| | Women | | Men | |
	M	SD	M	SD
Age (years)	31.30	11.95	33.80	11.84
Life satisfaction	16.30	2.11	15.90	2.23

If the data for a variable are skewed, it may also be worth mentioning this.

SUMMARY

- Score data can be summarised in terms of measures of central tendency, measures of dispersion and the shape of the distribution.
- The mean is the most commonly used measure of central tendency and the standard deviation the most commonly used measure of dispersion.
- The mean, median and mode are the same when the distribution of scores is symmetrical and peaked in the middle.
- About two-thirds (68.26 per cent) of scores fall within one standard deviation on both sides of the mean when the distribution of scores is normal.
- The frequency of score data can be displayed as a histogram, polygon or table.
- When there is a wide range of scores where scores are not represented or have low frequency, it may be useful to group scores together into larger units of equal size.

ANSWERS TO EXERCISES

Answers to Exercise 7.1

The mode is 17, which contains 3 of the 10 scores.
The median is also 17 because both the scores ranked 5th and 6th are 17.
The mean is 16.3 which results from the sum of 163 being divided by 10.

Answers to Exercise 7.2

The range is 7, varying from a minimum of 12 to a maximum of 19.
The standard deviation is 2.00.

8

—

Surveys and sampling

INTRODUCTION

By the end of this chapter you should be ready to start planning your research. We have covered a great deal of background and this hard work should be put to good use.

When carrying out a study it is impossible to test our ideas on everybody in the world. Instead, a sample of people is selected on the assumption that it is representative of people in general.

Generally in psychology the choice of sample tends to be opportunistic using convenient groups of people. This is often acceptable because psychologists tend to assume that their theories and ideas apply to people in general. As a consequence, it would not particularly matter who is in the sample. Hence a lot of psychological research in the past was carried out on university students who participated in their professors' research. So long as it is believed that one is studying a universal psychological process there is little wrong with this. However, this sort of thinking encourages potentially misleading assumptions such as that processes of memory are the same in university students as in elderly people. Despite the obvious difficulties with this approach it remains common. This chapter presents an overview showing how sampling can be done better and how to analyse the results of surveys based on samples.

EXAMPLES OF THE USE OF SURVEYS

Surveys are basically counts of the numbers or proportions of people who think a particular way about a topic, or have had particular sorts of experiences, or have a particular sort of lifestyle, or who differ in any number of ways.

Sometimes information from surveys can be vitally important. For example, surveys of domestic violence revealed far higher levels than once was thought to be the case, surveys of sexual behaviour revealed much that was unknown about sex and sexuality, and surveys have revealed useful information about the distribution of mental illness in the general population.

Surveys, then, can help to identify important findings about people and help establish priorities for more research.

WHAT IS SAMPLING?

This is a bit obvious. Sampling is the process of drawing samples.

A sample is a small selection from a population. There is a confusing feature to this. In statistics the sample is a small selection of all of the *scores* on a variable (i.e. the population of scores on that variable). Away from statistics, we tend to think of a sample as a number of people drawn from a population of people. Or perhaps, a sample of rats drawn from a population of rats. These two somewhat distinct ways of looking at samples are often spoken of as if they were more similar than they actually are.

Sampling is a very much neglected aspect of psychological research. Frequently, psychologists use any convenient group of participants in their research. Thus a great deal of research is based on students in an introductory psychology class, patients in the hospital where the researcher works, or youngsters in a local school.

Generally speaking, such groups cause no particular problems other than the fact that they are drawn from a very limited selection of the sorts of people who psychologists should be studying. The reason why this is more or less acceptable is that psychologists are often more interested in relationships between two or more variables than they are in getting precise estimates of how those variables are distributed in the population. So they are concerned about the size of, for example, the association between creativity and mental illness rather than how common creativity or mental illness is in the population.

BOX 8.1 WHAT IS RANDOM SAMPLING?

- In random sampling you need to have a list of all of the members of the population in question. This is the sampling frame.
- Random samples are subsets or subgroups of the population selected in a way which gives each member of the population an equal chance of being selected.
- Any other selection method is biased – meaning that some cases have a better chance of being selected than others.
- Drawing names out of a hat (provided that each name occurs only once) and the slips of paper feel the same and are well shaken is a good way of selecting a random sample since it ensures that each name has an equal chance of being selected.
- Notice that random sampling involves a degree of rigour and organisation. It is not a haphazard process but a carefully regulated one.
- Selecting a sample of people on the basis that they seem very varied or on the grounds that you think you are being unbiased is *not* random sampling. Random sampling must involve a demonstrably random selection process.

You may have noticed that some researchers take much greater care to obtain a wider selection of people than this. Think, for example, of the market research interviewers who approach you in the street or the public opinion pollsters who may telephone you. Their objectives are not satisfied by interviewing the most easily obtained group of people. They reject people who are not in their chosen categories and actively seek other types of people. This is because they require people representative of people in general and people representative of a particular type of consumer.

You may also remember seeing election broadcasts in which predictions are made about the likely election result from a public opinion poll of, say, one or two thousand voters. This sort of research requires precise estimates of the voting intentions of a sample of the population of voters.

TYPES OF SAMPLING

Sampling is an inescapable feature of most modern research. It is simply not practical to do research on all members of the population. Indeed it is one of the achievements of statistics that it has shown how ludicrous it would be to do so. Probably the only exceptions to this are the censuses of citizens periodically conducted by governments in which the entire population is contacted. These are such major undertakings that they are very infrequent.

A range of sampling methods is used in psychological research. They tend to trade off costs (money, labour and time) against precision (randomness/accuracy). It is then important to understand the various compromises inherent in the different sampling methods.

It is wrong to regard precision as the sole criterion for evaluating sampling methods. Precise estimates of population characteristics are not always an important requirement of research. Some of the less precise sampling methods have virtues in certain circumstances.

The main sampling methods are as follows:

1 convenience sampling;
2 snowball sampling;
3 simple random sampling (see Box 8.1);
4 stratified random sampling;
5 cluster sampling; and
6 quota sampling.

They differ largely according to whether (a) randomisation is employed, (b) whether the sampling is organised for the convenience of the researcher, and (c) whether the random sampling is restricted in some way to ensure better representativeness in the sample. Sampling methods are compared in Table 8.1.

Convenience sampling

The term convenience sample indicates a very casual way of obtaining participants for your research.

Table 8.1 Comparison of major sampling methods

	Simple random sampling	Convenience sampling	Snowball sampling	Quota sampling	Stratified random sampling	Cluster sampling
Example	Drawing names from a hat	Using students attending the same school or university	Asking stamp collectors to put you in touch with other stamp collectors	Approaching equal numbers of men and women in the street	Selecting men and women at random from a sampling frame but ensuring that there are equal numbers of each	Randomly selecting people but from a limited number of geographical areas
How random?	Definitely random	Not random	Not random	Not random	Approaches randomness but is not completely so	Approaches randomness but is not completely so
Cost	Can be costly. The list of names from which the sample is drawn may be expensive	Cheap	Relatively cheap	Relatively cheap	Costly	Reasonably costly
Travel	May involve much travel time to obtain each participant	Little or no travel time involved	In most cases the participant will name similar people close by so little travel involved	Reduces the amount of travel involved	May involve much travel time to obtain each participant	Travel is confined to certain areas or clusters but the researchers need to travel to these and within these
Precision	Highly precise estimates of population characteristics are possible	Often it is very unclear what the population is	Generally this is not a precise method of estimating the characteristics of the population	Difficult to estimate and dependent on the quality of the interviewer	The most precise estimates of population characteristics are possible	The precision depends on how well the clusters are chosen
Special comments	Might seem the ideal but it does have drawbacks	The sampling employed in most psychological studies	Only way of sampling with uncommon types of participant	Ensures that a variety of types of people are selected	For many purposes the best	Can be combined with stratified random sampling

Convenience samples consist of individuals who are readily available. As most psychological research is carried out at universities, usually the most convenient group to use in research is university students studying psychology. Psychology students are clearly not representative, say, of the nation's general population. Consequently, one could not use psychology students as a sample of the general population for a study of educational backgrounds.

However, when a psychologist is studying basic psychological processes such as memory or perception which are felt to be common throughout all people, there may be compelling reasons for thinking that a convenience sample is adequate.

The obvious difficulty is that one may wish to study psychological factors that differ greatly among people and groups of people.

Even when using a convenience sample, it is important to obtain basic demographic information such as the age, gender and other background factors. This is of some help in specifying the nature of the sample better.

Snowball sampling

So called because it is a sort of rolling sampling method in which more and more cases are gathered as the research proceeds. Rolling snowballs gather very little other than snow. Snowball samples are hoped to gather the same types of individuals as they go along.

It is very useful for categories of individuals that are relatively uncommon or for which there is no obvious source of suitable people of the desired type. It relies on the probability that people of a particular sort are most likely to know other people of that sort. Thus if one wished to obtain a sample of mothers of triplets then one could seek out a few mothers of triplets who could then be asked if they could help the researcher contact other mothers of triplets. If one wished to contact a sample of antique dealers, it is likely that other antique dealers are among the best source of such contacts.

The major problem with snowball sampling is that there is no guarantee that the mothers of triplets in your sample are typical of mothers of triplets in general. After all, your sample of mothers of triplets consists solely of mothers of triplets who know another mother of triplets.

Simple random sampling

This is the 'classic' approach to sampling a population. Ideally, it requires a sampling frame of *all* of the members of the desired population from which a sample is taken using a random sampling method. A sampling frame is merely a list of all members of the population (see Box 8.2 for more details).

Again ideally, each member of the population would be numbered and the appropriate size sample selected by generating random numbers (possibly using a computer or sequence of random numbers). When the sampling frame contains many cases – the electoral list of a city could include several million names – this is clearly a laborious process.

Sometimes labour saving shortcuts are employed – for example taking every 100th or 80th name on the list after a random starting point. This reduces the labour of sampling but is not truly random at every selection. Furthermore, if the list is structured in some way the selection may be biased. The selection interval used should be wide enough to cover the entire sampling frame. Thus if there are 50,000 people on the sampling frame, and the researcher wants a sample of 100 then every 500th name should be taken.

On geographically spread-out locations, random sampling may result in much travelling time on the researcher's part to collect data. This may be uneconomical especially as people may not be available when they are first contacted.

One further disadvantage of random sampling is that random samples may be very unrepresentative of the population. For example, it is possible with random sampling of a population that has men and women in equal proportions to pick a sample which contains only men and no women. In other words, there are no constraints with random sampling on selecting extreme samples. They may be rare but they are possible. Random sampling will yield representative outcomes only in the long run.

Stratified random sampling

Stratified random sampling is a modified version of random sampling which ensures that the final sample includes people ranging in characteristics and in the desired proportions.

For example, if it was decided that the sample should represent the general population distribution of the sexes, the sampling method has to be planned such that there are approximately equal numbers of men and women. If this is done the sample is said to be stratified by sex.

This is relatively easy conceptually speaking. One could have a hat with women's names in it and another one with men's names in it. If half of the names in the sample are randomly drawn from the men's hat and the other half randomly drawn from the women's hat then this would be a random sample stratified by sex.

In practice, one can randomly sample populations stratified by a range of variables – sex, age group and educational group, for example. This becomes a little exacting if the sampling frame contains no information on the stratifying variables. In these circumstances, a random sample is drawn but when the chosen number of people in a stratification category has been reached, this class of person is not interviewed on discovery they belong to that category. The alternative to this is to draw a random sample but then to weight the cases in ways that make the categories into the right proportions. This will make a difference to the outcome so long as the stratification variable is associated with the dependent variable.

Stratified random sampling is a good compromise between randomness and precision. Unfortunately, in itself, it does nothing to make the collection of data more efficient.

Cluster sampling

As we have seen, simple random sampling from populations in large geographical areas does nothing to reduce travel and related costs over these widespread locations. Cluster sampling confines the research to a limited number of relatively compact geographical areas thus reducing travel and related costs to a certain extent.

How the clusters are selected is of great importance. The usual approach is to choose locations that reflect key features of the diversity of the geographical area from which the clusters are being selected. Thus, a large city, a market town, a village and a rural

BOX 8.2 THE SAMPLING FRAME: THE ESSENTIAL STARTING POINT OF RANDOM SAMPLING

If we remember that drawing names from a hat is a good way of drawing random samples, it immediately becomes obvious that we can only draw a fully random sample if we have a list of all of the members of the population – the names in the hat.

But this list of members of the population is not easy to obtain. Where, for example, would we get a list of all the people living in London if we wished to obtain a random sample of 1,000 Londoners? Obviously we could knock on every door in London and find out the names of each person living at that address. The resulting list would have been time consuming and expensive to prepare. Furthermore, the list may not be that accurate – some people may have left London or died during the time the list was prepared.

Quite clearly, the list of members of the population to be sampled is crucial and hard to obtain. Generally speaking, researchers rely on ready-made lists. For example, if one wished to interview a sample of voters one could consult the electoral lists for an area. These are lists of people entitled to vote in current elections. One might decide to use the telephone directory as an easily available sampling frame or population list.

This is a good idea but not without problems. The electoral list becomes out of date because some households will move for example. Furthermore, for various reasons some people will avoid having their names on the list – to avoid local taxes or to hide from violent ex-partners for example. Telephone directories might seem to be a good sampling frame but they include only people who wish to be listed, one person usually per household, and only people who can afford a telephone. Thus, commonly available sampling frames only approximate the ideal. Skilled researchers have statistical adjustments that compensate for these deficiencies to some extent.

Of course, in some circumstances accurate sampling frames exist. For example, most schools, colleges and universities will have an accurate database on their students. In these and similar circumstances the sampling frame would be accurate for that population – that is students attending that school, college or university.

There are problems though with most sampling frames. They provide only the simplest of information about members of the population such as their name and address. If one required a sample of plumbers, for example, many people would have to be contacted in order to obtain the sample since plumbers are relatively uncommon in the population. Obviously in these circumstances it would be better to obtain a sampling frame of plumbers if that were available. In other words, random sampling can be very cumbersome when there are few of the desired category of individual in any available list. That is one reason why snowball sampling has some advantages.

area might be chosen to reflect this sort of diversity. Obviously, several large cities, several market towns, several villages and several rural areas may be selected as an improvement on the basic strategy. It is difficult to know what clusters should be chosen without having a clear idea of the purpose of the research. The clusters, of course, may be chosen at random but usually are not.

If it is known what the proportions of people are who dwell in the different types of locations it is possible to weight the sub-samples (clusters) in terms of their frequency in the geographical area.

Ideally, cases are selected from the clusters by random sampling.

Quota sampling

This is probably the sort of sampling the ordinary person is likely to be aware of. Many of us have been approached in the street by market research interviewers to take part in a survey or to answer a few questions.

Essentially the interviewer approaches people who appear to fit in categories specified by the interviewer's employer. Interviewers might be asked to obtain a sample of people of which 20 are males between 18 and 30 years, 20 are females between 18 and 30 years, 30 are males between 31 and 55 years, 30 are females between 31 and 55 years, 25 are males above 55 years and 25 are females above 55 years. These proportions will depend on the purpose of the research.

The interviewer does *not* randomly select people in the age and sex categories; the interviewer merely finds people who fit the category. Thus, although somewhat like stratified random sampling, quota sampling involves no random selection. The quotas allow the appropriate numbers in each stratum to be interviewed.

Usually interviewers stand in busy streets at busy times in order to maximise their potential recruits with the least effort. However, other locations could be specified.

Response rates in the selected sample are considered in Box 8.3.

BOX 8.3   RESPONSE RATES

- Response rates describe the proportions of people in the selected sample who finally contribute information to the research study.
- The response rates involve a number of factors:

  a people refusing to take part in the study;
  b failure to contact members of the sample;
  c inadequacies in the sampling frame.

- The percentage of people actually taking part in the study compared with the total number of people approached should be reported.
- The poorer the response rate, the less likely is the sample to reflect population characteristics. People who refuse to participate may be different from those who agree to participate.

STATISTICAL ANALYSIS APPROPRIATE TO SAMPLING

The obvious statistical analysis for the data from a survey is the arithmetic mean score for each of the variables measured. (This calculation is discussed earlier in Chapter 7, pp. 67–8.)

This is fine but there is a problem. Simply giving the arithmetic mean of a sample as the likely arithmetic mean of the population gives a misleading impression. It suggests a greater precision of the estimate of the population characteristics than is really the case. If the data from your sample indicate that people eat cornflakes on average 8.00 times per month there is some doubt as to the likely figure for the population. Since samples can fluctuate quite a lot from the population we are unlikely to be exact as to the population figure.

In these circumstances, we often express the population mean as a range of possible means. Thus, researchers might report that the average number of times people eat cornflakes for breakfast is 8.00 plus or minus 2. This tells us that the researchers think that the true mean of the population from which the sample came lies somewhere between 6.00 and 10.00 with the most likely value being 8.00.

This is known as the *confidence interval* and it is dependent on the variability in answers to the question in the sample (the more variability in the sample the greater will be the confidence interval) and the sample size (the bigger the sample the smaller will be the confidence interval). How do researchers know this?

Actually what they are doing is giving the range of means that includes 95 per cent of the most likely means that could be obtained if the population mean was actually the 8.00 found in the sample data. The population characteristics are assumed to be the same as those of the sample. Mathematics are then used to assess the distribution of means of random samples drawn from that population.

More technically, the variance of the sample of scores is used to estimate the variance of the population from which the sample came. This is known as the *variance estimate*. It is calculated in exactly the same way as the variance but the lower part of the formula tells us to divide by N–1 instead of N. We have already discussed this (Box 7.1) but it is worth emphasising. The formula for the variance estimate for a sample of scores is:

$$\text{Variance estimate} = \frac{\text{Sum of squared scores} - \dfrac{\text{Squared sum of scores}}{\text{Number of scores}}}{\text{Number of scores} - 1}$$

Once we have an estimate of the variance of the population it is a simple mathematical step to work out the likely distribution of the means of samples drawn from that population.

The variance in the means of samples is called the standard error. It is calculated simply by dividing the square root of the estimated variance of the population by the square root of the size of sample involved:

$$\text{Standard error} = \frac{\text{Square root of estimated variance}}{\text{Square root of sample size}}$$

$$= \frac{\text{Estimated standard deviation}}{\text{Square root of sample size}}$$

The final stage involves calculating the range within which the 95 per cent of randomly drawn samples will have their means. This is merely the standard error multiplied by the t-value for the 95 per cent range for the particular sample size in question. This can be obtained from tables. Generally the t-value is around 2.00 (especially with large samples) so roughly speaking the interval including 95 per cent of samples is plus or minus about two times the standard error. More precise values can be obtained from tables.

This 95 per cent range is known as the *confidence interval*. Sometimes one could employ the 99 per cent confidence interval which includes all but 1 per cent of randomly drawn samples.

All other things being equal, the confidence interval tends to *decrease* as the sample size increases. This corresponds to the common-sense view that, within reason, the bigger the sample size the better.

Worksheet 8.1 will help you calculate the confidence intervals for any data. We have included illustrative data. It is based on a survey of the study habits of a sample of university students. One of the questions is 'On average, how many hours do you devote to study in a typical week?' The data were collected from a small sample of ten students.

Some general points on random samples and statistics are given in Box 8.4.

STATISTICAL ANALYSIS FOR SURVEYS

All of the statistics we have dealt with so far arc of use in analysing surveys. Table 8.2 is a list to remind you of the most important statistical procedures for this purpose. One or two more advanced statistics are also listed which you might use as you get more skilled.

You cannot always use all of them but at least they should be considered.

SUGGESTIONS FOR PRACTICAL WORK

Plan a survey of people's attitudes towards or experience of a currently debated issue. For example, you might wish to research people's experience of road rage or their attitudes to a proposed local bypass road. Obviously the more interest you have personally in the topic the more you will gain from this exercise. The practical steps to take are the following:

- prepare a short questionnaire to measure aspects of the chosen issue (see pp. 38–45);
- decide who should be sampled;
- is there a sampling frame that could be used? (see Box 8.2);
- debate and decide on the best sampling method for your study. What does 'best' mean in this context? (see Table 8.1);
- how big a sample will you use?;
- carry out your interviews;
- statistically analyse your data;
- write a brief report of your study and its findings (see Chapter 21).

Worksheet 8.1 for confidence intervals

Step 1: Enter your scores in *Column 2* then square each of these scores separately and enter the value in the adjacent square in *Column 3*. Do the remaining calculations given at the bottom of the table and enter the values.

Column 1	Column 2	Column 3	Column 4	Column 5
Case	Score X	Square score X^2	t- for 95% range	Degrees of freedom ($N-1$)
1	20	400		
2	15	225	12.71	1
3	27	729	4.30	2
4	30	900	3.18	3
5	25	625	2.78	4
6	29	841	2.57	5
7	23	529	2.45	6
8	27	729	2.37	7
9	40	1600	2.31	8
10	26	676	2.26	9
11			2.23	10
12			2.20	11
13			2.18	12
14			2.16	13
15			2.15	14
16			2.13	15
17			2.12	16
18			2.11	17
19			2.10	18

20			2.09	19
21			2.09	20
22			2.08	21
23			2.07	22
24			2.07	23
25			2.06	24
26			2.06	25
27			2.06	26
28			2.05	27
29			2.05	28
30			2.04	29
	$\sum X$ = total of above scores = 262	$\sum X^2$ = total of above squares = 7254		
	$\left(\sum X\right)^2$ = above total squared = 262^2 = 68644	N = number of scores = 10		

N = the number of scores = 10

N–1 = the degrees of freedom = 10 – 1 = 9

$$\text{Mean} = \frac{\sum X}{N} = \frac{262}{10} = 26.2$$

Step 2: Substitute the above values into the standard deviation computational formula:

$$\text{Estimated standard deviation} \quad (\text{sd}) = \sqrt{\frac{\sum X^2 - \frac{\left(\sum X\right)^2}{N}}{N - 1}}$$

$$\text{Estimated standard deviation} \quad (\text{sd}) = \sqrt{\frac{7254 - \frac{262^2}{10}}{10 - 1}}$$

$$= \sqrt{\dfrac{7254 - \dfrac{68644}{10}}{9}}$$

$$= \sqrt{\dfrac{7254 - 6864.4}{9}}$$

$$= \sqrt{\dfrac{389.6}{9}}$$

$$= \sqrt{43.29}$$

$$= 6.57$$

Step 3: Divide the estimated standard deviation (sd) by the square root of the sample size (N) on which it was based to obtain the estimated *standard error* of means of sample size N drawn from that population:

$$\text{Standard error} \quad (\text{se}) = \dfrac{\text{estimated standard deviation}}{\text{square root of sample size}} = \dfrac{\text{sd}}{\sqrt{N}}$$

$$= \dfrac{6.57}{3.16}$$

$$= 2.08$$

Step 4: The standard error multiplied by the 5% significant t-value = the 95% confidence interval above or below the sample mean.

Step 5: To obtain the 95% confidence interval turn to a table of the t-distribution for the 5% two-tailed level of significance (e.g. Significance Table 18.1) and look up the value of t which corresponds to the *Row* for $N - 1$ or 9 in our example. A t- table is also built into the above Worksheet. The value of t for our sample with 9 degrees of freedom is 2.26.

Step 6: The 95% confidence interval is the mean ± (se × 2.26).

Step 7: This is 26.2 ± (2.08 × 2.26).

Step 8: Thus the 95% confidence interval = 26.2 ± 4.7
$$= 21.5 \text{ to } 30.9.$$

What does the confidence interval mean? Quite simply it is the range of means which would characterise 95% of random samples drawn from the population.

Reporting your findings

This is fairly straightforward. We would write something along the lines of the following: 'It was found that the mean hours spent studying each week were 26.2 (95% confidence interval = 21.5 to 30.9).'

Table 8.2 Statistical analyses for surveys

Statistical analysis	Purpose	Location in this book
Mean of scores	To indicate the typical or average values on the variable	Worksheet 7.1 pp. 67–8
Range of scores	To indicate the spread of scores	p. 70
Standard deviation of scores	To indicate the variability/spread of scores	Worksheet 7.3 p. 71
Standard error of scores	To indicate the variability in sample means drawn from the population	Worksheet 8.1 p. 92
Confidence interval or Margin of error	To indicate the upper and lower levels likely for the population mean	Worksheet 8.1 pp. 93, 94–6
Correlation*	To explore interrelationships between two or more sets of scores	Worksheet 10.1 pp. 110–23
Chi-square*	To explore interrelationships between two or more category variables	Worksheet 12.1 pp. 142–52

Note
* These are more advanced statistics which are dealt with later in the book.

BOX 8.4 RANDOM SAMPLES AND STATISTICS

Inferential statistics (Chapters 11 and 14) use the concept of random samples. This sometimes leads researchers to the erroneous view that samples need to be randomly drawn to allow statistical analysis to proceed.

However, this is a misunderstanding. Statistics only assumes randomness when testing the null hypothesis. Samples according to the alternative hypothesis are biased samples (as opposed to random samples). That is, in inferential statistics if the hypothesis is true then the sample is in fact a biased sample defined by the null hypothesis.

Null hypothesis testing simply asks the question whether the sample is likely if the null hypothesis is true. The population defined by the null hypothesis is assumed to be randomly sampled to assess the likelihood of the obtained sample coming from the null hypothesis defined population.

This means that it is misleading to suggest that research samples need to be random for statistical generalisation to be permissible. On the other hand, if one wishes to generalise from the sample to a precisely definable population then it is essential to employ random sampling.

Proper random samples are expensive to obtain which means that they are most likely to be used when precise population estimates are involved.

SUMMARY

- Because we cannot include everyone in our research, we have to select a sample of people.
- Fortunately, it has been shown that good estimates of statistical characteristics of the population can be obtained from relatively small samples of people.
- These estimates will vary less the bigger the sample.
- Most psychological research is based on convenience or non-random sampling.
- Random sampling assumes that everyone in the population has an equal and known probability of being selected.
- Random sampling is essential when we want to determine how common a particular characteristic is in the population.
- In most psychological research, however, we are simply interested in determining the extent to which two variables may be related or whether two or more groups differ.
- There are a wide variety of sampling methods ranging from snowball sampling to clustered random sampling. These each have their advantages and disadvantages which depend partly on the purpose of the research.

Part III

Exploring correlational relationships in survey/ non-experimental studies

9

—

Examining relationships between two variables

INTRODUCTION

So far we have examined individual variables dealt with one at a time. Much psychological research depends not on the analysis of variables taken in isolation but on the interrelationships between variables. More often than not, psychologists investigate the relationship between at least *two* variables. For example, is there a relationship between extraversion and criminality? Is there a relationship between age and speed of reaction time to a stimulus? Is there a relationship between intelligence and income? In each of these cases, there are two separate variables we wish to relate to each other. Statistics provides both numerical and graphical methods of describing the size of these relationships.

In this chapter we will explore the possible relationships between variables and the use of scattergrams to show visually the nature of the relationships. It cannot be emphasised too much how important it is to *examine visually* scattergrams of the relationships between your variables. It is a serious error to fail to do so.

POSSIBLE RELATIONSHIPS BETWEEN VARIABLES

Suppose, for example, we wanted to find out what the relationship is between working hard at school or university and being intelligent. We could hypothesise that there are four main possibilities as shown in Figure 9.1.

Possibility 1: Students who are more intelligent may work harder because they enjoy the work more

In this situation, people who obtain a high rank (or score) on intelligence would also obtain a high rank (or score) on working hard. Such a relationship is known as a *positive*

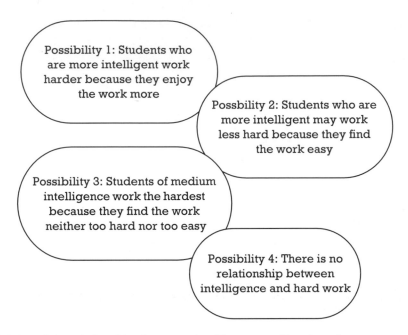

Figure 9.1 Possible relationships between intelligence and hard work

or *direct* relationship. If we hypothesised such a relationship we could say that working hard at school was expected to be positively (or directly) related to intelligence.

Suppose, for example, we have a small sample of five individuals who score in exactly the same order in terms of both intelligence and hard work. This means that the person who has the highest intelligence also has the highest score for hard work, the person who is scored second in intelligence scores second for hard work and so on as shown in Table 9.1. When two sets of scores are directly proportional to each other we have an example of a *perfect* linear relationship – in this case between intelligence and hard work.

Table 9.1 An example of a perfect positive linear relationship between intelligence and hard work

Individual	Intelligence	Hard work
1	1	1
2	2	2
3	3	3
4	4	4
5	5	5

This relationship could be presented as a *scattergram* or *scatterplot* as shown in Figure 9.2. In a scatterplot the vertical axis represents the values of one variable (say, working hard) while the horizontal axis represents the values of the other variable (intelligence). The position of each individual is plotted according to the values of the two variables.

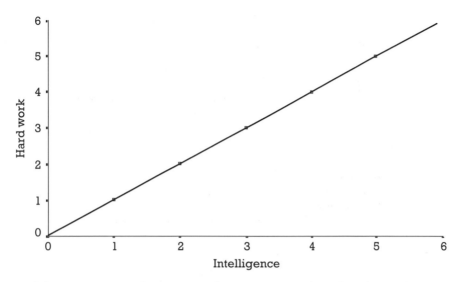

Figure 9.2 A scattergram showing a perfect positive relationship between intelligence and hard work

So, for example, Individual 1's scores on intelligence and hard work are represented by the first point on the left hand side. The point is at the intersection of a line drawn at right angles to a score of 1 on the vertical axis and a line drawn at right angles to a score of 1 on hard work. Scatterplots are best drawn on graph paper.

Notice how all of the points lie on a single straight line which can connect all of the points. This only happens when there is a perfect relationship between two variables. Because in this case there is a perfect relationship between the two variables, a straight line can be drawn to connect them.

A perfect linear relationship between two variables is highly unusual in psychology. So unusual that many researchers would check for errors if they found one. It is much more common for the points to be scattered quite widely about a line such as that shown in Figure 9.3 which is a visual representation of the data in Table 9.2. In such cases a straight line may be drawn which shows the general trend of these points.

This is an example of a positive relationship between two variables. In a positive relationship the scatter of points stretches across the scattergram from the lower left

Table 9.2 An example of a positive linear relationship between intelligence and hard work

Individual	Intelligence	Hard work
1	1	2
2	2	1
3	3	5
4	4	3
5	5	4

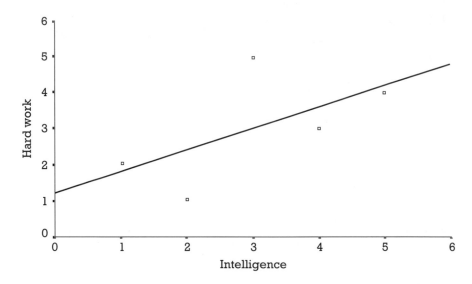

Figure 9.3 A scattergram showing a positive relationship between intelligence and hard work

corner to the upper right one. This is because values become progressively larger as we move from left to right on the horizontal axis and from the bottom to the top of the vertical axis.

Possibility 2: Students who are more intelligent may work less hard because they find the work easier

In this situation, people who obtain a high score on intelligence would obtain a low score on working hard. Such a relationship is known as a *negative* or *inverse* relationship. If we hypothesised such a relationship then working hard at school is expected to be negatively (or inversely) related to intelligence.

The data in Table 9.3 illustrate a negative relationship between intelligence and hard work. These data are presented in the scattergram in Figure 9.4. Note that with a negative relationship, the scatter (and the trend line that runs through it) extends across the scattergram from the upper left corner to the lower right one.

Table 9.3 An example of a negative linear relationship between intelligence and hard work

Individual	Intelligence	Hard work
1	1	4
2	2	5
3	3	3
4	4	1
5	5	2

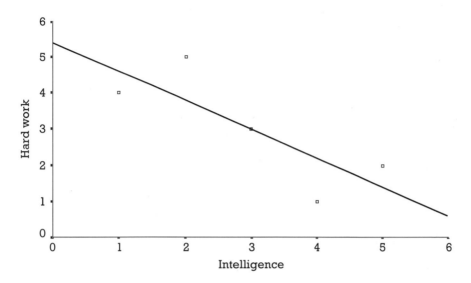

Figure 9.4 A scattergram showing a negative relationship between intelligence and hard work

Possibility 3: Students who are either not very intelligent or very intelligent may work less hard because either they find the work too difficult or too easy

In this situation, people who obtain either a high or a low rank (or score) on intelligence would obtain a low rank (or score) on working hard. Such a relationship is known as a *curvilinear* or *non-linear* relationship. If we hypothesised such a relationship then working hard at school is expected to be curvilinearly related to intelligence. People with high or low intelligence work less hard than people with intermediate intelligence.

The data in Table 9.4 demonstrate such a U-shaped curvilinear relationship between intelligence and hard work. These data are shown in the scattergram in Figure 9.5. There are numerous shapes of curvilinear relationship. Note that with a U-shaped curvilinear relationship, the 'best' fitting straight line runs more or less horizontally across the scattergram but the points fit the straight line extremely badly. Such a line does not show a real trend.

Table 9.4 An example of a curvilinear relationship between intelligence and hard work

Individual	Intelligence	Hard work
1	1	1
2	2	4
3	3	5
4	4	3
5	5	2

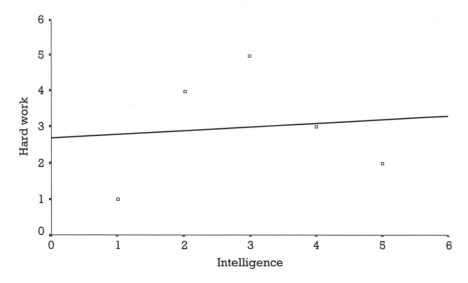

Figure 9.5 A scattergram showing a curvilinear relationship between intelligence and hard work

With a curvilinear relationship, there *may* be a good fitting line between the points of the scattergram but it will *not* be a straight line.

Possibility 4: There is no relationship between intelligence and hard work

The data in Table 9.5 show no relationship between intelligence and hard work. Figure 9.6 presents a scattergram of these. Note that there is no particular pattern to the scatter of points.

There is no good fitting straight line for a scattergram showing no relationship. Any line you draw will be as bad as any other line. The usual way of indicating no relationship between the two variables is to draw a straight line horizontally amidst the points of the scattergram.

Table 9.5 An example of no relationship between intelligence and hard work

Individual	Intelligence	Hard work
1	1	2
2	2	5
3	3	3
4	4	1
5	5	4

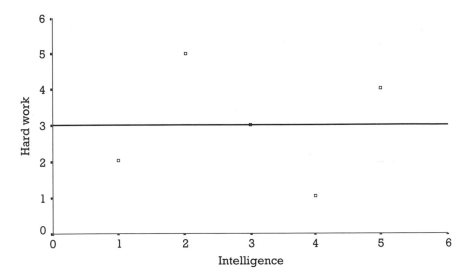

Figure 9.6 A scattergram showing no relationship between intelligence and hard work

Problems to consider

The scattergram is *essential* when interpreting relationships between two variables. *Without a visual examination of a scattergram the rest of this chapter can be extremely misleading.*

A scattergram is essential for the following reasons:

- You can instantly see from the scattergram whether you have a positive or negative relationship.
- By examining the scatter of the scattergram points around a straight line you can assess whether the relationship between the two variables is strong, moderate or weak. The more scatter the weaker the relationship.
- You can look out for signs that the relationship between the two variables departs from being a linear one. Do the points on the scattergram appear to be U-shaped or an inverted (upside down) U-shape for example? If they do then you should *not* attempt to fit a *straight* line to the scattergram.
- Finally you can look for the influence of *outliers* on the relationship.

Look at Figure 9.7 which illustrates these remarks on the apparent relationship between intelligence and hard work. Notice that we have added Individual 6 to the data in Table 9.5 to create Table 9.6 and redrawn Figure 9.6, which otherwise shows no relationship between intelligence and hard work. The influence of the outlier superficially suggests that there is actually a relationship between intelligence and hard work. This is shown in the scattergram for these data in Figure 9.7. However, without this outlier we see no relationship at all. Outliers are merely extreme cases which are exceptional and have unwarranted effects. Outliers such as this are easier to identify if you have larger volumes of data.

What to do about outliers is the problem. One approach is to redraw the scattergram based on the middle of the range of data (e.g. cutting out the extreme 10 per cent or so of cases at each end of the scattergram). If the relationship identified from this new scattergram is different from that found previously then outliers *are* having an unwarranted influence. This is not intended as a method of *distorting* your data to get the outcome you are seeking. You should only cut out the points at the extremes – *not* those in the middle as this would really be cooking the books so as to obtain a relationship which is not there.

Table 9.6 An example of data with the influence of an outlier affecting the relationship between intelligence and hard work

Individual	Intelligence	Hard work
1	1	2
2	2	5
3	3	3
4	4	1
5	5	4
6	8	9

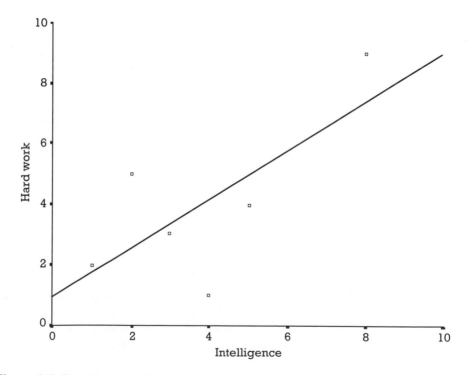

Figure 9.7 Scattergram with outlier

SUMMARY

- When investigating the relationships between variables it is essential to use scattergrams.
- The slope of a scattergram may be positive or negative according to whether there is a positive or negative relationship between the two variables.
- The greater the spread of the points of a scattergram around a straight line, the poorer the relationship.
- No relationship between two variables is indicated by a horizontal straight line.
- Great care should be taken to identify non-linear relationships by visual inspection.
- Equal care is needed to identify outliers (very unusual and extreme cases) which may spuriously create an apparent correlation between the variables.

10

Numerical ways of describing relationships

Correlation coefficients

INTRODUCTION

Although scattergrams are the best way of seeing what your data are like – they are *essential*, and a picture paints a thousand words – for many purposes numerical indices of relationships are useful.

We will show how to compute the following three statistical indices that describe a linear relationship between two variables:

- Pearson's (product moment) correlation;
- Spearman's (rank order) correlation; and
- phi.

These are very closely related and differ largely in terms of the kinds of data to which they are applied.

Pearson's correlation is often symbolised by the italicised letter r; Spearman's correlation by the Greek letter ρ (rho); and phi is the Greek letter ϕ.

Pearson's correlation, Spearman's correlation and phi can vary from a maximum negative value of –1.00 to a maximum positive value of 1.00. A value of –1.00 describes a perfect negative relationship while a value of 1.00 describes a perfect positive relationship.

A value of 0.00 or close to 0.00 may indicate either a curvilinear or no relationship in the case of case of Pearson's or Spearman's correlation. In the case of phi, it simply indicates no relationship since phi describes a relationship between two dichotomous variables (i.e. two variables having only two values each).

These values indicate both the direction and size of the relationship:

- a negative (–) value denotes a negative relationship on the scattergram; and
- a positive (+) value denotes a positive relationship on the scattergram.

SUMMARY

- When investigating the relationships between variables it is essential to use scattergrams.
- The slope of a scattergram may be positive or negative according to whether there is a positive or negative relationship between the two variables.
- The greater the spread of the points of a scattergram around a straight line, the poorer the relationship.
- No relationship between two variables is indicated by a horizontal straight line.
- Great care should be taken to identify non-linear relationships by visual inspection.
- Equal care is needed to identify outliers (very unusual and extreme cases) which may spuriously create an apparent correlation between the variables.

10

Numerical ways of describing relationships

Correlation coefficients

INTRODUCTION

Although scattergrams are the best way of seeing what your data are like – they are *essential*, and a picture paints a thousand words – for many purposes numerical indices of relationships are useful.

We will show how to compute the following three statistical indices that describe a linear relationship between two variables:

- Pearson's (product moment) correlation;
- Spearman's (rank order) correlation; and
- phi.

These are very closely related and differ largely in terms of the kinds of data to which they are applied.

Pearson's correlation is often symbolised by the italicised letter r; Spearman's correlation by the Greek letter ρ (rho); and phi is the Greek letter ϕ.

Pearson's correlation, Spearman's correlation and phi can vary from a maximum negative value of −1.00 to a maximum positive value of 1.00. A value of −1.00 describes a perfect negative relationship while a value of 1.00 describes a perfect positive relationship.

A value of 0.00 or close to 0.00 may indicate either a curvilinear or no relationship in the case of case of Pearson's or Spearman's correlation. In the case of phi, it simply indicates no relationship since phi describes a relationship between two dichotomous variables (i.e. two variables having only two values each).

These values indicate both the direction and size of the relationship:

- a negative (−) value denotes a negative relationship on the scattergram; and
- a positive (+) value denotes a positive relationship on the scattergram.

SUMMARY

- When investigating the relationships between variables it is essential to use scattergrams.
- The slope of a scattergram may be positive or negative according to whether there is a positive or negative relationship between the two variables.
- The greater the spread of the points of a scattergram around a straight line, the poorer the relationship.
- No relationship between two variables is indicated by a horizontal straight line.
- Great care should be taken to identify non-linear relationships by visual inspection.
- Equal care is needed to identify outliers (very unusual and extreme cases) which may spuriously create an apparent correlation between the variables.

10

Numerical ways of describing relationships

Correlation coefficients

INTRODUCTION

Although scattergrams are the best way of seeing what your data are like – they are *essential*, and a picture paints a thousand words – for many purposes numerical indices of relationships are useful.

We will show how to compute the following three statistical indices that describe a linear relationship between two variables:

- Pearson's (product moment) correlation;
- Spearman's (rank order) correlation; and
- phi.

These are very closely related and differ largely in terms of the kinds of data to which they are applied.

Pearson's correlation is often symbolised by the italicised letter r; Spearman's correlation by the Greek letter ρ (rho); and phi is the Greek letter ϕ.

Pearson's correlation, Spearman's correlation and phi can vary from a maximum negative value of –1.00 to a maximum positive value of 1.00. A value of –1.00 describes a perfect negative relationship while a value of 1.00 describes a perfect positive relationship.

A value of 0.00 or close to 0.00 may indicate either a curvilinear or no relationship in the case of case of Pearson's or Spearman's correlation. In the case of phi, it simply indicates no relationship since phi describes a relationship between two dichotomous variables (i.e. two variables having only two values each).

These values indicate both the direction and size of the relationship:

- a negative (–) value denotes a negative relationship on the scattergram; and
- a positive (+) value denotes a positive relationship on the scattergram.

SUMMARY

- When investigating the relationships between variables it is essential to use scattergrams.
- The slope of a scattergram may be positive or negative according to whether there is a positive or negative relationship between the two variables.
- The greater the spread of the points of a scattergram around a straight line, the poorer the relationship.
- No relationship between two variables is indicated by a horizontal straight line.
- Great care should be taken to identify non-linear relationships by visual inspection.
- Equal care is needed to identify outliers (very unusual and extreme cases) which may spuriously create an apparent correlation between the variables.

10

Numerical ways of describing relationships

Correlation coefficients

INTRODUCTION

Although scattergrams are the best way of seeing what your data are like – they are *essential*, and a picture paints a thousand words – for many purposes numerical indices of relationships are useful.

We will show how to compute the following three statistical indices that describe a linear relationship between two variables:

- Pearson's (product moment) correlation;
- Spearman's (rank order) correlation; and
- phi.

These are very closely related and differ largely in terms of the kinds of data to which they are applied.

Pearson's correlation is often symbolised by the italicised letter r; Spearman's correlation by the Greek letter ρ (rho); and phi is the Greek letter ϕ.

Pearson's correlation, Spearman's correlation and phi can vary from a maximum negative value of –1.00 to a maximum positive value of 1.00. A value of –1.00 describes a perfect negative relationship while a value of 1.00 describes a perfect positive relationship.

A value of 0.00 or close to 0.00 may indicate either a curvilinear or no relationship in the case of case of Pearson's or Spearman's correlation. In the case of phi, it simply indicates no relationship since phi describes a relationship between two dichotomous variables (i.e. two variables having only two values each).

These values indicate both the direction and size of the relationship:

- a negative (–) value denotes a negative relationship on the scattergram; and
- a positive (+) value denotes a positive relationship on the scattergram.

Stronger relationships between variables are represented by larger *numerical* values. As a rule of thumb:

- Values between 0.10 and 0.30 are usually described in words as being low and indicating a small or weak relationship.
- Values between 0.40 and 0.60 are described as indicating a modest or moderate relationship
- Values between 0.70 and 0.90 or larger are described as being high and indicating a large or strong relationship. For example, if we found a correlation of 0.80 between intelligence and hard work, we could say that intelligence was strongly positively related to hard work. Alternatively, we could say that there was a strong, positive correlation between intelligence and hard work.

Pearson's correlation

Ideally Pearson's correlation should be used to describe the relationship between two *score* variables that are both normally distributed. When there are a small number of cases, it might not be possible to determine whether the distribution of scores is normally distributed and it may be more appropriate to carry out a Spearman's correlation test. Spearman's correlation is simply a Pearson's correlation between continuous scores that have been ranked. The advantage of Spearman's correlation is that it ignores the absolute size of the scores and only takes account of their relative size in terms of their order. It is also less likely to be affected by outliers.

Pearson's correlation is the ratio of the variance shared between two variables over the square root of the *product* of the variances of the two variables. (The result of a multiplication is called a product.)

$$\text{Pearson's correlation} = \frac{\text{variance shared between 2 variables}}{\text{square root of the product of the variances of the 2 variables}}$$

If none of the variance is shared between the two variables, then the correlation will be 0.00. If all of the variance is shared between the two variables, the correlation will be −1.00 or 1.00.

Shared variance is simply the variation in variables that they have in common. So, for example, if you measure the height and weight of 20 people, you would expect a relationship between height and weight. However, height and weight do not have all their variation in common. Some people are overweight and others are underweight for their height so there is variation in weight which is not shared with height. Box 10.1 gives details of the formula for the correlation coefficient.

The data in Table 10.1 are used to illustrate the computation of Pearson's correlation as shown in Worksheet 10.1.

We suggest you now try Exercise 10.1.

Worksheet 10.1 for the Pearson correlation

Insert each of the pairs of scores (for variable X and variable Y) side by side in the first two columns below. Then do the calculations as indicated:

Number of pair	X-scores (intelligence)	Y-scores (hours worked)	X^2	Y^2	XY
1	150	12	22500	144	1800
2	110	15	12100	225	1650
3	100	6	10000	36	600
4	90	10	8100	100	900
5	80	8	6400	64	640
	$\sum X = 530$	$\sum Y = 51$	$\sum X^2 = 59100$	$\sum Y^2 = 569$	$\sum XY = 5590$

N = the number of *pairs* of scores = 5. Substitute the above values in the formula:

$$r \text{ (correlation)} = \frac{\sum XY - \dfrac{\sum X \sum Y}{N}}{\sqrt{\left(\sum X^2 - \dfrac{(\sum X)^2}{N}\right)\left(\sum Y^2 - \dfrac{(\sum Y)^2}{N}\right)}}$$

$$\frac{5590 - \dfrac{530 \times 51}{5}}{\sqrt{\left(59100 - \dfrac{530^2}{5}\right)\left(569 - \dfrac{51^2}{5}\right)}}$$

$$= 0.487$$

Or follow these steps

(a) $= \sum XY$ = final row of final column of table above = 5590

(b) $= \dfrac{\sum X \times \sum Y}{N}$ = multiply sum of column X above by sum of column Y above and divide by number of *pairs of* scores $= \dfrac{530 \times 51}{5} = \dfrac{27030}{5} = 5406$

(c) = (a) – (b) = 5590 – 5406 = 184 (*this can be a positive or a negative value*)

(d) $= \sum X^2$ = sum of third column in above table = 59100

(e) $= \dfrac{\sum X \times \sum X}{N}$ = multiply sum of first column by itself and divide by number of *pairs of* scores $= \dfrac{530}{5} \times \dfrac{530}{5} = 280900 = 56180$

(f) = (d) – (e) = 59100 – 56180 = 2920 (*this must be a positive value*)

(g) $= \sum Y^2$ = sum of fourth column in above table = 569

(h) $= \dfrac{\sum Y \times \sum Y}{N}$ = multiply sum of second column by itself and divide by number of *pairs of* scores $= \dfrac{51}{5} \times \dfrac{51}{5} = 2601 = 520.20$

(i) = (g) – (h) = 569 – 520.20 = 48.80 (*this must be a positive value*)

(j) $= \sqrt{(f) \times (i)}$ = square root of (f) multiplied by (i) $= \sqrt{2920 \times 48.80} = \sqrt{142496} = 377.486$

The Pearson correlation coefficient $= \dfrac{(c)}{(j)} = \dfrac{184}{377.49} = 0.487$

Remember!

1 The correlation should be between –1.00 and +1.00.
2 A scattergram should always be produced in conjunction with a correlation coefficient.
3 Although this comes later, it is important to report the statistical significance of your correlation coefficient.

(See Chapter 11 for the statistical significance of the correlation coefficient.)

Reporting your findings

It is not necessary to go into much detail about your statistical analysis when reporting your findings. In this case, we would write something along the lines of the following: 'The correlation between intelligence and the number of hours worked was positive but not statistically significant ($r = 0.49$, $N = 5$, not significant).' Unless the correlation coefficient is statistically significant then we do not claim a relationship between the two variables. Statistical significance for the correlation coefficient is dealt with in Chapter 11. Although the correlation coefficient is moderately large in this example, the small sample size is perhaps worthy of comment.

Table 10.1 Intelligence scores (X) and number of extra hours worked (Y)

Individual	Intelligence score (X)	Hours worked (Y)
1	150	12
2	110	15
3	100	6
4	90	10
5	80	8

EXERCISE 10.1 CALCULATING PEARSON'S CORRELATION

Calculate Pearson's correlation for the hours worked and the intelligence scores of the following five individuals

Individual	Hours worked	Intelligence score
1	6	100
2	12	105
3	8	95
4	10	97
5	15	103

BOX 10.1 THE CONCEPT OF THE CORRELATION COEFFICIENT

As explained in Chapter 7, variance is the mean of the squared differences of the mean from each score. The computational formula for variance is

$$\text{Variance} = \frac{\text{Sum of squared scores} - \dfrac{\text{Squared sum of scores}}{\text{Number of scores}}}{\text{Number of scores}}$$

The variance shared between two variables is calculated by multiplying the difference from the mean for the score of one variable by the difference from the mean for the score of the other variable for each person and then averaging the sum of these products. This shared variance is known as the *covariance*.

If we call one variable X and the other variable Y, the computational formula for covariance is

$$\text{Covariance} = \frac{\text{Sum of products of variables } X \text{ and } Y - \dfrac{\text{Sum of variable } X \times \text{ Sum of variable } Y}{\text{Number of paired scores}}}{\text{Number of paired scores}}$$

Putting together the formulae for covariance and variance we obtain the computational formula for Pearson's correlation as follows:

$$\frac{\dfrac{\text{Sum of products of variables } X \text{ and } Y - \dfrac{\text{Sum of variable } X \times \text{ Sum of variable } Y}{\text{Number of pairs of scores}}}{\text{Number of pairs of scores}}}{\text{Square root of} \left[\left(\dfrac{\text{Sum of squared scores of } X - \dfrac{\text{Squared sum of scores of } X}{\text{Number of pairs of scores}}}{\text{Number of pairs of scores}} \right) \times \left(\dfrac{\text{Sum of squared scores of } Y - \dfrac{\text{Squared sum of scores of } Y}{\text{Number of pairs of scores}}}{\text{Number of pairs of scores}} \right) \right]}$$

Although not immediately apparent, fortunately we can simplify this computational formula algebraically as follows:

$$\frac{\text{Sum of products of variables } X \text{ and } Y - \dfrac{\text{Sum of variable } X \times \text{ Sum of variable } Y}{\text{Number of pairs of scores}}}{\text{Square root of} \left[\left(\text{Sum of squared scores of } X - \dfrac{\text{Squared sum of scores of } X}{\text{Number of pairs of scores}} \right) \times \left(\text{Sum of squared scores of } Y - \dfrac{\text{Squared sum of scores of } Y}{\text{Number of pairs of scores}} \right) \right]}$$

If we do this, the covariance now becomes known as the sum of products and the variance becomes known as the sum of squares. Normally the above formula is given in symbols as

$$r = \frac{\sum XY - \dfrac{\sum X \sum Y}{N}}{\sqrt{\left(\sum X^2 - \dfrac{\left(\sum X\right)^2}{N} \right) \left(\sum Y^2 - \dfrac{\left(\sum Y\right)^2}{N} \right)}}$$

where
r is the symbol for the Pearson correlation coefficient,
X represents the scores on variable X and Y represents the scores on variable Y,
N is the number of pairs of scores,
$\sum$ is sigma or the summation sign which tells you to add several components,
$\sqrt{}$ is the square root sign.

Spearman's correlation

Spearman's correlation can be used when the data are not normally distributed or where the values are too few to determine whether the distribution of values is normal. Spearman's correlation is a Pearson's correlation on data that have been rank ordered. Consequently, begin computing a Spearman's correlation by giving each score on the first variable a rank, and then give each score on the second variable a rank. You then simply calculate a Pearson correlation between these ranks or use the quicker computational formula in Worksheet 10.2.

The data in Table 10.1 will be used to demonstrate the calculation of Spearman's correlation. The outcome of this may be compared with that from the Pearson correlation coefficient.

Rank ordering the scores of the two variables X and Y is done as follows:

- To assign rank orders to the scores of variable X (intelligence), find the lowest score (80 for individual 5) and give this the rank of 1. Next find the second from lowest score (90 for individual 2) and give that the next lowest rank of 2 as shown in Worksheet 10.2. In this case ranking is fairly easy as the scores are in decreasing order of size anyway.
- Assign rank orders to the scores of variable Y (hours worked). Once again find the lowest score (6 for individual 3) and give that the rank of 1. Then find the next lowest score (8 for individual 5) and give that the next rank of 2 and so on as shown in Worksheet 10.2.

Dealing with *ties* is important If two or more scores have the same value (say, 110) then they have *tied scores*. To deal with this situation, add the ranks that would be given to these scores if you could separate them and then divide by the number of scores to give the average of the ranks. Suppose we had two intelligence scores of 110 in Table 10.1 instead of the scores of 110 and 100. The ranks of the two scores would be added together to give a sum of 5 (2 + 3 = 5) which divided by the number of scores (2) would give an average rank of 2.50 (5/2 = 2.50).

We recommend you carry out Exercise 10.2 at this point.

EXERCISE 10.2   CALCULATING SPEARMAN'S CORRELATION

Calculate Spearman's correlation for the hours worked and the intelligence scores of the following five individuals

Individual	Hours worked	Intelligence score
1	6	100
2	12	105
3	8	95
4	10	97
5	15	103

The calculations and answer to this exercise are given at the end of this chapter.

Phi coefficient (correlation)

It is also possible to describe the relationship between two dichotomous category variables such as sex (female and male) and employment status (e.g. full-time employment versus other categories).

With a category variable such as employment status which has more than two categories (e.g. full-time, part-time, homework, student and seeking work), it is necessary either to select the two categories of most interest or to re-categorise the data to create the two categories of interest.

For example, we may be interested in determining whether there is a relationship between sex and full-time work in that females may be less likely to be working full-time. In dichotomising employment status, one of the two categories would be full-time work. The other category could be one of four categories such as part-time work or it could be some combination of the other four categories, such as excluding the category of student but including the other three categories of part-time, homework and seeking work.

The phi correlation is simply the Pearson correlation calculated between the two sets of dichotomous scores of 1 and 2. Its calculation can be shown by the relationship between sex and employment status for the data in Table 10.2.

Employment status will be categorised as full-time versus part-time, homework and seeking work. In other words for the purpose of this analysis, students will be excluded.

For the newly created dichotomous variable of employment status, full-time employment will be coded as 1 and the other three categories of part-time, homework and seeking work as 2. For the dichotomous variable of sex, females will be coded as 1 and males as 2.

Table 10.2 Sex and employment status coded as two numerical values

Individual	Sex	Sex coded	Employment status	Employment status coded
1	Female	1	Student	
2	Female	1	Student	
3	Female	1	Student	
4	Female	1	Seeking work	2
5	Female	1	Seeking work	2
6	Female	1	Full-time	1
7	Female	1	Full-time	1
8	Female	1	Part-time	2
9	Female	1	Homework	2
10	Female	1	Homework	2
11	Male	2	Student	
12	Male	2	Student	
13	Male	2	Student	
14	Male	2	Seeking work	2
15	Male	2	Seeking work	2
16	Male	2	Full-time	1
17	Male	2	Full-time	1
18	Male	2	Full-time	1
19	Male	2	Full-time	1
20	Male	2	Part-time	2

Worksheet 10.2 for Spearman's rho

Remember that this is merely a speedy computational formula which becomes increasingly inaccurate the more ties there are. A tie is merely two or more scores on a variable that have the same values. There may be several values which have tied scores.

Insert your X and Y scores as *pairs* in the first two columns.

X-scores	Y-scores	X[r] Rank each score in the 1st column	Y[r] Rank each score in the 2nd column	D or difference between ranks in the third and fourth column	D² Square the difference
150	12	5	4	1	1
110	15	4	5	−1	1
100	6	3	1	2	4
90	10	2	3	−1	1
80	8	1	2	−1	1
					$\sum D^2 = 8$

N = the number of pairs of scores = 5

Now simply substitute the values of N and $\sum D^2$

$$r\left[\text{Spearman}\right]=1-\frac{6\sum D^2}{N\left(N^2-1\right)}$$

$$=1-\left[\frac{6\times 8}{5\left(5^2-1\right)}\right]=1-\left[\frac{48}{5\left(25-1\right)}\right]=1-\left[\frac{48}{5\left(24\right)}\right]=1-\frac{48}{120}=1-0.400$$

$$=0.60$$

Reporting your findings

It is not necessary to go into much detail about your statistical analysis when reporting your findings. In this case, we would write something along the lines of the following: 'The correlation between intelligence and the number of hours worked was positive but not statistically significant (rho = 0.60, N = 5, not significant).' Unless the correlation coefficient is statistically significant then we do not claim a relationship between the two variables. Statistical significance for correlation coefficients is dealt with in Chapter 11.

The potential relationship between sex and employment status may be more readily seen if we re-organise Table 10.2 as a 2 × 2 contingency table as shown in Table 10.3.

In terms of our hypothesis we are expecting a negative phi value because the higher value of sex (males coded as 2) is thought to be associated with the lower value of employment status (full-time work coded as 1).

The two cells in the contingency table that have the highest frequencies are 'male full-time' and 'female other' suggesting that there is a negative relationship. Note that the total number of individuals is now 14 because the 6 students have been excluded.

Table 10.3 A 2 × 2 contingency table showing the relationship between sex and employment status

| | | Employment status | |
		Full-time (1)	Other (2)
Sex	Female (1)	2	5
	Male (2)	4	3

To calculate phi we simply compute a Pearson's correlation between the numerical values of sex and employment status in Table 10.2 (i.e. excluding the students). This calculation is illustrated in Worksheet 10.3 on pages 120–1.

We suggest you now carry out Exercise 10.3.

Worksheet 10.3 for phi (Pearson's correlation between two sets of dichotomous scores)

Insert each of the pairs of scores (for variable X and variable Y) side by side in the first two columns below. Then do the calculations as indicated:

Number of pair	X-scores Sex	Y-scores Employment status	X^2	Y^2	XY
1	1	1	1	1	1
2	1	1	1	1	1
3	1	2	1	4	2
4	1	2	1	4	2
5	1	2	1	4	2
6	1	2	1	4	2
7	1	2	1	4	2
8	2	1	4	1	2
9	2	1	4	1	2
10	2	1	4	1	2
11	2	1	4	1	2
12	2	2	4	4	4
13	2	2	4	4	4
14	2	2	4	4	4
	$\sum X = 21$	$\sum Y = 22$	$\sum X^2 = 35$	$\sum Y^2 = 38$	$\sum XY = 32$

N = the number of pairs of scores = 14

$$r\left(\text{correlation}\right)=\frac{\sum XY-\dfrac{\sum X\sum Y}{N}}{\sqrt{\left(\sum X^2-\dfrac{\left(\sum X\right)^2}{N}\right)\left(\sum Y^2-\dfrac{\left(\sum Y\right)^2}{N}\right)}}$$

$$=\frac{32-\dfrac{21\times22}{14}}{\sqrt{\left(35-\dfrac{21^2}{14}\right)\left(38-\dfrac{22^2}{14}\right)}}=\frac{32-\dfrac{462}{14}}{\sqrt{\left(35-\dfrac{441}{14}\right)\left(38-\dfrac{484}{14}\right)}}$$

$$=\frac{32-33.00}{\sqrt{\left(35-31.5\right)\left(38-34.571\right)}}=\frac{-1.00}{\sqrt{\left(3.500\right)\left(3.429\right)}}=\frac{-1.00}{\sqrt{12.002}}=\frac{-1.00}{3.464}=-0.289$$

Reporting your findings

In this case, we would write something along the lines of the following: 'The phi correlation between sex and employment status was small (phi = −0.29, N = 14, not significant).' Unless the correlation coefficient is statistically significant then we do not claim a relationship between the two variables. The negative sign in the phi coefficient indicates that males are more likely than females to be in full-time employment. Statistical significance for correla-

---

EXERCISE 10.3   CALCULATING PHI

Work out for the following data the relationship between passing one's coursework and one's exams. Passing is coded as 1 and failing as 2. Begin by summarising the data in a 2×2 contingency table.

Individual	Coursework	Exam	Individual	Coursework	Exam
1	1	1	6	1	2
2	1	1	7	1	2
3	1	1	8	2	1
4	1	1	9	2	2
5	1	1	10	2	2

The calculations and answer to this exercise are given at the end of this chapter.

Point-biserial correlation

Finally, it is possible to compute a Pearson's correlation between a *single* dichotomous variable (such as sex) and a *single* score variable (such as exam marks). The procedure for doing this is exactly the same as that for working out Pearson's correlation although the correlation is usually referred to as the point-biserial correlation.

There is a faster computational formula for computing the point-biserial correlation. However, this was developed before people had computers to help them with repetitive calculations. Nowadays a computer would be used if there were many point-biserial correlations to be calculated.

STEPS WHEN DECIDING ABOUT CORRELATION

There are a number of decisions to be made when using the correlation coefficient. These are summarised in Figure 10.1. It is essential to work through this guide to decide the most appropriate test for your purpose and your data.

SUMMARY

- The minimum requirement for determining a linear relationship between two variables is that the values of the two variables should be capable of being rank ordered.
- Pearson's correlation should be used to describe the linear relationship between two variables whose values are normally distributed.
- Spearman's correlation should be used to describe the linear relationship between two variables whose values are not normally distributed or where the number of values is too few to determine whether they are normally distributed.
- Both Pearson's and Spearman's correlation can vary from −1.00 through 0.00 to 1.00.
- Negative correlations indicate that high values on one of the two variables tend to be associated with low values on the other variable.
- Positive correlations show that high values on one of the variables tend to be associated with high values on the other variable.
- Correlations that are zero or close to zero mean either that there is no relationship between the two variables or that the relationship is non-linear.
- To determine which of these two possibilities applies, it is necessary to draw a scattergram and to look at the plot of the points.
- Correlations between 0.10 and 0.30 indicate a weak relationship; correlations between 0.40 and 0.60 a moderate relationship; and correlations between 0.70 and 0.90 or more a strong relationship.
- Spearmans's correlation is simply a Pearson's correlation on two variables whose values have been ranked.
- The relationship between two dichotomous variables can be indicated with phi, which is a Pearson's correlation.

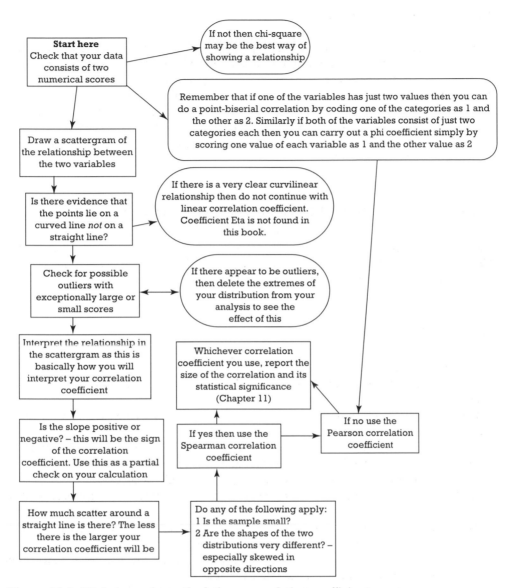

Figure 10.1 Vital steps when calculating a correlation coefficient

- The relationship between a dichotomous variable and a score variable can be described with a point-biserial correlation, which is also a Pearson's correlation.

ANSWERS TO EXERCISES

Answer to Exercise 10.1

Pearson's correlation is 0.61.

Answer to Exercise 10.2

Spearman's correlation is 0.60. This Spearman's correlation is the same as that previously calculated because the rank order of the two data sets is the same.

Answer to Exercise 10.3

Phi is 0.36, indicating that students who pass their coursework tend to pass their exams.

11

Statistical significance of the correlation coefficient

INTRODUCTION

This chapter introduces a crucial concept in research – significance testing. It addresses the basic problem of how we know whether what we find in a sample of data can be generalised to people in general. As research is almost always carried out on samples, this is an essential dilemma of almost all research.

Statistical significance testing is only one aspect of a good statistical analysis of data. It is no more important than carefully examining your data to understand what they imply about your hypothesis.

PROBABILITY OF FINDING A RELATIONSHIP

Regardless of how a sample is selected, how likely is it that the findings apply to what happens to people at large? In other words, what is the likelihood that a research finding is generally true and not simply true for a particular sample?

Suppose, for example, we knew from previous research that there was *no* relationship between how neurotic people were and how introverted they were. That is, neurotic people were no more likely to be introverted than stable people. If we were to measure neuroticism and introversion in a new sample of people, we would generally expect to find the same results as previous researchers had found.

However, if we were to do this on a large number of samples, in a few samples we would find that there was a relationship. In some of these samples neurotic people would tend to be introverted whereas, in other samples they would tend to be extraverted.

We can illustrate this idea with the data in Table 11.1 that represent a population of 20 people. In this population, there is no relationship between introversion and neuroticism.

Table 11.1 The personality of 20 people described in terms of stability (S)/neuroticism (N) and introversion (I)/extraversion (E)

Case	SI, NI, SE or NE	Case	SI, NI, SE or NE
1	SI	11	SE
2	NI	12	NE
3	SE	13	SI
4	NE	14	NI
5	SI	15	SE
6	NI	16	NE
7	SE	17	SI
8	NE	18	NI
9	SI	19	SE
10	NI	20	NE

Each person in this population is either introverted (I) or extraverted (E) and either neurotic (N) or stable (S). In other words, we have four personality types:

1 stable introverts (SI);
2 neurotic introverts (NI);
3 stable extraverts (SE); and
4 neurotic extraverts (NE).

In Table 11.1 there are five stable introverts, five neurotic introverts, five stable extraverts and five neurotic extraverts. Because neuroticism is associated the same number of times with introversion (i.e. 5) as it is with extraversion (i.e. 5) and because stability is also associated the same number of times with introversion (i.e. 5) as it is with extraversion (i.e. 5), there is no association between neuroticism and introversion. This relationship is easier to see if we arrange the data into a 2 × 2 contingency table as shown in Table 11.2. If we calculated phi (pp. 120–21) for the relationship between neuroticism and introversion, we would find it was 0.00, indicating no relationship between the two variables. Remember that phi is just the Pearson correlation between binary category variables *each* scored 1 for one category and scored 2 for the second category.

If, for example, we draw a sample of 8 people at random from this population of 20 individuals, our sample is likely to contain equal numbers of stable introverts, neurotic introverts, stable extraverts and neurotic extraverts because there are equal numbers of these personality types in the population. Do try Exercise 11.1 now.

Table 11.2 A 2 × 2 contingency table showing no relationship between neuroticism and introversion in cases 1–20 of Table 11.1

	Introverted (1)	Extraverted (2)
Stable (1)	5	5
Neurotic (2)	5	5

EXERCISE 11.1 SELECTING 10 RANDOM SAMPLES OF 8 INDIVIDUALS EACH FROM A POPULATION OF 20 PEOPLE

Select 10 random samples of 8 individuals each from the population of 20 people in Table 11.1.

You can use one of two methods for selecting a random sample:

1 Write the numbers 1 to 20 on separate cards or bits of papers. Thoroughly shuffle the cards or bits of paper. Note the first 8 numbers that are selected. Select the 8 individuals from Table 11.1 that have these numbers.
2 Use the random number Appendix in Table 11.A1. Decide which way you are going to work through the table (e.g. moving across each row from left to right down the page). Place your finger on one of the values, then work in your chosen direction. Note the first 8 numbers that range from 1 to 20, ignoring the other numbers. Select the 8 individuals from Table 11.1 that have these numbers.

For each sample, enter below the number of stable introverts (SI), neurotic introverts (NI), stable extraverts (SE) and neurotic extraverts (NE)

Sample 1:   —— SI; —— NI; —— SE; —— NE
Sample 2:   —— SI; —— NI; —— SE; —— NE
Sample 3:   —— SI; —— NI; —— SE; —— NE
Sample 4:   —— SI; —— NI; —— SE; —— NE
Sample 5:   —— SI; —— NI; —— SE; —— NE
Sample 6:   —— SI; —— NI; —— SE; —— NE
Sample 7:   —— SI; —— NI; —— SE; —— NE
Sample 8:   —— SI; —— NI; —— SE; —— NE
Sample 9:   —— SI; —— NI; —— SE; —— NE
Sample 10:   —— SI; —— NI; —— SE; —— NE

Count the number of samples that have an equal number in each group.

However, some samples may contain very unequal numbers of the four personality types, even though they have been randomly selected. So, for example, one sample may consist of the following order of 8 individuals:

Order	Number	Personality
1	10	NI
2	7	SE
3	19	SE
4	2	NI
5	13	SI
6	3	SE
7	6	NI
8	14	NI

This sample consists of 1 stable introvert, 4 neurotic introverts, 3 stable extraverts and no neurotic extraverts as shown in the 2 × 2 contingency table in Table 11.3. A contingency table is merely a way of showing the numbers of cases in the categories defined by two (or more) variables. There is more about contingency tables in Chapter 12.

As there are more neurotic introverts and stable extraverts than stable introverts and neurotic extraverts, there is a relationship between neuroticism and introversion. Because introversion is coded 1 and neuroticism is coded 2, the relationship is a negative one as low scores on one of the variables tend to be associated with high scores on the other variable. If we calculated phi for this sample, it would be –0.77.

Remember that this correlation was obtained solely through chance and that really this sample came from a population where there was truly no relationship.

Table 11.3 A 2 × 2 contingency table showing a negative relationship between neuroticism and introversion

	Introverted (1)	Extraverted (2)
Stable (1)	1	3
Neurotic (2)	4	0

The important point is that even if there is no relationship between two variables in a population, there will be a relationship in some of the samples drawn at random from that population. These samples are not representative of that population. The probability of obtaining such samples is relatively small. However, if our sample was biased in this way and if we did not know what the relationship was in the population, we would falsely conclude that there was a relationship between neuroticism and introversion when there was no such relationship in the population. In most situations, we will not know what the relationship is in the population because if we did there would be no point in trying to determine it. Consequently, we would assume that there was a relationship between the two variables because the probability of this occurring by chance was so remote.

STATISTICAL SIGNIFICANCE

In statistical analysis, we almost always work from the *null hypothesis* (Chapter 1, p. 7) that there is no relationship between two variables. Thus the null hypothesis for our example says that there is no correlation between the introverted/extraverted dimension and the stable/neurotic dimension. In other words, the null hypothesis basically suggests that the correlation between introversion and neuroticism is 0.00.

In significance testing we simply assess from the sample that we have the likelihood that the null hypothesis is true compared with the likelihood that the *alternative hypothesis* (Chapter 1, p. 7) is true.

So in significance testing we work out the likelihood of obtaining a relationship between two variables if there is actually *no* relationship in the population. This population is the one for which the null hypothesis of no relationship is true.

If the chances of a relationship being found between two variables are five times or less out of a hundred, that relationship is unlikely to have occurred by chance. It suggests that a relationship actually exists in the population.

This probability is usually expressed as being less than the proportion of 0.05 (5/100 = 0.05) and is normally abbreviated as '$p < 0.05$' where p stands for 'probability', < for 'less than' and 0.05 for 'five times out of a hundred'.

When a relationship is found which is estimated to occur five times or less out of a hundred, if the null hypothesis was actually true of the population, it is described as being *statistically significant* (or simply as *significant*).

In these circumstances, the relationship obtained in our sample is so unlikely if the null hypothesis of no relationship is true that we prefer to accept that the null hypothesis is probably wrong. If the null hypothesis is probably wrong then the alternative hypothesis is probably correct. So, for the relationship shown in Table 11.3, we would state that there was a statistically significant negative correlation between neuroticism and introversion.

When a relationship is obtained which is estimated to occur by chance more than five times out of a hundred, it is described as being *statistically non-significant* (or simply as *non-significant*). Note it is *not* appropriate to describe such a relationship as insignificant.

Sometimes 0.05 is described as the 5 per cent level of significance, since a probability of 0.05 out of 1 is the same as 5 out of 100 (i.e. 5%). Do try Exercise 11.2 now.

Relationships between two variables can be either positive or negative. The probability of obtaining a relationship between two variables in a sample when there is no relationship in the population takes the general form of the bell-shaped curve or distribution shown in Figure 11.1. The correlation between the two variables will be 0.00 or close to 0.00 most of the time. The likelihood of the correlation being positive or negative is equal so we are as likely to obtain a positive correlation as a negative one. The probability of obtaining a correlation greater than 0.00 decreases with its size since large correlations are much less likely to occur than small correlations if the null hypothesis is true. It is possible to obtain a correlation of +1.00 or −1.00 although it is extremely unlikely. Because bigger correlations are less likely to occur by chance, they are more likely to be statistically significant.

EXERCISE 11.2 DETERMINING STATISTICAL SIGNIFICANCE

Circle which of the following probabilities are statistically significant at the 0.05 level:

(1) 0.0031   (2) 0.0734   (3) 0.1505   (4) 0.0217   (5) 0.0498   (6) 0.0510

Answers to this exercise are given at the end of this chapter.

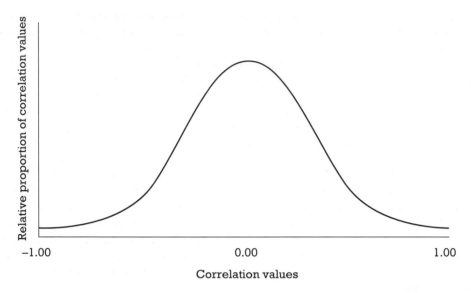

Figure 11.1 Bell-shaped distribution of correlation values when there is no relationship between two variables in the population

What affects significance levels?

Three main factors influence whether or not a relationship is statistically significant:

- The size of the relationship in the population. The bigger the relationship the more likely that tests of significance will identify the sample as *not* coming from a population with a relationship of 0.00 between the two variables.
- The size of the sample used. The bigger the sample we use the better we can estimate what the characteristics of the population are. This is common sense – if you wished to survey how many people live in households with two or more televisions we would put more faith in a sample of 2,000 than a sample of 200 all other things being equal. For example, at the 0.05 two-tailed level a Pearson's correlation of ± 0.30 will not be statistically significant in a sample of 43 or less but will be statistically significant in a sample of more than 44.
- The measure of correlation used. Some measures of correlation are better at detecting differences than others. Usually this is described as the *power* of the test.

It should be obvious, then, that small samples are poor at detecting small relationships whereas large samples will result in us finding small relationships statistically significant.

Thus whether or not you need a small or large sample for your research depends on how strong you estimate the relationship to be and if you are interested in small relationships. This is not an easy decision for beginners to make.

Calculating statistical significance

The calculation of the statistical significance of correlation coefficients is usually done simply by consulting a table which gives the *minimum* sizes of correlation which are significant. If you like, these are minimum cut-off points between statistical significance and statistical non-significance. We will adopt this approach as it is by far the simplest and quickest.

The one slight complication is caused by the fact that the sample size employed has an influence on whether or not a particular correlation will be statistically significant. In practical terms this means that we need cut-off values for different sample sizes.

Some psychologists prefer to use something called *degrees of freedom* rather than sample size. However, this is a rather abstract concept so we have preferred sample size instead. The degrees of freedom for a correlation are two less than the sample size. This will only be useful to you when using significance tables in some other books.

The Appendix Table 11.A2 gives the table of the critical values of the Pearson correlation coefficient for the 0.05 or the 5 per cent level of significance. It includes values for directional and non-directional hypotheses. These are usually referred to as 1-tailed (directional) and 2-tailed (non-directional) tests respectively. Always choose the 2-tailed (directionless) test *unless* you have strong reasons for believing that the relationship will be in a particular direction (that the correlation between the variables will be, for example, negative). Figure 11.2 is a flow chart which should enable you to decide whether to use a directional test.

We suggest you try Exercise 11.3 on page 133 now.

For your particular Pearson correlation coefficient, you simply find the row for your sample size. Put a ruler or pencil mark under that row. Then find the column which corresponds to the 0.05 (or 5 per cent) significance level for a *two-tailed test*. Follow this column down until you reach the marked row. The value given here is the minimum value of the Pearson correlation coefficient which is statistically significant with a two-tailed test at the 0.05 (or 5 per cent) level of significance.

If your correlation coefficient took a negative value then ignore the negative sign briefly while you look up the significance of the correlation in Table 11.A2. However, remember that this is simply a temporary matter while consulting the table and that the sign should remain when reporting the actual value of the correlation coefficient.

Worked example 11.1

- Take the Pearson's correlation of 0.49 in Worksheet 10.1 which is between intelligence and the number of hours worked for five people.
- We go to a sample size of 5 in the first column of Table 11.A2.
- Looking in the second column of Table 11.A2 we can see that Pearson's correlation has to be 0.81 or bigger to be statistically significant at the one-tailed 0.05 level.
- Because our correlation of 0.49 is smaller than this value of 0.81 we would conclude that our correlation is not statistically significant at the one-tailed 0.05 level.
- In other words, intelligence is not related to the number of hours worked at the one-tailed 0.05 level.
- Looking in the third column of Table 11.A2 we can see that Pearson's correlation has to be 0.88 or bigger to be statistically significant at the two-tailed 0.05 level.
- In other words, to be statistically significant at the 0.05 level the correlation has to be bigger at the two-tailed level (0.88 or larger) than at the one-tailed level (0.81).
- Since our correlation is not significant at the one-tailed level, it will not be significant at the two-tailed level.

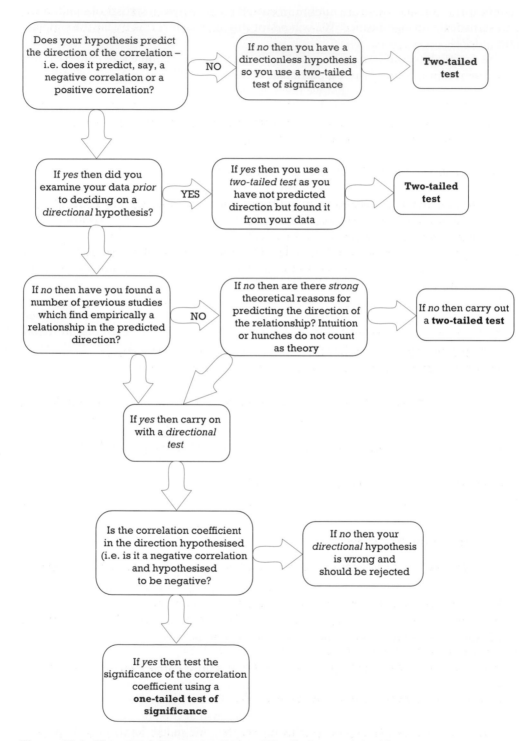

Figure 11.2 Choosing between 1-tailed and 2-tailed tests of significance

- We only use the one-tailed level if we are able to predict the direction of the correlation on the basis of the research literature and if we made this prediction before we collected the data.

We recommend trying Exercise 11.4 now.

EXERCISE 11.3 CHOOSING BETWEEN A ONE- OR TWO-TAILED LEVEL OF SIGNIFICANCE

Which tailed test should you choose if you predicted that being:

1 religious would be related to being superstitious but you did not know if the relationship would be positive or negative;
2 anxious would be positively related to being depressed;
3 extraverted would be negatively related to wearing subdued colours; and
4 popular would not be related to being physically attractive but found it to be positively related.

EXERCISE 11.4 WORKING OUT THE STATISTICAL SIGNIFICANCE OF PEARSON'S CORRELATION

What is the one-tailed t-value for a Pearson's correlation of 0.37 for a sample of 22?

Is this correlation statistically significant at the one-tailed 0.05 level?

Answers to this exercise are given at the end of this chapter.

Reporting your findings

When reporting statistical significance, it is usual to mention the following five features:

- the statistical test used – e.g. Pearson correlation coefficient;
- the statistical value of the test used – i.e. the size of the correlation coefficient obtained including its sign;
- the sample size (or alternatively the degrees of freedom);
- the significance level obtained or an indication that the analysis was non-significant; and
- whether the significance level was 1- or 2-tailed.

You will find that psychologists tend to do this in a standardised form which varies little.

You find statements like:

- 'The correlation between neuroticism and extraversion was calculated using the Pearson correlation coefficient. The correlation was significant ($r = .36$, $d.f. = 38$, two-tailed $p < 0.05$). Thus the alternative hypothesis that neuroticism and extraversion are related was supported.'
- 'It was found that there was no relationship between neuroticism and extraversion ($r = .36$, $d.f. = 23$, two-tailed $p > 0.05$). This supports the null hypothesis and leads us to reject the alternative hypothesis that there is a relationship between neuroticism and extraversion.'
- 'The Pearson correlation between neuroticism and extraversion indicated a significant negative relationship ($r = -.43$, $d.f. = 28$, two-tailed $p < 0.05$). Thus the null hypothesis of no relationship was rejected in favour of the hypothesis that neuroticism is inversely related to extraversion.'

Statistical significance of the Spearman correlation

The Spearman correlation is not quite so powerful as the Pearson correlation coefficient at detecting significant findings. This is because the use of ranks causes a loss of information from the data. Consequently, a larger Spearman correlation is needed in order for it to be as statistically significant as the Pearson correlation calculated on the same data.

The minimum or critical values for a Spearman correlation to be significant are found in Appendix Table 11.A3 which is used exactly as Table 11.A2.

Worked example 11.2

- Take the Spearman correlation of 0.60 in Worksheet 10.2, which is between intelligence and the number of hours worked for five people.
- We go to a sample size of 5 in the first column of Table 11.A3.
- Looking in the second column of Table 11.A3 we can see that Spearman's correlation has to be 0.90 or bigger to be statistically significant at the one-tailed 0.05 level.
- Because our correlation of 0.49 is smaller than this value of 0.90 we would conclude that our correlation is not statistically significant at the one-tailed 0.05 level.
- In other words, intelligence is not related to the number of hours worked at the one-tailed 0.05 level.
- Looking in the third column of Table 11.A3 we can see that Spearman's correlation has to be 1.00 to be statistically significant at the two-tailed 0.05 level.
- In other words, to be statistically significant at the 0.05 level the correlation has to be bigger at the two-tailed level (1.00) than at the one-tailed level (0.90).
- Since our correlation is not significant at the one-tailed level, it will not be significant at the two-tailed level.
- We only use the one-tailed level if we are able to predict the direction of the correlation on the basis of the research literature and if we made this prediction before we collected the data.

SUMMARY

• We calculate the statistical significance of an association between two variables to indicate the probability of that association occurring by chance.
• Associations having a probability of 0.05 or less ($p < 0.05$) of occurring by chance are described as being statistically significant and are assumed not to be chance findings.
• Associations having a probability of more than 0.05 ($p > 0.05$) of occurring by chance are described as being statistically non-significant and are assumed to be chance findings.
• The statistical significance of correlation coefficients can be assessed by consulting significance tables.
• The (negative) sign of the correlation is ignored when doing this.
• A one-tailed test may be used when the direction of the association is predicted with strong justification.
• The following information should be given when reporting an association: (1) the direction of the association; (2) the test used and its value; (3) the sample size, (4) the tailedness of the probability level; and (5) whether the probability level is greater than or equal to and less than 0.05.
• Associations are more likely to be statistically significant with bigger samples.

ANSWERS TO EXERCISES

Answers to Exercise 11.2

Findings with the probability of:

1 0.0031 are significant (because this probability is smaller than 0.05)
2 0.0734 are non-significant (because this probability is larger than 0.05)
3 0.1505 are non-significant (because this probability is larger than 0.05)
4 0.0217 are significant (because this probability is smaller than 0.05)
5 0.0498 are significant (because this probability is smaller than 0.05)
6 0.0510 are non-significant (because this probability is larger than 0.05)

Answers to Exercise 11.3

You should use a:

1 two-tailed level because the direction of the relationship has not been predicted
2 one-tailed level because the direction of the relationship has been predicted
3 one-tailed level because the direction of the relationship has been predicted
4 two-tailed because no relationship has been predicted

However, answers 2 and 3 are only correct if there are strong reasons for making the prediction. For example, if similar previous research has also shown the predicted relationship or if there are justifications on the basis of well-established theory. Chapter 12 has more about this.

Table 11.A1 Random number table

Decide which way you are going to work through the table (e.g. moving across each row from left to right down the page). Place your finger on one of the values (keep your eyes shut to choose this 'random' starting point), then work in your chosen direction until you have found all of the numbered cases you need. 00 represents 100.

66	21	32	77	24	71	59	15	15	31	44	22	69	76	6	24	92	54	96	51	98	69	19	14	16
60	65	81	40	47	15	35	48	44	98	61	52	28	98	32	51	41	99	74	43	68	88	23	46	07
43	10	50	81	00	59	62	26	20	18	82	18	42	46	78	83	34	93	96	93	60	89	27	83	97
32	02	16	30	60	65	09	14	57	70	17	60	58	24	33	79	79	17	16	13	50	51	74	10	39
13	20	94	45	87	04	86	06	07	15	58	14	11	10	81	10	06	15	55	97	46	59	76	20	03
99	28	12	46	17	64	91	94	14	04	71	56	04	99	27	30	85	59	17	25	72	63	52	01	18
45	84	52	96	25	91	57	80	43	73	05	42	54	84	57	88	28	65	55	94	05	50	92	24	07
50	11	00	90	81	88	72	11	37	47	29	26	97	70	72	30	03	93	85	16	74	30	55	85	74
91	59	74	01	01	19	64	64	76	96	58	64	99	13	38	62	89	78	33	81	54	43	01	59	73
00	99	36	20	83	59	08	08	40	76	68	18	37	81	72	59	83	06	72	85	04	37	44	46	01
79	79	76	88	77	27	92	23	29	51	75	79	24	57	88	09	93	26	55	11	40	30	94	46	74
74	42	24	23	58	69	45	53	29	48	32	81	65	65	55	04	08	90	73	61	23	74	27	43	86
91	77	86	65	77	57	85	20	58	33	10	08	67	97	04	52	97	13	93	66	53	44	49	00	64
64	75	40	92	18	29	34	67	03	03	49	68	50	31	52	56	23	77	90	57	16	28	37	77	50
91	71	93	83	26	49	98	93	82	10	35	05	43	91	75	35	69	73	10	25	46	83	98	94	51
61	23	89	18	40	91	76	33	04	18	94	30	04	35	81	41	99	60	44	84	04	92	53	71	40
88	33	01	86	90	86	80	68	46	79	22	96	27	00	35	33	12	06	40	61	44	54	03	44	75
07	86	99	85	20	59	41	56	54	50	16	62	20	61	67	22	69	98	75	14	47	32	42	10	09

Table 11.A1 continued

19	59	79	10	18	64	94	42	80	07	84	73	35	84	64	66	89	32	48	56	97	45
88	21	08	74	31	53	96	93	92	66	85	53	47	05	86	81	41	52	58	44	83	36
52	13	40	67	78	69	49	71	99	73	40	96	24	12	07	63	54	95	41	73	61	79
28	62	22	25	66	20	23	08	35	76	82	35	02	38	88	07	63	84	97	92	76	58
39	82	94	57	26	50	16	86	65	89	71	67	94	44	81	95	39	23	41	40	28	91
54	90	07	12	95	28	82	59	16	03	49	84	99	00	02	94	43	82	67	11	70	06
25	99	86	62	35	68	35	41	20	09	70	94	99	71	93	49	01	77	29	39	04	05
34	49	37	13	64	52	32	46	30	52	96	37	00	85	68	24	44	51	73	45	40	43
08	89	06	64	81	55	41	16	02	34	09	02	97	29	10	12	55	61	38	97	97	42
41	48	65	83	85	00	28	36	24	76	84	08	37	16	14	05	66	07	03	41	61	91
55	32	03	67	66	00	47	52	46	32	26	86	54	37	63	14	12	23	32	53	20	99
57	04	44	18	67	32	08	72	03	10	08	53	25	19	89	71	26	49	89	97	02	46
24	30	04	50	01	40	01	97	69	66	70	92	33	15	42	27	03	61	23	78	68	95
63	82	58	89	32	83	88	98	63	59	80	25	66	10	79	36	59	91	37	64	35	78
81	53	96	90	04	05	88	85	25	24	90	70	09	06	39	03	47	02	62	30	60	38
53	27	58	20	82	13	21	04	99	59	33	61	29	73	26	03	26	24	82	36	59	76
33	93	32	98	00	98	29	50	82	52	86	61	02	35	77	60	31	84	65	28	88	12
69	72	37	11	55	05	38	50	57	74	59	46	87	12	83	54	58	13	12	37	25	69
40	84	27	24	65	67	98	95	21	90	14	61	22	30	82	59	13	06	33	45	89	62
09	57	16	49	06	81	71	39	96	11	91	52	07	58	69	11	57	13	23	32	21	82
82	83	71	70	12	05	36	30	69	94	17	29	76	72	01	11	20	77	73	08	32	74
99	29	29	46	94	68	01	94	29	27	63	14	11	20	60	40	28	12	49	25	57	41
13	75	68	49	79	02	18	77	60	25	26	74	29	39	28	68	09	45	28	64	86	02
67	44	08	18	34	92	37	52	59	77	94	84	00	32	11	04	69	89	94	44	56	24
04	80	03	43	16	77	45	16	40	19	17	19	35	15	89	57	25	75	70	35	80	94

Table 11.A1 continued

18	34	21	82	20	97	91	81	35	96	01	24	85	82	39	96	37	15	37	88	74	32
74	28	18	26	79	02	43	27	54	30	10	26	43	05	82	31	00	57	42	46	07	62
23	80	06	21	52	52	49	87	53	56	40	33	64	93	68	20	78	60	77	50	65	12
40	94	28	26	73	91	10	03	36	38	44	56	67	07	35	55	73	27	79	89	44	48
10	87	02	57	73	84	13	79	05	35	84	34	44	99	61	64	86	18	41	86	32	92
11	02	06	72	82	73	29	50	58	04	89	74	43	20	85	36	93	80	77	59	92	74
40	66	17	22	86	57	78	55	91	94	34	38	32	73	85	76	27	17	67	65	56	76
39	44	76	83	69	90	95	22	74	60	34	77	43	53	93	74	74	57	88	00	22	09
77	89	29	87	86	41	87	24	96	04	12	33	42	84	50	27	12	32	27	07	61	88
87	59	45	63	76	11	09	44	91	30	05	24	80	00	87	52	19	10	53	48	97	40
52	45	27	83	36	41	28	64	03	57	33	55	38	40	82	40	17	60	89	79	98	52
33	26	21	75	46	17	22	56	54	52	12	15	61	97	64	75	89	61	62	15	98	15
86	99	77	06	23	73	96	26	99	69	92	93	34	82	47	16	83	25	94	26	43	42
93	23	47	77	96	71	82	03	09	54	35	48	96	50	71	29	23	90	47	59	61	50
81	47	08	15	88	99	06	31	09	46	67	87	70	32	68	00	91	78	96	78	82	11
27	15	40	75	76	67	95	80	24	31	56	44	40	27	78	74	34	51	70	84	07	65
59	91	19	12	35	00	03	67	28	89	46	73	53	85	86	69	40	86	84	27	73	15
44	77	60	02	44	11	77	74	82	44	76	64	61	54	76	76	42	15	53	10	08	78
90	97	33	73	01	97	35	44	82	47	40	42	18	58	42	67	28	40	28	63	91	39
73	73	22	99	60	52	14	14	50	24	70	00	60	87	41	06	93	52	27	20	73	72
14	08	10	41	46	26	28	23	59	78	24	73	79	16	19	26	54	04	38	23	88	14
01	43	24	00	42	57	97	24	06	06	30	49	44	10	58	35	71	13	27	53	34	35
41	88	24	87	64	32	21	40	53	57	55	84	83	73	49	93	03	88	24	37	89	96
67	43	60	39	17	63	77	64	73	33	23	51	00	11	38	05	42	63	66	80	28	35
40	67	72	15	95	19	89	39	38	18	43	82	88	27	91	89	02	41	08	13	86	05

Table 11.A1 continued

30	08	67	49	24	71	86	62	49	52	79	02	22	18	46	73	54	75	34	68	97	67	56	18	25
93	26	72	95	54	27	28	50	68	72	22	61	22	77	65	33	52	62	12	35	50	75	01	04	05
58	20	86	20	41	64	37	42	85	16	99	37	79	00	83	28	58	95	26	06	90	48	30	79	27
14	72	59	55	86	50	62	10	27	93	90	07	18	08	74	68	83	71	41	26	53	33	82	77	14
64	86	43	49	38	90	69	23	84	02	70	69	16	38	79	28	12	44	03	08	78	66	27	53	42
82	22	40	90	37	97	81	42	80	43	51	49	88	86	66	51	25	68	22	47	49	07	15	60	98
82	39	20	82	94	87	49	18	23	23	18	55	89	12	59	12	83	54	88	04	77	62	46	17	76
07	19	21	46	93	97	34	77	82	01	12	65	85	12	68	72	06	15	83	26	03	24	68	03	43
86	74	75	87	79	67	72	21	25	00	99	34	44	49	46	24	54	49	87	96	15	51	75	69	69
83	98	77	89	42	27	51	46	80	42	05	23	67	38	25	01	84	99	14	44	44	13	95	20	31
31	52	16	95	07	18	36	77	14	60	57	67	44	24	71	22	59	34	15	45	32	39	80	07	61
85	11	82	50	72	81	37	17	41	57	77	68	67	96	38	23	05	89	12	20	58	93	46	15	46
79	09	74	36	40	49	38	98	75	41	75	50	44	66	58	93	87	53	15	08	14	24	25	13	35
93	93	14	79	87	41	27	32	38	57	32	49	42	10	21	10	25	47	64	40	85	04	51	93	42
79	87	15	64	53	67	44	87	91	63	35	34	96	18	48	93	33	27	75	41	60	38	67	58	90
92	41	32	68	56	30	00	01	75	40	33	52	07	38	02	05	51	63	83	11	97	78	75	76	26
00	09	90	77	62	13	94	38	38	78	35	81	45	37	44	60	09	34	11	29	15	30	64	21	56
04	06	27	21	78	51	63	97	93	98	81	29	07	51	36	83	25	50	28	18	76	26	56	70	66

Note

This table was compiled by the authors.

Table 11.A2 One- and two-tailed 0.05 significance levels for Pearson's correlation

If your sample size is not listed, then use the values for the next smaller sample size. If your correlation coefficient (ignoring any negative signs) is equal to or larger than the listed value for your particular sample size, then you reject the null hypothesis and accept the hypothesis that there is a relationship between the two variables.

Sample size	One-tailed 0.05 level	Two-tailed 0.05 level
3	0.99	1.00
4	0.90	0.95
5	0.81	0.88
6	0.73	0.81
7	0.67	0.75
8	0.62	0.71
9	0.58	0.67
10	0.55	0.63
11	0.52	0.60
12	0.50	0.58
13	0.48	0.55
14	0.46	0.53
15	0.44	0.51
16	0.43	0.50
17	0.41	0.48
18	0.40	0.47
19	0.39	0.46
20	0.38	0.44
25	0.34	0.40
30	0.31	0.36
35	0.28	0.33
40	0.26	0.31
45	0.25	0.29
50	0.24	0.28
60	0.21	0.25
70	0.20	0.24
80	0.19	0.22
90	0.17	0.21
100	0.17	0.20
200	0.12	0.14
300	0.10	0.11
400	0.08	0.10
500	0.07	0.09
1000	0.05	0.06

Note
The above table was calculated by the authors.

Table 11.A3 One- and two-tailed 0.05 significance levels for Spearman's correlation

If your sample size is not given, use the values for the next smaller sample size. If your correlation coefficient (ignoring any negative signs) is equal to or larger than the listed value for your particular sample size, then you reject the null hypothesis and accept the hypothesis that there is a relationship between the two variables.

Sample size	1-tailed 0.05 level	2-tailed 0.05 level
5	0.90	1.00
6	0.83	0.89
7	0.71	0.79
8	0.64	0.74
9	0.60	0.68
10	0.56	0.65
11	0.52	0.62
12	0.50	0.59
13	0.48	0.57
14	0.46	0.54
15	0.44	0.52
16	0.43	0.51
17	0.41	0.49
18	0.40	0.48
19	0.39	0.46
20	0.38	0.45
25	0.34	0.40
30	0.31	0.36
35	0.28	0.34
40	0.26	0.31
45	0.25	0.30
50	0.24	0.28
60	0.21	0.26
70	0.20	0.24
80	0.19	0.22
90	0.17	0.21
100	0.17	0.20
200	0.12	0.14
300	0.10	0.11
400	0.08	0.10
500	0.07	0.09
1000	0.05	0.06

Note
The above table was calculated by the authors.

12

Differences and associations among two sets of categories

Chi-square

INTRODUCTION

It was explained in Chapter 6 that category (i.e. nominal or category data) variables are analysed differently from score variables. This chapter deals with the circumstances in which both of the variables under investigation are nominal (i.e. category) variables.

The only exceptions to this occur when both of the nominal variables are categorised in binary fashion. That is both variables are restricted to only two different categories each. In these circumstances you have a choice – either follow through this chapter or use the phi coefficient (see Chapter 10 also).

CONCEPTUAL BACKGROUND

An example of data suitable for chi-square is sex of person and choice of favourite leisure entertainment. Sex is a variable with just two different categories – male or female. Favourite leisure entertainment as measured in this case is between going to a disco, going to the cinema or playing with a computer. Everyone in the study makes the choice of one favourite entertainment. The data are as in Table 12.1.

Looking at Table 12.1, there does seem to be a difference between males and females in terms of their favourite leisure entertainment. Discos are more popular with females and computers with males. Another way of putting this is to say that there is a relationship (or association) between a person's favourite leisure entertainment and their sex. In other words, chi-square shows differences between groups but these differences can also be regarded as relationships or associations. This is true of any correlation coefficient

Table 12.1 Sex differences in favourite leisure entertainment

	Males	Females
Disco	f = 20	F = 45
Cinema	f = 24	F = 17
Computer	f = 35	F = 12

too – people scoring highly on the first variable are different on the second variable from those who have low scores on the first variable. That is true as long as there is a significant correlation.

Chi-square is a statistic which determines whether the frequencies of cases in different categories differ from the pattern we would expect by chance under the null hypothesis. Chi-square is sometimes represented by the Greek letter χ^2. It is most commonly used in psychology when the relationship between two variables is being investigated.

When referring to analyses with two category variables, it is convenient to indicate the number of categories in each variable. In the simplest case where each variable is dichotomous in the sense of only having two categories, we would refer to the analysis as a two-by-two analysis which is usually written as 2 × 2. A 2 × 3 analysis would be one where one variable had only two categories and the other variable had three categories. A 3 × 3 analysis would be one where both variables had three categories, and so on.

It is important to make a distinction between unrelated and related data. The chi-square test is used with unrelated data where the data come from different cases and where one of the two variables is seen as representing two or more samples. For example, this variable may consist of the two unrelated samples of females and males or the three unrelated samples of members of the Labour, Conservative and Liberal Democratic parties.

We shall begin by describing the chi-square for a 2 × 2 unrelated analysis. This will be followed by a chi-square for an unrelated analysis where the two variables have more than two categories initially.

To carry out a chi-square test it is necessary that the number of cases which are expected to fall by chance in the cells of the contingency table formed by the two variables exceed a certain number. This requirement varies somewhat for the three kinds of analyses:

- With a 2 × 2 unrelated analysis, the minimum expected number in any of the four cells is 5.
- With a larger unrelated analysis the minimum expected number in any one cell must be 1 or larger and more than 80 per cent of the cells should have a minimum expected number of 5.
- With a 2 × 2 related analysis, the average minimum number of cases falling in the two cells representing change should be 5.

So, before carrying out any of these three kinds of analyses we have to check whether the minimum expected frequencies have been met. Calculating expected frequencies is the first step in computing chi-square and allows us to determine whether the minimum expected frequencies have been satisfied.

Chi-square test for a 2 × 2 unrelated analysis

Suppose we wanted to find out whether women and men differed in the extent to which they had fallen in love at first sight with their current partner. Chi-square considers two different aspects of the situation:

- The actual numbers of men and women who fall in love at first sight compared with those who do not.

- The expected frequencies of men and women who fall in love at first sight and those who do not as predicted by the null hypothesis that men and women do not differ in the tendency to fall in love at first sight.

The expected frequencies are obtained by combining the men and women's data on falling in love at first sight. If the null hypothesis is true then we expect the same proportion of men as women to fall in love at first sight. The only problem is that we may have different numbers of men and women in our research. Consequently we have to adjust the expected frequencies so that they take into account the different numbers in the male and female samples.

We can work out the expected proportions of women and men who would be expected by chance to have fallen in love at first sight or later by simply combining the male and female data. Imagine, for instance, that we had a sample of 50 women and another sample of 30 men and that 20 of these 80 people had fallen in love at first sight while the remaining 60 had fallen in love later, as shown in Table 12.2.

Table 12.2 Row and column totals of a 2 × 2 contingency table

	First sight love	Later love	Row total
Women			50
Men			30
Column total	20	60	80

Note that this information is presented in what are called the *row* and *column totals* (or *marginal totals*) of the 2 × 2 contingency table in Table 12.2. It does not matter which of the two category variables forms the rows and which forms the columns. In this case, the rows represent sex and the columns falling in love. Using these row and column totals provides us with an easier way of doing the calculations of expected frequency. Note also that at this stage we do not need to know the actual number of women and men falling in love at first sight.

If the null hypothesis that men and women do not differ in falling in love at first sight is true, then we would expect that 20 out of every 80 men had fallen in love at first sight; similarly 20 out of every 80 women had fallen in love at first sight.

As we have 30 men we would expect that 20/80 of the 30 men (i.e. 7.5) would have fallen in love at first sight if the null hypothesis were true and the rest would have fallen in love later.

Similarly, since we have 50 women we would expect 20/80 of the 50 women (i.e. 12.5) to have fallen in love at first sight whereas the remainder would have fallen in love later.

Working out these expected frequencies simply involves multiplying the appropriate row total by the appropriate column total of Table 12.2 and dividing by the grand total or total number of participants.

- Thus to calculate the expected number of women falling in love at first sight we simply multiply the women's row total (50) by the first sight love column total (20) and divide by the overall total (80). This is $\frac{50 \times 20}{80} = 12.5$.

- Similarly, to calculate the expected frequency of later love in men we would multiply the men's row total (30) by the later love total (60) and divide by the overall total (80). This gives us $\frac{30 \times 60}{80} = 22.5$.

The general formula for working out the expected number or frequency of people falling in a particular cell of the contingency table is as follows:

$$\text{Expected frequency} = \frac{\text{Appropriate row total} \times \text{Appropriate column total}}{\text{Grand total}}$$

We can enter our calculations of the expected frequencies in the 2 × 2 contingency table as shown in Table 12.3.

Table 12.3 Expected numbers or frequencies for a 2 × 2 contingency table

	First sight love	Later love	Row total
Women	12.5	37.5	50
Men	7.5	22.5	30
Column total	20	60	80

The minimum expected number in any of the four cells is 7.5 (for men falling in love at first sight). Because this minimum expected frequency is not less than 5, we can carry out a chi-square on these data. The more that the actual or observed number of people falling in these four cells differs from the frequency that would be expected by chance, the greater is the probability that the results will differ from chance.

At this point do try Exercise 12.1.

EXERCISE 12.1   CALCULATING EXPECTED FREQUENCIES FOR A 2 × 2 CONTINGENCY TABLE

Of 20 Psychology graduates and 30 English graduates, 10 received First Class degrees.

Based on these figures what number of English graduates would be expected to obtain a First Class degree?

Would it be possible to carry out a chi-square test on these data?

The formula for obtaining chi-square is as follows:

$$\text{Chi-square} = \sum \frac{(\text{Observed frequency in a particular cell} - \text{Expected frequency in that cell})^2}{\text{Expected frequency in that cell}}$$

Or more commonly the following formula is used which means exactly the same:

$$\text{Chi-square} = \sum \frac{(O - E)^2}{E}$$

Basically the above formula means that the bigger the difference between the observed (*O*) and expected (*E*) frequencies, the bigger the value of chi-squared. That is another way of saying that the bigger the value of chi-square then the less likely is the null hypothesis to be true. The summation sign means that several smaller calculations have to be carried out and the outcomes of these summed.

Calculating chi-square

Worksheet 12.1 sets out the steps in calculating any chi-square up to four rows by four columns. Simply delete any unwanted columns or rows. Figure 12.1 shows you when to use chi-square.

After going through Worksheet 12.1 do try Exercise 12.2.

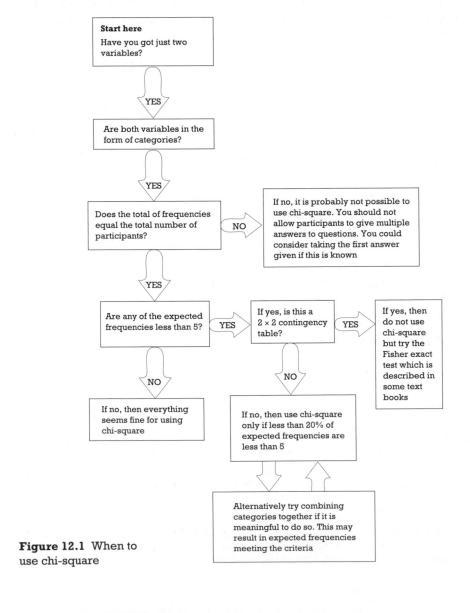

Figure 12.1 When to use chi-square

Worksheet 12.1 for chi-square

For each cell in the chi-square table you calculate the following:

$$\text{Chi-square} = \frac{(O-E)^2}{E}$$

where
  O = observed frequency
  E = expected frequency.

Step 1: Using the data given in Table 12.4 (concerning attitudes to fox hunting), enter your frequencies in Table 12.5 (up to four categories and four cells). If you cannot decide which are the categories and which are the samples don't worry since an arbitrary choice will make no difference to the analysis:

Table 12.4 Observed numbers or frequencies in a 4 × 3 contingency table

Political party	Attitude towards fox hunting			Row totals
	For	Against	Don't know	
Labour	8	40	7	55
Conservative	30	9	5	44
Liberal-Democrat	5	7	7	19
Other	2	7	4	13
Column totals	45	63	23	131

a   delete any rows and columns you are not using;
b   calculate the sum of the frequencies for each of the columns;
c   calculate the total of the frequencies for each of the rows; and
d   calculate the overall total by adding together all of the column totals.

Table 12.5 The observed data and row, column and overall totals

	Sample 1	Sample 2	Sample 3	Sample 4	
Category A	8	40	7		Row 1 = 55
Category B	30	9	5		Row 2 = 44
Category C	5	7	7		Row 3 = 19
Category D	2	7	4		Row 4 = 13
	Column 1 = 45	Column 2 = 63	Column 3 = 23	Column 4 =	Overall total = 131

Step 2: Insert the row and column *totals* in Table 12.6. Then calculate the expected frequency for *each* cell by multiplying its *row total* by its *column total* and then dividing by the *overall total*.

Table 12.6 The expected frequencies and row and column totals

	Sample 1	Sample 2	Sample 3	Sample 4	
Category A	18.89	26.45	9.66		Row 1 = 55
Category B	15.11	21.16	7.73		Row 2 = 44
Category C	6.53	9.14	3.34		Row 3 = 19
Category D	4.47	6.25	2.28		Row 4 = 13
	Column 1 = 45	Column 2 = 63	Column 3 = 23	Column 4 =	Overall total = 131

Step 3: Check Table 12.6 for violations of the rules for chi-square which say that none of the expected frequencies should be under 1.00 and that no more than 20 per cent of expected frequencies should be under 5. In this case we are fortunate as the rules are not broken. If the rules had been broken then the offending category or sample could be deleted from the analysis or samples and/or categories could be combined if it is reasonable to do so.

Step 4: We then simply substitute the above values in the chi-square formula. This means that you simply sum the individual calculations to obtain the chi-square value:

$$\text{Chi-square} = \sum \frac{(O - E)^2}{E}$$

Do this for each individual cell as in Table 12.7. Enter your calculations in this table.

Table 12.7 The chi-square calculation for each cell

	Sample 1	Sample 2	Sample 3	Sample 4
Category A	6.28	6.94	0.73	
Category B	14.67	6.99	0.96	
Category C	0.36	0.50	4.01	
Category D	1.36	0.09	1.30	

Step 5: Sum the individual calculations in Table 12.7 to give the value of chi-square. The value of chi-square = 44.19.

Step 6: The degrees of freedom are (the number of columns of data −1) × (the number of rows of data −1) = (3 − 1) × (4 − 1) = 2 × 3 = 6.

Step 7: We then check the table of the critical values of chi-square to see whether or not our samples differ among each other so much that they are unlikely to be produced by the population defined by the null hypothesis. The value must equal or exceed the tabled value to be significant at the listed level of significance.

Step 8: For our value of the degrees of freedom (6), Table 12.A1 tells us that we need a minimum value of chi-square of 12.59 to be significant at the 5 per cent (or 0.05) level with a two-tailed test. Our value of 44.19 is above this minimum which means that overall our distribution of data is statistically significant. This means that the frequencies in the cells are not what would be predicted under the null hypothesis.

Reporting your findings

- If your value of chi-square is *larger* than or equal to the listed value: Your chi-square value is statistically significant at the 5 per cent level. In these circumstances we might write 'The frequency data in cross-tabulation Table 12.5 were examined to test whether attitudes towards fox hunting are related to political party affiliation. The relationship was statistically significant (chi-square = 44.19, *d.f.* = 6, $p < 0.05$).'
- If your value of chi-square is *smaller* than the listed value: Your chi-square value is *not* statistically significant at the 5 per cent level. In these circumstances we might write 'The frequency data in cross-tabulation Table 12.5 were examined to test whether attitudes towards fox hunting are related to political party affiliation. The relationship was not statistically significant (chi-square =   , *d.f.* =   , n.s.) indicating that there is no relationship between attitudes towards fox hunting and political party affiliation.'

EXERCISE 12.2 CALCULATING CHI-SQUARE FOR A 2 × 2 TABLE

To determine whether cohabiting prior to marriage was associated with marital break-up, 50 divorced and 70 still married couples were asked whether they had cohabited prior to marriage. Of the divorced couples, 20 had cohabited compared with the married couples. Do these data show that there is an association between cohabiting before marriage and divorce?

1 What are the expected frequencies of divorce for couples cohabiting and not cohabiting prior to marriage?
2 What is the value of chi-square?
3 Should the one- or two-tailed critical value be used?
4 How many degrees of freedom should be used?
5 Is this value statistically significant.
6 Do these data show that people who cohabit prior to marriage are more likely to divorce than people who do not cohabit?
7 How would you write up these results?

Chi-square and phi

There is a simple relationship between chi-square for a 2 × 2 table and phi (discussed in Chapter 10). If we know one of these values we can easily work out the other value using the more appropriate of the following two formulae:

$$\text{phi} = \sqrt{\frac{\text{Chi-square}}{\text{Number of Cases}}}$$

chi-square = phi squared × number of cases

To illustrate the relationship between chi-square and phi, we will convert the chi-square of 13.52 to its phi value of 0.41.

$$\text{phi} = \sqrt{\frac{13.52}{80}} = \sqrt{0.169} = 0.41$$

Because chi-square can only take a positive value, phi will always be positive when calculated from chi-square.

ANSWERS TO EXERCISES

Exercise 12.1

Of 20 Psychology graduates and 30 English graduates, 10 received First Class degrees.

The number of English graduates expected to obtain a First Class degree would be 6.

$$\frac{\text{Number of English graduates} \times \text{Number of Firsts}}{\text{Total number of graduates}}$$

$$= \frac{30 \times 10}{50} = \frac{300}{50} = 6.0$$

It would not be possible to carry out a chi-square test on these data because the number of Psychology graduates expected to obtain a First is 4.

$$\frac{\text{Number of Psychology graduates} \times \text{Number of Firsts}}{\text{Total number of graduates}}$$

$$= \frac{20 \times 10}{50} = \frac{200}{50} = 4.0$$

Although chi-square's assumptions concerning expected frequencies are violated in this case, if we could increase the sample of Psychology graduates by five or so then the expected frequency would be likely to increase sufficiently.

Exercise 12.2

1 The observed (*O*) and expected (*E*) frequencies of divorce for couples cohabiting and not cohabiting prior to marriage are:

	Cohabited	Not cohabited	Row total
Divorced	*O* = 20 *E* = 16.7	*O* = 30 *E* = 33.3	50
Married	*O* = 20 *E* = 23.3	*O* = 50 *E* = 46.7	70
Column total	40	80	120

2 The calculation of the value of chi-square involves the following steps:

		Cell 1 Divorced/ cohabiting	Cell 2 Divorced/not cohabiting	Cell 3 Married/ cohabiting	Cell 4 Married/ not cohabiting
Step 1:	Subtract	$\dfrac{(20-16.7)^2}{16.7}$	$\dfrac{(30-33.3)^2}{33.3}$	$\dfrac{(20-23.3)^2}{23.2}$	$\dfrac{(50-46.7)^2}{46.7}$
Step 2:	Square	$\dfrac{3.3^2}{16.7}$	$\dfrac{-3.3^2}{33.3}$	$\dfrac{-3.3^2}{23.3}$	$\dfrac{3.3^2}{46.7}$
Step 3:	Divide	$\dfrac{10.89}{16.7}$	$\dfrac{10.89}{33.3}$	$\dfrac{10.89}{23.3}$	$\dfrac{10.89}{46.6}$
Step 4:	Sum	0.65	0.33	0.47	0.23

chi-square = 1.68.

3 The two-tailed critical value should be used because the direction of any difference was not specified.

4 The degrees of freedom are 1.

5 It is not statistically significant because 1.68 is smaller than the two-tailed 0.05 level of 3.84.

6 No, the data do not show that people who cohabit prior to marriage are more likely to divorce than people who do not cohabit.

7 One way would be like this: 'Divorced couples were not significantly more likely than still married couples to have cohabited prior to marriage ($\chi^2 = 1.68$, $d.f. = 1$, two-tailed p n.s.).'

Table 12.A1 Two-tailed 0.05 critical values for chi-square

For your value of chi-square to be statistically significant at the 5 per cent (0.05) level it has to equal or exceed the tabled critical value for the degrees of freedom for your analysis.

Degrees of freedom	Critical values	Degrees of freedom	Critical values
1	3.84	9	16.92
2	5.99	10	18.31
3	7.82	11	19.68
4	9.49	12	21.03
5	11.07	13	22.36
6	12.59	14	23.68
7	14.07	15	25.00
8	15.51	16	26.30

Note
The above table was calculated by the authors.

13

Conducting survey/ non-experimental studies

INTRODUCTION

By now readers should be able to conduct a wide variety of non-experimental research. The objectives of much research are met by demonstrating the relationships between two or more variables. The correlation coefficients from Chapter 10 along with chi-square allow you to carry out a basic statistical analysis of any study based on the correlations between variables. Of course, as you advance your understanding of research you may need more sophisticated statistical analyses. Many of these are to be found in other sources (e.g. Cramer 1998; Howitt and Cramer 2000). Nevertheless, the basics of a correlational analysis covered so far will allow you to answer a wide variety of research questions.

Survey/non-experimental research can take a wide variety of forms. Perhaps the commonest approach in psychology involves the use of structured questionnaires of the sort discussed in Chapter 4, but practically any measurement technique can be used in a correlational analysis. However, since students are most likely to use this form of analysis for the analysis of questionnaire data, we shall concentrate on the use of questionnaires in this chapter. (Of course, questionnaires are often used to measure variables in experiments also.)

Survey/non-experimental research, as we saw in Chapter 2, faces the fundamental dilemma that it is difficult to use a correlation to demonstrate that one variable *causes* the other. So it is always important to be cautious about any statement which implies cause in survey/non-experimental research. At best, the findings of a correlational analysis may be consistent with a causal explanation.

EXAMPLES OF POTENTIAL SURVEY/NON-EXPERIMENTAL STUDIES

The following are all examples of relatively straightforward studies using survey/non-experimental methods:

- Is there a relationship between drivers' age and how frequently they have experienced road rage?
- Do neurotic individuals smoke more?
- Do feelings of jealousy decline with the length of the relationship?
- Is there a relationship between a person's physical attractiveness and the attractiveness of their partners?
- Does ability to memorise names decline with age?
- Does co-operative behaviour increase with children's age?
- Are people who cohabit before marrying less likely to divorce?
- Are people who watch more violence on television more aggressive?
- Is personality related to birth signs?
- Are women more compliant than men?
- Are only children more selfish than those who have siblings?
- Do children with separated or divorced parents do less well at school than children with parents who are still married?
- Are friends similar in personality?
- Are people who are afraid of spiders generally anxious?

Each of these is easily turned into a hypothesis and a null hypothesis.

Some of the variables you will find standard measures for, others you will not (refer to Box 4.1 again).

COLLECTING SURVEY/NON-EXPERIMENTAL DATA

Review Chapter 8 on simple surveys since all the basics described there are important considerations now we have moved on to correlational analysis.

Figure 13.1 outlines some of the basic steps that you should *consider* when contemplating doing research of this sort. This does not mean that each of the steps will have to be done and done to the highest standard for all research, but they each need deliberating upon.

Some of the steps or their order will be a surprise to some. Our emphasis on planning the analysis of the data before the data have been collected, for example. But it is important to know that your data can be analysed and only by pre-planning in this way can you be sure to avoid the problem that the data you have collected cannot be analysed statistically.

Another consideration which might be a surprise is the importance of reviewing the relevant research literature for suitable questionnaires and other measures. There is no guarantee that the measures that you want exist so you may have to design them yourself. Also do not fall into the trap of assuming that if a measure exists it will be suitable for your purposes. Sometimes questions may be too American for another country or designed for a different age group or include rather old-fashioned language, etc. In these circumstances modification will be necessary. Sometimes a questionnaire may be far too long for your purposes so may need shortening.

It is also important to remember that large amounts of data can be easily collected in surveys/non-experimental research. As your research skills develop, it becomes more and more necessary to use a computer to help you in the statistical analysis of your

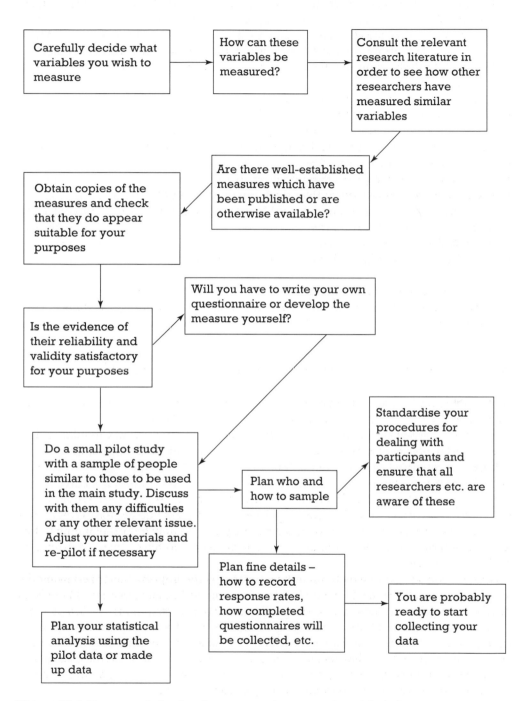

Figure 13.1 Key aspects in planning a survey/non-experimental study

data. There are various books which may help you do this (e.g. Bryman and Cramer 1999; Howitt and Cramer 1999). It is important to plan your questionnaires with computer analysis in mind if you intend to do your analysis by computer. Many questionnaires include numbered boxes in which the data can be recorded as they are to be entered into the computer.

STATISTICAL ANALYSIS

It cannot be re-emphasised too often how important it is to plan the statistical analysis from the earliest stages. This can forewarn you of potential problems with the data in the way you are proposing to collect them. Modifications can be made as a consequence before it is too late. Pilot work can include a pilot data analysis.

As in all statistical analyses, no matter how complex, a basic step is to calculate appropriate descriptive statistics for each of your variables. A summary of the important descriptive statistics is to be found in Chapter 8 (Table 8.2). Remember that the classification of each of the variables in your research as nominal category or numerical score variables is essential to deciding which descriptive statistics to use. There is a far richer variety for numerical score data.

The statistical analysis of data involving correlations, as we have seen, is dependent on the statistical nature of the variable. For each pair of variables you are correlating, you need to decide whether we are dealing with a numerical score or a nominal category. Once this is done then the selection of appropriate statistics is generally routine.

Never forget the importance of examining the distribution of the data for each of your variables. The main considerations you should look for are as follows:

- Extreme skewness or lop-sidedness in the distribution of any of the variables (which may make non-parametric statistics such as Spearman's rho more appropriate). This was discussed earlier (Chapter 10, p. 116)
- Signs from scattergrams that the correlation between two variables is a curve rather than a straight line (Chapter 9, pp. 105–6).
- The influence of outliers – extreme points on a scattergram that are having an undue influence on the correlation since they do not reflect the trend in the main body of the data (Chapter 9, pp. 107–8).

The more correlations you do, the more significant results you would expect. Remember that you expect 5 per cent of your correlations to be significant by chance. Thus for every 20 correlations one should be significant by chance.

When presenting correlations always give the mean and the standard deviation for each variable. The mean will indicate whether the scores are bunched at either the high or low end of the scale, showing that either the group is atypical or the measure is insensitive. The standard deviation indicates whether the range of scores may be too restricted for a reasonable correlation to be obtained.

Figure 13.2 shows major aspects of the statistical analysis required and Table 13.1 gives advice on choices of statistics according to the types of variable concerned.

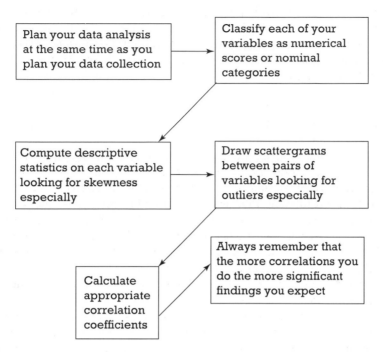

Figure 13.2 Major aspects of the statistical analysis of a survey/non-experimental study

Table 13.1 Appropriate statistics according to the type of each variable

Variable A	Variable B	Statistic	Location
Numerical score	Numerical score	Pearson correlation	Worksheet 10.1
		Spearman's correlation	Worksheet 10.2
Numerical score	Dichotomous variable	Point-biserial correlation	Worksheet 10.1
Dichotomous variable	Dichotomous variable	Phi-coefficient	Worksheet 10.3
Nominal categories	Nominal categories	Chi-square	Worksheet 12.1
Numerical score	Nominal categories	If there are just a few nominal categories then the One-way ANOVA (Chapter 20) might be used. This, however, compares the means of the numerical score variable for the various nominal categories	Worksheet 20.1
Nominal categories	Numerical score	As above	

SUMMARY

- The correlational analysis of survey/non-experimental data builds on the material on surveys in Chapter 4.
- No matter how the data are collected, survey/non-experimental research needs to be treated with caution when making claims about which variables have causal influences on other variables.
- Planning this sort of research involves a number of considerations. The flow diagrams can help you organise your planning.
- Statistical analysis should be planned at an early stage of the research.

Part IV

Exploring differences between group means

14

Testing for differences in means
More on significance testing

INTRODUCTION

We have already looked at significance testing in Chapter 11. However, significance testing is used whenever research is based on samples – which is all of the time.

The most typical research question is to ask whether two groups differ in some characteristic. For example, are French men better lovers than English men? Are students more liberal in their views than others of the same age? Are vegetarians less aggressive than meat eaters? Each of these questions is easily answered if we obtain people in the two groups and measure their scores on the variable on which they possibly differ. So, a group of French men, a group of English men and a measure of their ability as lovers are basically all we need to answer the first question.

But as we are only using samples, any differences that we obtain between French and English men could be the result of real differences in love making but, alternatively, it could be that French men and English men do not differ in this way. Any differences between our samples may be due to chance factors which have resulted from us selecting samples that just happen to differ as lovers.

The task of deciding which of these alternatives is the more likely is the job of inferential statistics.

Explaining inferential statistics and significance testing is not easy. They refer to rather abstract ideas and the explanation risks getting a little long-winded. Consequently most of the material in this chapter will repay a repeated reading. Do not be surprised if you do not grasp some of the points the first time. Everyone struggles with these ideas.

WHAT IS THE PROBLEM?

As we already have learnt, the problem is that in psychological research we deal with only samples of data. This raises the issue of just how far we can rely on findings based on samples since samples from a population vary somewhat.

Inferential statistics tries to estimate the degree of reliance we can place on the findings from our samples.

Inferential statistics uses the information available in a sample to estimate just how variable we expect samples to be.

> Samples from a population can vary greatly. The amount of variability is dependent on the variability in the population. Only if all of the scores in the population were identical would this not be true.

THE HYPOTHESIS AND NULL HYPOTHESIS

We will repeat ourselves a little but many concepts bear repetition.

A *hypothesis* in psychological research is almost invariably a statement that there is a relationship between two different variables. Examples of this are 'There is a relationship between people's social class (i.e. variable 1) and their feelings of job security (i.e. variable 2)'; or 'There is a relationship between receiving training in memorisation techniques or not (i.e. variable 1) and ability on multiple choice tests (i.e. variable 2)'. Of course, hypotheses can appear to be much more sophisticated than these but at root all of them are similar. Sometimes the hypothesis is called the alternative hypothesis.

For every *hypothesis* in research there is a *null hypothesis* which says that there is *no* relationship between the two variables. Thus the equivalent null hypothesis for the above hypotheses might read 'There is *no* relationship between people's social class and their feelings of job security.' and 'There is *no* relationship between receiving training in memorisation techniques or not and ability on multiple choice tests.' Again, the wording can be much more sophisticated than this.

Significance testing is the process by which one decides whether it is the hypothesis that is most likely to be correct or the null hypothesis that is most likely to be correct. Both cannot be correct.

Inferential statistics is the branch of statistics which uses the characteristics of your data in order to help you decide in favour of the hypothesis or the null hypothesis.

Research findings are said to be statistically significant if the data convincingly support the hypothesis.

Research findings are said to be statistically non-significant if the data do *not* support the hypothesis convincingly.

Statistical significance is expressed as a probability. Thus the 5 per cent level of significance merely means that there are 5 chances in 100 of getting your data *if* your null hypothesis is in reality correct. (Usually this is written as a probability out of 1 such as 0.05, which is the same as 5 per cent.)

Statistical tests are used on your obtained data on the assumption that the null hypothesis is correct. Mathematical procedures then allow the researcher to say whether the obtained data are likely to have been found if the null hypothesis were true.

Statistical significance is usually claimed only if the 5 per cent criterion has been met. However, 5 per cent is the conventional minimum level to claim statistical significance and to accept the hypothesis. If the 1 per cent level of significance is reached this means that the hypothesis is far more likely to be true than the null hypothesis. In fact, there is just 1 chance in 100 of getting your findings *if* the null hypothesis were true. This is even more convincing evidence that the hypothesis is correct.

TYPE 1 AND TYPE 2 ERRORS

Significance testing relies on probabilities of the hypothesis being correct. This reliance on probabilities means that there is a chance that we have made the wrong decision.

Type 1 Errors occur when the hypothesis is accepted as correct when in fact the *null* hypothesis is correct.

Type 2 Errors occur when the *null* hypothesis is accepted as correct when in fact the hypothesis is correct.

By and large these are conceptual or theoretical matters. Usually the researcher has no idea whether or not she or he has made a Type 1 or a Type 2 Error – or neither of these.

2-tailed and 1-tailed tests again

2-tailed tests really refer to the characteristics of the hypothesis being tested. In a 2-tailed test the hypothesis merely states that there is some sort of relationship between two variables. So, the hypothesis 'There is a relationship between people's social class and their feelings of job security' is an example of a hypothesis for which 2-tailed testing is appropriate. The hypothesis does *not* stipulate the direction of the relationship between social class and job security. Thus if the data show that middle class people are more likely than working class people to feel insecure about their job then this supports the hypothesis. But equally, if it is found that it is in fact the working class people who feel the most insecure about their job then this would also confirm the hypothesis. Thus 2-tailed testing merely examines whether there is any sort of relationship between the two variables. So long as there is a relationship, the directionless hypothesis is supported.

As a rule of thumb, stick with 2-tailed testing unless you have a *very* good reason for doing otherwise.

1-tailed tests are based on hypotheses which state the direction of the relationship. So, if our hypothesis were 'feelings of job insecurity are higher in working class individuals' then the data have to show this precise pattern for us to accept the hypothesis. Otherwise we accept the null hypothesis that job insecurity is *not* higher in working class individuals.

Generally speaking, 1-tailed testing requires convincing theoretical and empirical arguments in its support. If this is not available then use the 2-tailed test. (See Table 14.1).

The practical importance of all of this is that the directional hypothesis is accepted with a lower trend in the data. Thus the 1-tailed test is more likely to give significant findings if the data are in the predicted direction.

If in doubt, it is safer to stick with 2-tailed testing.

Table 14.1 Criteria for 1- and 2-tailed tests

Criterion	1- or 2-tailed test	Explanation
1 Is there a *very* strong line of theory which supports the relationship predicted by the hypothesis?	If *yes* then 1-tailed significance testing is likely to be appropriate	The strong theory which is likely to have empirical support means that one requires less of a trend in the data to be convinced that there is a trend
2 Has previous research generally supported the predicted direction of the relationship?	If *yes* then 1-tailed significance testing is likely to be appropriate	Because of the previously established relationship, one would not need such a strong trend in the data to convince one that the trend is there
3 Have you seen the pattern of results in your data prior to deciding to do a 1-tailed test?	If *yes* then stick to 2-tailed significance testing as you are merely opting for what you have seen to be the case	You are not predicting the outcome but merely reflecting what you have observed in the data
4 Was it just a subjective feeling or hunch which caused you to write a directional hypothesis?	If *yes* then stick to 2-tailed significance testing as you are just guessing	

SIGNIFICANCE TESTS

There are numerous significance tests available. The most famous are the *t*-test, chi-square, the Mann-Whitney test, the Wilcoxon matched-pairs test, and the Analysis of variance. Each of these is explained elsewhere in this book.

They all work in different ways and are applicable to different types of research. The later chapters present what are generally the best significance tests for the research method in question.

Virtually all significance tests involve calculating what is known as a *statistic*. A statistic is merely a characteristic of a sample.

Virtually all significance tests used in psychology have Tables of Significance. These tables tell you for particular sample sizes what value of the statistic is needed if the hypothesis is correct.

For many, the discussion so far may be sufficient for their immediate purposes. The next section explains the general process of significance testing. It is designed to help you achieve a more practical understanding of the concepts.

AN ILLUSTRATION OF SIGNIFICANCE TESTING

A typical study in psychological research

Perhaps the most concrete way of learning about inferential statistics and significance testing is to apply the concepts to a simple research study. There are plenty of books which will take you through the formulae involved instead if you feel up to that.

It is good practice to start every study with a clear research question. For our study the research question is 'Do men and women differ in terms of their fine motor skill (such as the number of errors they make when typing into a word processor)?'

Many research questions suggest hypotheses. Ours might be: 'Men and women have different levels of fine motor skill.'

In psychological research jargon this does not mean '*All* men have different levels of fine motor skills to those of *all* women'. What it really means is that 'The average level of fine motor skill in men is different from the average level of fine motor skill in women.'

There is also a null hypothesis. Ours might be: 'Men and women do not differ in terms of their fine motor skill.'

How could we conduct a research study to explore our research question? Essentially you need a sample of men (Sample A) and a sample of women (Sample B) and a measure of fine motor skill. This might be measured *operationally* using the percentage number of word-processing errors people make when copying a particular page from a book over a one-minute period.

An *operational definition* of a variable is merely a way of defining a concept by the way in which it is measured. Operational definitions often include more variables than the one we want to specify. For example, the ability to type words will include variables other than motor skills such as the ability to read, the ability to type, tiredness and the motivation to do well.

The independent variable for this study is gender and the dependent variable is word-processing errors.

Imagine that we collected data in this study from ten men and ten women. (The actual size of samples is arbitrary for the purposes of explaining inferential statistics and statistical significance.)

The data obtained from our sample of ten women were as in Table 14.2:

Table 14.2 The scores for the ten women studied

2	2	2	3	4	4	4	5	6	8

Remember that the ten numbers in Table 14.2 are the percentages of errors made by the ten different women. We have arranged the scores from smallest to largest just so that you can quickly see how frequent the different scores are. Usually this would *not* be done.

The mean or arithmetic average of these ten women's scores is the total of the ten scores divided by ten. This is 40/10. Thus the sample of women's mean score is 4.0.

The data obtained from the other sample, the ten men, were as in Table 14.3:

Table 14.3 The scores for the ten men studied

3	4	4	5	6	6	6	7	9	10

The mean or arithmetic average of the ten men's scores is the total of the ten scores divided by ten. This is 60/10. Thus the men's mean is 6.0.

The difference between the men's mean and the women's mean is therefore $6.0 - 4.0 = 2.0$.

This shows that our sample of men, on average, is making more errors than the sample of women. The question is whether this difference of 2.00 is the result of a clear difference between men and women or whether it is merely the outcome of sampling fluctuations.

In other words, does the average difference of 2.00 between the men and women suggest that the hypothesis is correct? Or does it suggest that the null hypothesis is correct and that the differences are merely chance fluctuations inherent in sampling?

ESTIMATING THE CHARACTERISTICS OF THE POPULATION OR WHY THE NULL HYPOTHESIS IS IMPORTANT

At first sight, we seem to be faced with an impossible task. All we have are two samples but we want to know about the populations from which they came. Can we use the information from samples to make useful inferences about the populations from which they are samples?

The short answer is yes provided we make some reasonable additional assumptions.

Actually a rather neat 'trick' is employed which you need to understand before the process will make much sense. The 'trick' is that we try to estimate the population which would be involved if the null hypothesis were correct. The null hypothesis always indicates that there is no difference between the two samples. In our study, the null hypothesis says that there are no differences between men and women in terms of the number of word-processing errors they make. Thus the null hypothesis suggests that on average the difference between the sample of men and the sample of women will be zero. This can be put another way: the male and female samples come from the same population of scores. They must do if the samples, according to the null hypothesis, do not differ apart from sampling variations.

Given that any sampling involves a certain amount of fluctuation in the characteristics of the samples, we would expect a certain degree of variability in the differences between the means of the samples. Although theoretically the difference between the means of two samples should be zero if the null hypothesis is true, in practice we would only expect it to be more or less true because of sampling fluctuations. In the long run the differences between the means of the two samples should average at zero if we repeat the study many times *and* the null hypothesis is true. (Remember that sometimes the difference will be positive, sometimes the difference will be negative, and occasionally it will be exactly zero. The net results of this over *many* pairs of samples should be zero *if* the null hypothesis is true.)

The first stage of the inference process is to get our best estimate as to the population of scores. The only information we have is from our sample of men and our sample of women. So all we do is to combine these two samples to give us our best guess as to the distribution of scores in the population. This is shown in Table 14.4 using *italics* for the female scores and **bold** for the male scores.

Table 14.4 The male and female samples combined to give an estimate of the population characteristics

2	*2*	*2*	*3*	*4*	*4*	*4*	*5*	*6*	*8*
3	**4**	**4**	**5**	**6**	**6**	**6**	**7**	**9**	**10**

The trouble with this estimate of the population characteristics is that it is unclear whether the population is the one which supports the null hypothesis or not. It could be that we have combined together two very different samples which actually come from different populations. (Remember that the hypothesis suggests that they do come from different populations.)

What we do is to make sure that the samples are combined in a way which ensures that they come from the same population of scores. This is simply a matter of adjusting each score in each sample so that the sample means become equal. In other words, we can make the sample means the same as the population mean. If the sample means are the same then the samples represent what we would expect under the *null hypothesis*.

The mean score of the estimated population in Table 14.4 is 5.0 (that is 100/20 = 5.0).

On average, the scores of the women in the data are 4.0 so in order to make the mean of the women's sample the same as the population mean of 5.0 we need to *add* 1.00 to each of the women's scores.

Similarly, since the mean of the men's sample in our data is 6.0, we need to *subtract* 1.00 from each man's score to make the mean of the sample of men's scores the same as the population mean of 5.0.

The result of these two steps is shown in Table 14.5. We have left the male and female scores identified by different type faces.

Table 14.5 The estimated population adjusted to meet the requirements of the null hypothesis

3	*3*	*3*	*4*	*5*	*5*	*5*	*6*	*7*	*9*
2	**3**	**3**	**4**	**5**	**5**	**5**	**6**	**8**	**9**

Now, you will find, that the mean male score (those in **bold**) and the mean female score (those in *italics*) in Table 14.5 are identical at 5.0.

Remember, what we have done is to take the male and female samples and adjust them so that they have identical means. This mean is 5.0. These adjustments ensure that the population in Table 14.5 is the one specified by the null hypothesis which says the male and female means should be identical. In other words, the null hypothesis suggests that the male and female scores come from one population of scores.

The 'adjusted' scores in Table 14.5 are based on the actual data as far as the variability in scores goes. However, what differences are due to sex have been removed as required by the null hypothesis.

This set of adjusted scores can be turned into a frequency table such as Table 14.6. As can be seen, most of the scores are between 3 and 7 inclusive. Relatively few scores

Table 14.6 Frequency table of the population of scores of 'adjusted' to meet the requirements of the null hypothesis

Frequency

Frequency	1 or less	2 to 3	4 to 6	7 to 8	9 or more
10			6		
9			6		
8			5		
7			5		
6		3	5		
5		3	5		
4		3	5		
3		3	5		
2		3	4	8	9
1		2	4	7	9

are more that 7 or less than 3. With a little bit of imagination, one might suggest that the histogram is relatively symmetrical (well roughly so) and sort of bell shaped (very roughly so!).

The estimated population of scores in Tables 14.5 or 14.6 can be used to discover the variability in the means of samples taken from this adjusted population. That is, we can randomly select samples from this estimated population of scores to obtain an indication of what the variability in means of samples taken from that population is. This may not be a particularly good estimate of the variability in scores (we never know for certain since we never know the characteristics of the population) but it is the only one we have – unless we run the study many times again.

Take a break. These ideas are complicated and abstract so you might wish to reread the above section. Remember that all we have done so far is to take two samples of scores and combine them in such a way that they fulfil the requirements of the null hypothesis.

SAMPLING FROM THE ESTIMATED POPULATION

So far we have estimated (using the available information from our samples of data) what the characteristics of the population would be if the null hypothesis is true. The variability around the mean reflects the extent to which the samples are likely to vary. The more variability in the population, the more will be the variability in the means of the samples.

Remember that the data we have collected concern a pair of samples – one for a group of men and the other for a group of women. These differ in their means. The men's mean is 6.00 and the women's mean is 4.00. The difference between the two means is 6.00 – 4.00 or 2.00. At face value this supports the hypothesis that men and women differ in terms of their fine motor skills as assessed by typing ability. Women seem to make fewer errors.

We need to know how likely it is that the men and women have means 2.00 apart if the null hypothesis is true that there really is zero difference between samples of men and women.

The estimated population of scores conforming to the requirements of the null hypothesis (Tables 14.5 or 14.6) can be used to assess what happens if a random sample of ten scores is taken from the population. Assume that this represents a sample of ten men. This is a perfectly reasonable step given that the estimated population in Tables 14.5 or 14.6 is assumed to be the same for men and women according to the null hypothesis. The sample consists of scores 2 3 3 3 5 5 9 5 5 1. Thus the male mean is 41/10 = 4.1.

The process is then repeated for another sample of ten scores from the estimated population in Tables 14.5 or 14.6. Assume that this second sample represents a sample of ten women. Again this is perfectly reasonable as this estimated population is one in which there are no differences between the men's scores and the women's scores. We know this to be true because we made it so. The 'female' scores are 2 2 3 3 4 5 6 7 7 8. Thus the female mean is 47/10 = 4.7.

The difference between the means of the two samples is then calculated. This is 4.1 – 4.7 = –0.6.

The last three steps are repeated over and over again until many pairs of samples have been collected. Scores are replaced in the population as soon as the score has been selected at random (see Box 14.1). This ensures that our small population does not decline in size.

BOX 14.1 RANDOM SAMPLING WITH REPLACEMENT

Random sampling with replacement means that once a case is selected at random, say by drawing lots from a bag, it is then replaced into the sample. Thus the same case can be selected more than once.

This form of random sampling is actually used in statistical theory.

In psychology, when we draw samples, we do not replace the cases into the population. When the population is small this can make a difference. When the population is large, random sampling with or without replacement gives virtually the same outcomes.

In a sense, then, psychological practice and statistics are different on the issue of replacement. However, in practice the difference is of little consequence.

> Random sampling gives each member of the population an equal chance of being selected for inclusion in a sample. Each of the scores in the population in Tables 14.5 or 14.6 could be written on a separate piece of paper and placed in a hat. If the slips of paper are then stirred and selected blindfold one at a time this is a random sampling method. The slip should be replaced in the hat and the slips stirred around before the next slip is selected.

These repeated pairs of samples and differences between the sample means of men and women are given in Table 14.A1. There are fifty pairs presented in total. It could be many more if we had time and patience. These differences have been plotted as a histogram. This represents the sampling distribution of *differences* between sample means (Table 14.7). In this case it is pairs of samples of size 10. The reason for choosing samples of size ten is that this is the size of both samples in our data.

Table 14.7 A histogram giving the differences in the means of pairs of means taken from the null-hypothesis defined population in Tables 14.5 and 14.6

Frequency

	−1.3 or less	−1.2 to −0.9	−0.8 to −0.5	−0.4 to +0.4	+0.5 to 0.8	+0.9 to +1.2	+1.3 or more
15				+0.4			
14				+0.4			
13				+0.4			
12				+0.4			
11				+0.3			
10			−0.5	+0.3			
9		−0.9	−0.5	+0.2			
8		−0.9	−0.5	+0.2			
7		−0.9	−0.6	0.0			
6		−1.0	−0.6	−0.1	+0.8		
5		−1.0	−0.6	−0.2	+0.8		
4	−1.3	−1.1	−0.6	−0.3	+0.7	+1.2	
3	−1.3	−1.1	−0.6	−0.3	+0.6	+1.1	
2	−1.5	−1.1	−0.7	−0.3	+0.6	+0.9	+1.8
1	−1.7	−1.2	−0.8	−0.4	+0.5	+0.9	+1.4

Table 14.7 is very important. It represents the likely pattern of differences between sample means that would occur if we could sample at random from the population from which the two samples in our study were drawn. The population in question is that in which the null hypothesis is correct. The differences can be positive or negative in value.

The question now is as follows: How likely is it that we would obtain the difference between the two samples we did (i.e. 2.0) if they actually came from the population defined by the null hypothesis? Table 14.7 gives us indications of the likelihood. As we can see there, most differences between pairs of samples cluster around 0.00. This is just as we would expect as the population from which the pairs of samples were drawn came from the same population. Only a few samples depart by more than +1.5 or –1.5 from the null hypothesis population mean of 0.00.

What we do next is to say that the 95 per cent of differences between the means of pairs of samples which are closest to the population mean of zero probably support the null hypothesis that the two samples are drawn from a population in which the mean is zero. In Table 4.7, since we have only 50 differences between pairs of sample means, the middle 95 per cent of scores covers the middle 48 differences (more or less since the middle 48 equals the middle 96 per cent which is as near to 95 per cent as we can get).

This middle '95 per cent' covers the scores of –1.5 to + 1.4.

Anything more negative than –1.5 or more positive than +1.4 is in the extreme 5 per cent.

However, this remaining 5 per cent of extreme differences between the means of the two samples of scores seems rather unlikely if we are indeed sampling from a population with a mean of zero (the null hypothesis population). Since they are unlikely to come from such a population, they are more likely to support the hypothesis that the two samples actually come from different populations which have different means. This is the assumption underlying the research hypothesis. That is, men as a whole and women as a whole differ in terms of their fine motor skills as assessed by errors made in typing into a word processor.

The decision to use the extreme 5 per cent of differences as supporting the hypothesis and as rejecting the null hypothesis is somewhat arbitrary although it is conventional in statistics. It just keeps the risk of falsely adopting the hypothesis as true at a fairly low level.

Other significance levels are used including the 1 per cent level.

With the greater use of computers, significance levels are often reported as exact values such as 0.035 or 0.87. Nevertheless the 5 per cent level is generally the key significance level in all research.

Remember the difference between the sample of men and the sample of women obtained in our research was +2.0. This is bigger than +1.4 so it is in the extreme 5 per cent of differences drawn from the null hypothesis population. Thus we reject the null hypothesis in favour of the hypothesis that men and women differ in their fine motor skills.

In the rather curious language used to describe this outcome we say the null hypothesis that men and women have equally fine motor skills was not supported and,

BOX 14.2 WHAT ACTUALLY HAPPENS IN SIGNIFICANCE TESTING

In 'real' statistics a more mathematical approach is taken although this involves many of the steps we have described in our illustration. The big difference is that many of our steps are hidden by the superficial mathematics of the process. The point of using mathematical formulae is that they greatly speed up the process of assessing statistical significance compared with our method. Our method applies only to a particular pair of samples and we would have to begin from scratch for any other data. Mathematical formulae make the process more general. There are two methods used to develop formulae. One involves ranking the scores (i.e. non-parametric statistics) which instantly converts a set of very different scores to a common set of ranks. This speeds up the process enormously.

The other approach is parametric statistics. The t-tests described later are good examples of these. Instead of working with a sample of scores, parametric statistics turn them into a set of z-scores or standard scores. Standard scores are merely scores put on to a standard scale of measurement. Once this is done the calculations become quick and straightforward. Instead of working with the actual scores as we did, the t-test works with the variances of the scores. The variances of the two sets of scores are combined to give an estimate of the variance of the combined samples or 'population'. The estimated variance of the population is known as the variance estimate.

Once the variance estimate has been calculated, this can be used mathematically to work out the deviations of samples from the mean of that population. The 'average' of these deviations is called the standard error. The standard error is merely the standard deviation of the means of samples drawn from the population. The maths is very simple: the variance estimate divided by the square root of the sample size gives you the standard error. The standard error can also be used to calculate the standard error of the differences between two sample means. The difference between the sample means obtained in the research divided by the standard error of the difference between two sample means is distributed like a statistical distribution called t. The distribution of t can then be used to assess how likely the obtained difference between the sample means is if the null hypothesis of zero difference between the samples is true.

The data in Table 14.4 were also analysed using conventional tests of statistical significance. They resulted in exactly the same conclusion as our test. That is, that the keyboard errors of men and women when word-processing are significantly different at the 5 per cent level.

The only drawback of using our method is that it is very time consuming. Obtaining many random samples from a population is not the quickest of processes. Consequently statisticians have used much more mathematical ways of doing what we did.

consequently, the hypothesis that men have poorer fine motor skills than women was accepted.

We can also speak of a statistically significant difference. This merely indicates that our obtained difference between sample means is *not* in the middle 95 per cent of differences that would be obtained if the null hypothesis were correct. This is all that 'significant at the 5 per cent level' means.

EXERCISE 14.1   TESTING THE NULL HYPOTHESIS

The methods described in this chapter can be used on any data where there are two groups. It is a practical proposition to use these methods in class to test significance and to learn better the processes involved. It is probably too time consuming if you are working alone.

Collect your data from two different samples. The method works best if you have equal sample sizes. For convenience, the sample sizes should not exceed 12 each.

Work out the mean of both samples combined. Add or subtract appropriate amounts to the scores in each sample such that each sample mean equals the combined sample mean.

Each member of the class should carry out the following steps:

•   Write each of these 'adjusted' scores on a slip of paper, using a different slip for each adjusted score. This is the estimated null hypothesis population.
•   Put the slips of paper into a hat and draw out a number of them corresponding to the size of your first sample. Each slip should be replaced into the hat once the score written on it has been noted.
•   Now draw out a number of slips from the hat corresponding to the size of your second sample, replacing as above.

Calculate the mean of the first sample minus the mean of the second sample. This is the difference between the sample means. Make a note of the difference including the positive or negative sign.

Carry on drawing slips and calculating the differences between the sample means. Stop the process when you are getting short of available time or when you have 100, 200 or 300 differences between sample means.

Using the mean differences from all members of the class carry out the following:

•   Draw a histogram plotting the distribution of differences between the means. This is best if it is similar to Table 14.7 although the ranges used for each bar may be modified depending on your data.
•   Work out which scores account for the middle 95 per cent of difference scores.

Does your empirical data support the hypothesis or the null hypothesis at the 5 per cent level of significance?

Of course, the difference between the two samples may have been close to the 0.00 that we would have expected if the null hypothesis was true. If the difference is in the middle 95 per cent of differences then we accept the null hypothesis as likely to be true and reject the hypothesis. In these circumstances, the difference between our sample means is non-significant.

See Box 14.2 for information on significance testing in 'real' statistics.

Now carry out Exercise 14.1.

SUMMARY

- Inferential statistics are the techniques by which information available from samples is generalised to populations.
- It tends to be not the easiest set of ideas to assimilate so take time and care to understand them.
- All research in psychology uses samples; no research is carried out on all of the population. Consequently the question is whether information from samples can usefully be used to make generalisations to populations.
- Significance testing uses inferential statistics to help you decide whether your hypothesis or your null hypothesis is more likely to be true.
- Five per cent significance means that your data are in the most unusual 5 per cent of samples if the population defined by the null hypothesis is sampled. It is taken to mean that it is more likely that your data do not support the null hypothesis. Thus we speak of rejecting the null hypothesis at the 5 per cent level in favour of the hypothesis.
- Later chapters return to significance testing as it is carried out in practice.

Table 14.A1 Table of means of 'samples of men' and 'samples of women' selected at random from the estimated population under the null hypothesis (Table 14.5)

Pair number	Scores in sample A Men	Sample A mean	Scores in sample B Women	Sample B mean	Difference between means
1	2 3 3 3 5 5 9 5 5 1	4.1	2 2 3 3 4 5 6 7 7 8	4.7	−0.6
2	3 3 3 5 5 5 6 6 8 9	5.3	2 2 5 5 5 6 8 8 9 9	5.9	−0.6
3	1 3 3 4 5 5 5 7 8 9	5.0	3 3 3 5 5 5 6 3 6 9	4.8	+0.2
4	1 2 3 3 4 4 4 5 5 6	3.7	2 4 5 5 5 5 6 6 7 7	5.2	−1.5
5	3 3 4 4 5 5 5 5 7 9	5.0	2 3 3 4 4 5 5 5 5 6	4.2	+0.8
6	3 3 5 5 5 6 6 8 9 9	5.9	3 3 4 5 5 7 8 9 9 9	6.2	−0.3
7	3 3 3 4 5 5 5 5 7 9	4.7	3 4 4 5 8 9 9 4 5 9	6.0	−1.3
8	2 3 3 3 3 4 5 5 9 9	4.6	3 4 5 5 5 5 5 6 7 8	5.3	−0.7
9	3 3 3 4 5 5 5 5 6 9	4.8	4 4 4 5 5 5 6 8 9 9	5.9	−1.1
10	3 3 3 5 5 6 6 7 9 9	5.6	2 3 4 5 5 5 6 6 7 9	5.2	+0.4
11	2 3 3 3 4 5 5 5 7 8	4.5	2 4 5 5 5 5 6 6 8 9	5.5	−1.0
12	2 3 3 3 3 4 5 6 8 9	4.6	3 3 3 3 4 4 5 5 5 6	4.1	+0.5
13	3 3 3 5 5 5 5 5 6 7	4.7	3 3 4 5 5 5 5 6 7 8	5.1	−0.4
14	2 3 3 3 4 4 4 5 5 9	4.2	3 3 5 5 5 5 5 6 7 9	5.3	−1.1
15	2 4 9 3 3 5 5 6 7 9	5.3	3 3 3 3 5 5 5 7 8 9	5.1	+0.2
16	3 4 5 5 5 5 6 6 9 9	5.7	2 2 3 3 4 5 6 7 8 9	4.9	+0.8
17	3 3 3 3 4 4 4 5 7 9	4.4	2 3 3 4 5 5 5 7 9 9	5.2	−0.8
18	3 3 3 5 5 5 5 6 8 9	5.2	2 3 3 4 3 5 5 6 9 9	4.9	+0.3
19	3 3 3 4 5 5 5 5 6 6	4.5	3 3 4 5 5 5 5 5 9 9	5.1	−0.6
20	2 3 3 3 4 5 5 6 7 9	4.7	3 3 4 5 5 5 5 5 6 8	4.9	−0.2
21	2 3 5 5 5 5 5 5 6 8	4.7	2 3 3 5 6 7 8 8 9	5.6	−0.9
22	3 4 5 6 6 7 8 9 9 9	6.6	2 3 3 4 5 5 5 6 6 9	4.8	+1.8
23	2 3 3 3 3 6 6 6 8 9	4.9	2 3 4 4 4 5 5 5 5 9	4.3	+0.6
24	3 3 3 3 3 5 6 6 9 9	5.0	3 3 3 4 4 5 5 6 7	4.3	+0.7
25	3 3 3 4 5 5 5 5 6 7	4.4	3 3 3 5 5 5 5 5 6 7	4.5	−0.1
26	2 4 4 5 6 6 6 7 8 9	5.6	3 4 4 5 5 5 6 7 8 9	5.6	0.0
27	3 3 3 4 5 5 5 6 7 9	4.8	2 3 3 4 5 6 6 7 9 9	5.4	−0.6
28	3 4 5 5 5 6 6 7 9 9	5.9	2 3 3 4 5 5 5 8 9 9	5.3	+0.6

Table 14.A1 continued

Pair number	Scores in sample A Men	Sample A mean	Scores in sample B Women	Sample B mean	Difference between means
29	2 3 3 3 5 5 6 6 7 8	4.8	3 3 4 4 8 7 9 9 9 9	6.5	−1.7
30	2 3 3 4 4 4 5 5 8 9	4.7	3 3 4 5 5 5 5 6 8 9	5.3	−0.6
31	4 4 5 5 6 6 6 7 9 9	6.1	2 3 3 4 5 5 5 6 8 9	5.0	+1.1
32	3 3 4 5 5 5 6 6 9 7	5.3	2 3 3 3 3 5 5 5 6 9	4.4	+0.9
33	2 2 3 4 6 7 7 8 9 9	5.7	2 3 3 3 3 5 5 5 6 8	4.3	+1.4
34	2 3 4 5 5 5 6 8 8 9	5.5	3 3 4 5 5 5 5 5 5 6	4.6	+0.9
35	2 3 3 3 3 4 5 5 7 8	4.3	3 3 3 5 5 5 6 8 9 9	5.6	−1.3
36	3 4 4 5 5 6 6 6 9 9	5.6	3 3 4 5 6 6 7 7 9 9	5.9	−0.3
37	2 3 3 3 4 5 5 5 6 7	4.3	3 4 4 5 5 5 5 6 8 9	5.4	−1.1
38	2 3 3 4 6 6 8 9 9 9	5.5	3 3 3 3 5 5 5 6 9 9	5.0	+0.5
39	2 3 3 3 3 5 5 5 5 6	4.0	2 3 3 3 4 5 5 6 6 8	4.5	−0.5
40	3 3 3 3 4 5 6 7 9	4.6	3 3 3 5 5 5 8 9 9	5.5	−0.9
41	2 3 3 3 4 5 5 6 7 9	4.7	3 3 3 3 4 5 5 8 9 9	5.2	−0.5
42	3 3 4 5 5 5 6 8 9 9	5.7	2 3 3 4 5 5 5 6 9	4.5	+1.2
43	3 3 4 4 5 5 5 6 9 9	5.3	3 3 3 5 5 5 5 5 6 9	4.9	+0.4
44	2 3 3 3 5 5 6 8 9	4.7	3 3 4 5 5 5 5 8 9	5.0	−0.3
45	2 3 3 6 4 5 5 7 9 9	5.3	3 3 3 5 5 5 7 9 9 9	5.8	−0.5
46	3 3 4 5 5 5 6 8 9 9	5.7	3 4 4 5 5 5 5 6 9	5.1	+0.6
47	3 3 3 3 4 4 5 5 8 9	4.7	3 4 5 5 5 6 6 7 9 9	5.9	−1.2
48	2 3 4 5 5 5 6 6 6 7	4.9	3 4 4 5 5 5 7 8 9 9	5.9	−1.0
49	2 3 3 3 3 4 4 5 5 6	3.8	2 3 3 3 4 5 5 5 8 9	4.7	−0.9
50	2 3 3 4 5 5 5 6 9 9	5.1	3 3 3 3 4 5 5 6 6 9	4.7	+0.4

15

Comparing the scores of two groups of people

Mann-Whitney U-test

INTRODUCTION

Questions such as: 'Are women better drivers than men?'; 'Do children who are beaten for misbehaviour grow into criminals?'; 'Do vegans have a better developed sense of social responsibility than vegetarians?; 'Are country music fans less intelligent than opera lovers?'; and 'Can young people memorise things better than older people?', are familiar in everyday conversation as well as research.

They also imply hypotheses such as: 'Women and men differ in their driving ability'; 'Beating children is related to criminality'; 'Vegans have different levels of social responsibility than vegetarians'; 'Country music fans have lower intelligence test scores than do opera lovers', and 'Age is related to memory ability'.

All of these different questions and hypotheses can be addressed using the same basic research design. They each involve (or imply) two different groups of people – women drivers and men drivers, beaten children versus non-beaten children, vegans and vegetarians, country music fans and opera lovers, and younger people and older people.

They also involve a variable or measure on which the two groups supposedly differ: driving ability; criminal behaviour; social responsibility; intelligence; and memory ability.

All of these questions imply very much the same sort of research design. Any of them could be adapted to the generalised research design given in Table 15.1.

Table 15.2 shows how the general design can be applied to two of the questions mentioned above. Try figuring out how the tables would look for the research question 'Are country music fans less intelligent than opera lovers?'

The numbers in the boxes in Table 15.2 are scores on the dependent variable. So, in the study of women drivers versus men drivers the dependent variable is driving ability and the numbers represent scores on a measure of driving ability. Driving ability is called the dependent variable because it is believed that driving ability is dependent upon whether a driver is a woman or a man.

Table 15.1 General research design for comparing two groups

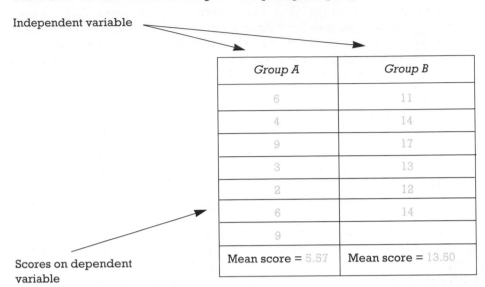

Independent variable

Scores on dependent variable

Group A	Group B
6	11
4	14
9	17
3	13
2	12
6	14
9	
Mean score = 5.57	Mean score = 13.50

Table 15.2 Illustrating how the general research design in Table 15.1 can be used for the women versus men drivers and the beaten versus non-beaten children investigations

Group A	Group B	Women drivers	Men drivers	Beaten children	Non-beaten children
6	11	59	30	9	4
4	14	40	27	7	2
9	17	55	20	5	3
3	13	43	51	8	1
2	12	70	43	5	4
6	14	65	35	7	5
9					1
Mean = 5.6	Mean = 13.5	Mean = 55.3	Mean = 34.3	Mean = 6.8	Mean = 2.9

The gender of the driver is known as the *independent variable*. It is called the independent variable because driving ability obviously cannot cause the driver's sex.

This categorisation into dependent and independent variables only applies to a particular study. In another study, driving ability might be the independent variable.

The numbers in the columns of Table 15.2 are scores on the dependent variable. That is to say, they are measures of an individual's driving ability or criminal behaviour.

Finally, the tables contain the means of the columns of scores for each group. The reason for this is that when we say things like 'women are better drivers than men' we actually mean to say that the average woman is a better driver than the average man. We do *not* think that *all* women drivers are better than *all* men drivers. Consequently, we usually compare the average of the scores for one group with the average of the scores for the other group. See Boxes 15.1 and 15.2.

BOX 15.1 USEFUL ADVICE

Although this is not essential, if you can it is usually better for statistical reasons to have equal or nearly equal numbers of participants in both your groups. If you cannot, then you need to be extra careful about checking that the variances of both groups are similar and that their distributions are symmetrical rather than skewed.

Statistical significance in such designs only shows that the two groups differ from each other. This does not explain why the two groups differ. So, if it turns out in your research that women are indeed better drivers than men, then do not make unsupported claims that this is because men are reckless or that women are slow drivers. These claims would require additional research to substantiate them.

Of course you may *speculate* why there is this difference but you should make it absolutely clear that you are aware that you cannot test your explanations at the present time. For example, 'There are a number of *possible* reasons why women show better driving skills than men. These include: that women have a greater sense of social responsibility; that women tend to be taught to drive by professional driving instructors more often than men; that women tend to drive their children around more often than men do; and that women are less likely to overestimate their driving ability than men are. These possibilities require further research in order to establish their viability.'

BOX 15.2 STRENGTHS AND WEAKNESSES OF THIS DESIGN

This is a straightforward and uncomplicated research design.

If you obtain a significant difference between your two groups you can conclude that the hypothesis is supported and that the null hypothesis should be rejected. There is a difference between the two groups.

However, you must go no further than stating that there is a difference. To say what caused the difference is to go beyond the data collected.

THE ANALYSIS OF TWO GROUPS OF SCORES

Although we could take any of our examples, let us take the familiar, vexed old question of whether women or men make the better drivers.

All we need is a group of men and a group of women drivers. Gender is the *independent variable*.

Ideally they will be similar to each other in all respects except for their gender. Probably the researcher would wish to ensure that the male and female drivers are similar in age range, have been driving for a similar number of years, and do similar amounts and types of driving. Of course, there may be other variables which the researcher should have taken into account but failed to do.

We also need a measure of good driving. This sounds straightforward but it is likely that few of us could agree on a single definition. Some might argue that it should be the number of accidents they have had each year they have been driving. Some might argue that it should be the number of fines they have had for potentially hazardous activities such as speeding and driving recklessly. Others might suggest that the drivers' ratings of themselves would be a useful measure, and yet others might argue that it should be a more standardised measure such as the number of errors made when driving around a standard obstacle course. You might have your own ideas. All of these measures are *dependent variables*. However, for the purposes of simple statistical analysis, these should be dealt with separately.

It is useful to design a data collection sheet for your data. We give an example in Table 15.A1. Notice that we have identified the independent variable and several separate dependent variables. We have also included a number of additional variables which might be pertinent to any gender differences we find.

Refer to Table 15.3 for the statistical analyses you are likely to need to present in your report. The table also gives the location of more information on these analyses in this book.

The relevant data from the data collection sheet need to be entered on to Worksheet 15.1 (see pages 181–2). Mostly when doing research, your data collection sheet will not match exactly the format required for your tables and statistical analysis.

We will compare the male and female scores on dependent variable 1 (driving ability). So the scores for the females on dependent variable 1 should be entered into Column 1 of the Worksheet. Then the scores for males on dependent variable 1 should be entered into Column 3 of the Worksheet.

The steps for the Worksheet can now be followed.

Look at Boxes 15.3 and 15.4 on the Mann-Whitney *U*-test and the ideal dependent variable, then carry out Exercise 15.1.

Table 15.3 Important statistical analyses to include in your report

Statistical analysis	Purpose	Location in this book
Compute the mean (average) score for both Group 1 and Group 2 separately	It indicates which group has the highest average score on your dependent variable. The difference between the two means indicates the degree of difference between the two groups.	pp. 66–7 Worksheet 7.1
Compute the variance of Group 1 and the variance of Group 2.	To determine if the variances are similar	pp. 72–3 Worksheet 7.2
	If the variances are similar then it is appropriate to use parametric tests such as the unrelated *t*-test instead of the Mann-Whitney *U*-test	pp. 224–8 Worksheet 18.1
Draw separate histograms of the Group 1 scores and the Group 2 scores. Alternatively a compound histogram can be used	This will help you detect very skewed distributions which suggest the Mann-Whitney *U*-test is the more appropriate	pp. 181–2 Worksheet 15.1

BOX 15.3   WHAT IS THE MANN-WHITNEY *U*-TEST?

- The Mann-Whitney *U*-test is a test of statistical significance.
- It is a *non-parametric* test. As such, you do not have to have bell-shaped data which are symmetrical when plotted on a histogram or frequency curve.
- You use it when you have two groups of scores from separate groups of individuals. That is, the scores are *unrelated* to each other.
- You use it when you want to know whether the typical (or averaged ranked) scores in the two groups differ from each other.
- It tells you whether it is safe to generalise from your data that are collected from samples of people to the population of people from which your samples come.
- The Mann-Whitney *U*-test involves ranking all of the scores from the smallest to the largest. The use of ranks standardises the statistical analysis.
- In itself, the test does not tell you which of your two groups has the largest scores. In order to know which group has the largest scores, you need to work out the average of the scores for the first group and then the average of the scores for the second group.

Worksheet 15.1 for the Mann-Whitney U-test

The data used are based on the study of men and women drivers in Table 15.2.

Step 1: Put the scores for the *larger* group in Column 1.

Step 2: Put the scores for the *smaller* group in Column 3. (In this example both groups are the same size so the male drivers' scores have been arbitrarily placed in Column 1.)

Column 1	Column 2	Column 3	Column 4
Larger group scores Men drivers	Larger group ranks	Smaller group scores Women drivers	Smaller group ranks
30	3	59	10
27	2	40	5
20	1	55	9
51	8	43	6.5
43	6.5	70	12
35	4	65	11
	Sum the above ranks. This is $R_1 = 24.5$		

Step 3: *Irrespective of whether the score is in the larger or smaller group*, rank all of the scores from the smallest to the largest (p. 116). Put these ranks in Column 2 and Column 4 as appropriate, next to the scores to which they refer.

Step 4: Scores which tie are given the average of the ranks they would otherwise have received (p. 116)

Step 5: Add up the ranks in Column 2. This is $R_1 = 24.5$

Step 6: N_1 = the *number* of scores in the *larger group* = 6

Step 7: N_2 = the *number* of scores in the *smaller group* = 6

Step 8: We then test the statistical value of U (23.5) by consulting Table 15.A2.

Step 9: Draw an (imaginary) pencil line down from the column of Table 15.A2 which corresponds to our value of N_1 (in the present case 6).

Step 10: Draw a horizontal pencil line through the row of Table 15.A2 which corresponds to our value of N_2 (in the present case 6).

Step 11: The cell at the intersection of the vertical and horizontal lines gives the *two* ranges of sums of ranks which are significant. Circle these lightly in pencil.

Step 12: Your value of R_1 has to be within either of the two ranges to be statistically significant at the 5 per cent level (two-tailed test). If your value of R_1 is not within either range then it is not statistically significant.

Step 13: Table 15.A2 tells us for sample sizes of 6 and 6, the significant ranges are 21 to 26 or 52 to 57. Our value of $R_1 = 24.5$. This is therefore within one of the significant ranges. In other words, we reject the null hypothesis that the independent variable is unrelated to the dependent variable in favour of the view that the independent variable has an influence on the scores on the dependent variable (see pp. 162–3).

Reporting your findings

- If your value of R_1 is within one of the listed ranges for your sample sizes, your Mann-Whitney value is statistically significant at the 5 per cent level. In these circumstances we might write 'The mean score for the women drivers on the test of driving ability was 55.33 and for the men drivers 34.33 indicating that the men tended to have poorer driving ability. The Mann-Whitney U-test indicated that this difference was statistically significant ($R = 24.5$, $N = 6, 6$, $p < 0.05$. Thus we accept the hypothesis that there is a gender difference in driving skill.'

- If your value of R_1 is *not* within one of the listed ranges for your sample sizes, your Mann-Whitney value is *not* statistically significant at the 5 per cent level. In these circumstances we might write 'The mean score for the women drivers on the test of driving ability was ___ and for the men drivers ___ indicating that ___.
However, a Mann-Whitney U-test showed that this difference was not statistically significant ($R = $ ___, $N = $ ___, n.s.). Thus we reject the hypothesis that there is a gender difference in driving skill.'

BOX 15.4   THE IDEAL DEPENDENT VARIABLE

Dependent variables are normally measured by numerical scores in psychological research. Ideally in research, the measure of the dependent variable should be examined for the following:

- *Validity* What sort of evidence is there that it measures what it is supposed to measure. This is most likely to be a problem where you develop your own measure since assessing validity can be expensive of time and money. Validity is much less of a problem where you use standard psychological tests and measures for which there is available published evidence of their validity. Similarly, if you are adopting other people's dependent variables from published research, they may provide evidence for the validity of their measure.
- *Reliability* Some measurements are more prone to errors than others. For example, income may be assessed by inspecting people's pay slips over a year. This is likely to be a very reliable measure as it is fairly free from imprecision. However, asking a person's partner to state their yearly income may be very error prone. The partner may have never asked, they may have been misled, they may confuse gross income with net income after deductions and so forth. Unreliable measures may be valid in the sense that they measure what they are supposed to measure but they introduce considerable error which reduces the trends in the data. Again reliability is a major unknown factor if you are using your own measures. It is more easily assessed from published data on fairly standard and common measures.

Try to avoid measures which have only a small range of possible scores. For example, to measure attitude to abortion on a five-point scale such as: 'I am strongly against abortion'; 'I am against abortion'; 'I am neither for nor against abortion'; 'I am in favour of abortion'; and 'I am strongly in favour of abortion', would provide a restricted range of scores from 1 to 5. This can cause problems in statistical analysis based on ranks since there will be many tied ranks. It may also be too crude to allow changes and variations in opinion to be addressed.

Try to ensure that measures do not have a 'ceiling'. This means avoiding scores that in general are high so that 'improvement' is difficult or impossible. For example, a test of mathematical ability may be too easy for the age group to which you are administering it. Most of the children score at the top end of the distribution. This means that this test will not be very useful for measuring improvements in mathematical ability. Ceiling effects can occur in virtually any sort of measure. They have the further disadvantage of skewing the distribution of scores.

Also remember that there may be a 'floor' to the measure. This would have the effect of preventing scores getting lower. They, also, may produce skewed distributions.

EXERCISE 15.1 CALCULATING A MANN-WHITNEY *U*-TEST

Analyse the data in Table 15.1 with the Mann-Whitney *U*-test to determine whether beaten children are more likely to show criminal behaviour than non-beaten children. Higher scores denote greater criminal behaviour.

- What is the sum of ranks of the beaten group?
- What is the sum of ranks of the non-beaten group?
- Is the level of significance one- or two-tailed?
- Are beaten children significantly more likely to show criminal behaviour than non-beaten children?

The answers to this exercise are at the end of this chapter.

SUMMARY

- This chapter explains how to compare scores on a single (dependent) variable from two distinct groups of people.
- This is known as an independent groups design.
- Essentially the researcher needs to know if there is a difference between the scores of one group and those of another. For example, does the average score of Group 1 differ from the average score of Group 2?
- The chapter describes the use of histograms, basic descriptive statistics and the Mann-Whitney *U*-test to compare the scores of two (unrelated) groups of people.
- Care should be taken about inferring causes of any significant difference found.
- Speculative interpretations should be presented as such.

ANSWERS TO EXERCISE

Answers to Exercise 15.1

The sum of ranks of the beaten group is 62.

The sum of ranks of the non-beaten group is 29.

The level of significance is one-tailed because beaten children are expected to have higher criminal scores than non-beaten children.

Beaten children are significantly more likely to show criminal behaviour than non-beaten children.

Table 15.A1 Data collection sheet

	Case	Dependent variable 1	Dependent variable 2	Dependent variable 3	Additional information		
					Age	Years driving	Annual mileage
	1						
	2						
	3						
	4						
	5						
Group 1	6						
Males	7						
	8						
	9						
	10						
	11						
	12						
	13						
	14						
	15						
	16						
	17						
	18						
	19						
	20						
	21						
Group 2	22						
Females	23						
	24						
	25						
	26						

Table 15.A1 Data collection sheet continued

		Dependent variable 1	Dependent variable 2	Dependent variable 3	Additional information		
	Case				Age	Years driving	Annual mileage
	27						
	28						
	29						
	30						
	31						
	32						
	33						
	34						
	35						
	36						
	37						
	38						
	39						
	40						

Table 15.A2 5 per cent two-tailed significance table for the sum of ranks in the Mann-Whitney *U*-test

- Find the column and row where your larger and smaller sample sizes intersect.
- In the cell you will find two sets of ranges. If your sum of ranks for the larger sample size is in either of these inclusive ranges then your findings are statistically significant at the 5 per cent level with a two-tailed test. That is you reject the null hypothesis.
- If the sample sizes are equal, it does not matter which you select for the larger group.
- Values can also be used as a 2.5 per cent one-tailed significance table.

Sample size for larger group

	6	7	8	9	10	11	12	13	14	15	16	17	18	19	20
6	21–26	28–34	36–44	45–55	55–66	66–79	78–92	91–107	105–122	120–139	136–157	153–175	171–195	190–215	210–237
	52–57	64–70	76–84	89–99	104–115	119–132	136–150	153–169	172–189	191–210	211–232	233–255	255–279	279–304	303–330
7		28–36	36–46	45–57	55–69	66–82	78–96	91–111	105–127	120–144	136–162	153–181	171–201	190–222	210–244
		69–77	82–92	96–108	111–125	127–143	144–162	162–182	181–203	201–225	222–248	244–272	267–297	291–323	316–350
8			36–49	45–60	55–72	66–85	78–100	91–115	105–131	120–149	136–167	153–187	171–207	190–228	210–251
			87–100	104–117	118–135	135–154	152–174	171–195	191–217	211–240	233–264	255–289	279–315	301–1342	329–370
9				45–62	55–75	66–89	78–104	91–119	105–136	120–154	136–173	153–192	171–213	190–235	210–258
				109–126	125–145	142–165	160–186	180–208	200–231	221–255	243–280	267–306	291–333	316–361	342–390
10					55–78	66–92	78–107	91–124	105–141	12–159	136–178	153–198	171–219	190–242	210–265
					132–155	150–176	169–198	184–221	209–245	231–270	254–296	278–323	303–351	328–380	355–410
11						66–96	78–111	91–128	105–145	120–164	136–183	153–204	171–226	190–248	210–272
						157–187	177–210	197–234	219–259	241–285	265–312	289–340	314–369	341–3399	368–430

Table 15.A2 continued

	C1	C2	C3	C4	C5	C6	C7	C8	C9
12	78–115	91–132	105–150	120–169	136–189	153–210	171–232	190–255	210–279
	185–222	206–247	228–273	251–300	275–328	300–357	326–387	353–418	371–450
13		91–136	105–155	120–174	136–195	153–216	171–238	190–263	210–286
		215–260	237–287	261–315	285–344	311–374	338–405	366–438	394–470
14			105–160	120–179	136–200	153–220	171–245	190–269	210–293
			246–301	271–330	296–360	324–391	349–423	379–457	407–490
15				120–184	136–206	153–228	171–251	190–276	210–300
				281–345	306–376	335–408	361–441	391–476	420–510
16					136–211	153–234	171–257	190–283	210–308
					317–392	344–425	373–459	403–495	432–530
17						153–240	171–264	190–290	210–315
						355–442	384–477	415–514	445–550
18							171–270	190–297	210–322
							396–495	427–533	458–570
19								190–304	210–329
								439–552	471–590
20									210–337
									483–610

Note
The above table was calculated by the authors.

16

Comparing scores from the same group of people on two occasions

Wilcoxon matched-pairs test

INTRODUCTION

There are many circumstances in which you might wish to measure changes in a group of people's scores obtained at two different points in time. For example, do children use more adjectives in their speech when they are six years old than when they are five? Does the intelligence of a group of people decline between the age of 70 and 75 years? Have the mathematics scores of a group of children changed over the last six months?

These questions imply hypotheses such as: 'Children use more adjectives in speech at age six than age five'; 'Intelligence scores decline from age 70 to age 75'; and 'Mathematical ability increases over time'. All of these hypotheses conform to the same basic research design which is illustrated in Table 16.1 which also shows the data for the 'adjectives in children's speech study'.

Table 16.1 Some of the change over time studies illustrated in a general schematic form

	Time 1	*Time 2*
Person A		
Person B		
Person C		
Person D		
Person E		
Person F		
Mean score		

	Number of adjectives at five years	*Number of adjectives at six years*
Child A	8	17
Child B	12	20
Child C	3	15
Child D	14	22
Child E	4	13
Child F	9	18
Mean score		

Try drawing up a similar table to illustrate the study of the decline in intelligence between 70 and 75 years of age.

In all of the examples, the researcher studies change in a *single* group of people from an earlier to a later point in time. This is known as a *related* design because the two sets of scores are obtained from exactly the *same* group of people at two different points in time.

Always in these designs there must be equal numbers of scores for each time period. This has to be the case with related designs. There is a risk that you cannot measure everyone at the two different stages. Those without the two scores measured at different times must be omitted from the analysis.

The *independent variable* is time in all of these studies. However, sometimes the researcher may prefer to point to some variable that has changed over time. For example, the independent variable might be the introduction of a new mathematics curriculum in school.

The *dependent variable* is measured by the numerical scores on the variable that is being investigated. For example, in the above examples the dependent variables might be the number of adjectives spoken by the child in a five minute interview, the IQ scores, and scores on a standard test of mathematical ability.

A further example

Suppose it is important to know how effective psychotherapy is. For example, does Gestalt psychotherapy improve mental health?

One obvious way of finding this is to obtain from a group of people scores on a measure of mental health *before* they undergo a course of Gestalt psychotherapy, and to measure their mental health *after* the course of Gestalt psychotherapy. This design is represented in Table 16.2.

This is known as a before-and-after study or a pre-test–post-test study.

The *independent variable* is time. However, since the study is intended to assess the effects of Gestalt psychotherapy it is assumed that changes over time are due to the effects of Gestalt psychotherapy.

The *dependent variable* is measured by the numerical scores on the measure that is being investigated. In our example, the dependent variable is mental health. These are scores on a measure of mental health called the *Howitt and Cramer Happiness with Life Index*.

To analyse the data, one checks whether the mean (average) score on the dependent variable changes from the first to the second measurement time.

Sometimes a researcher may have *two or more dependent variables*. For example, the researcher might use the mental health measure and a depression measure. In this kind of circumstance the data are analysed as if they were two separate experiments. In other words, one goes through the analysis for the mental health measure and then again for the depression measure. This is a very important point which can help avoid much confusion. Having many dependent variables does not mean that you have to use complex statistical techniques. The simple statistical tests in this book used repeatedly are often a satisfactory approach.

Table 16.2 Improvement in mental health following Gestalt psychotherapy

	Time 1 (January – before psychotherapy)	Time 2 (March – after Psychotherapy)
	Scores on dependent variable – mental health	
Anthony*	8	13
Cheri	3	7
Winston	5	5
Jenny	9	7
Malcolm	5	8
Samantha	6	11
Carrie	8	14
Sanjit	4	9
Buster	7	13
Alice	5	9

Note
*Names have been inserted as a reminder that this is a related design in which scores have been obtained from the one group of people at two different points in time. For ethical reasons, real names would not be given in research actually carried out.

Analysis of data from the Gestalt psychotherapy study

In our example, the researcher is investigating the effects of Gestalt psychotherapy (the independent variable) on a measure of psychological well-being (the dependent variable). The measure of psychological well-being was taken in January before the psychotherapy began and then again in March after the course of psychotherapy was finished.

The *hypothesis* is 'There is a relationship between time of measurement and scores on the dependent variable *Happiness with Life*'. Another way of putting this is to say that there will be a change in the mean score on the dependent variable *Happiness with Life* following Gestalt psychotherapy.

The *null hypothesis* is 'There is *no* relationship between the time of measurement and scores on the dependent variable *Happiness with Life*'. The null hypothesis indicates that there should be no difference between the means at Time 1 and Time 2 in Table 16.2. However, sampling fluctuations will ensure that some differences will be different from zero.

The Wilcoxon matched-pairs test is a simple significance test for this sort of data. We will use it for our statistical analysis in Worksheet 16.1. The related *t*-test (Chapter 19, pp. 238–40) probably could be used as an alternative. However, it is computationally somewhat more difficult and its use can be avoided until you have developed your skills in research a little more.

Box 16.1 highlights some problems with assessing changes over time, and Boxes 16.2 and 16.3 give more information on the Wilcoxon matched-pairs test. Now carry out Exercise 16.1.

BOX 16.1 PROBLEMS IN ASSESSING CHANGES OVER TIME

A design with a single pre-test–post-test comparison cannot involve random assignment of participants to conditions because there is only one condition. Consequently it is difficult to know precisely what factors lead to changes over time.

Many different factors may be associated with the elapse of time. Children grow and mature which leads to all sorts of developmental changes; adults mature and age which may lead to changes in memory, experience and so forth; unusual events may happen after the first measurement and before the final measurements – the death of a celebrity may affect everyone's mood; all participants in the research will have had experience in the first phase of the study which leads to changes in the second phase – for example, having completed an IQ test, people may be better at the test simply as a consequence of this practice. All of these factors – and others – lead to uncertainty about just why the average scores for the group have changed over time.

Because the study is happening over time, some participants in the first stage of the study may not take part in the second phase of the study. For example, clients who feel that their psychotherapy is not effective may leave psychotherapy and the study. Thus there is a bias towards obtaining apparent improvements in the study. This is sometimes referred to as *differential dropout* or *attrition*.

When testing the effects of any therapy, it is possible to confuse the effects of psychotherapy with those of spontaneous remission. *Spontaneous remission* is the natural tendency for people to recover without treatment. Hence, time is a great healer!

Even if no changes seem to occur between Time 1 and Time 2, this may be because the factor being studied prevented scores declining! For example, psychotherapy may stop the clients' mental health from declining without appearing to improve mental health.

This does not mean that such designs are useless. It merely means that care needs to be exercised about making *causal* interpretations of your data.

Worksheet 16.1 for the Wilcoxon matched-pairs test

Step 1: Enter the data into the Time 1 and Time 2 columns of the following table. The values were taken from the data described in Table 16.2.

Pair	Column 1 Time X_1	Column 2 Time 2 X_2	Column 3 Difference $D = X_2 - X_1$	Column 4 Rank of difference ignoring sign during ranking
1	8	13	+5	6^+
2	3	7	+4	3.5^+
3	5	5	0 (ignore)	(ignore)
4	9	7	−2	1^-
5	5	8	+3	2^+
6	6	11	+5	6^+
7	8	14	+6	8.5^+
8	4	9	+5	6^+
9	7	13	+6	8.5^+
10	5	9	+4	3.5^+
11				
12				
13				
14				
15				
16				
17				
18				
19				

20				
21				
22				
23				
24				
25				
26				
27				
28				
29				
30				
Means	$\bar{X}_1 = 6.0$	$\bar{X}_2 = 9.6$		Sum of + ranks = 44 Sum of − ranks = 1

Step 2: Subtract the scores in Column 1 from the scores in Column 2. Enter these difference scores in Column 3. Any difference score which is *zero* should be ignored, i.e. deleted from the analysis.

Step 3: Rank the difference scores in column 3 *ignoring the sign of the difference*. That is, treat the difference scores as if they were all positive when ranking.

Remember that where scores are tied, the average of the ranks which otherwise would have been given is used for each of the scores. So, for example, there are two ranks of 3.5 which means that there are two identical scores which if they could be separated would be ranked 3 and 4. Because they cannot be separated they are ranked as the average of 3 and 4 which is 7/2 = 3.5. Similarly, three scores tie which otherwise would be ranked 5, 6 and 7. They are therefore all given the average of 5, 6 and 7 which is 18/3 = 6.

A positive sign is given to the ranks in Column 4 if they are based on a positive difference score in Column 3. A negative sign is given to the ranks if they are based on a negative difference score.

Step 4: Sum the positively signed ranks and then sum the negatively signed ranks in Column 4.

Step 5: Select which is the smaller – the sum of the positively or the sum of the negatively signed ranks. The smaller sum is the value of *T*.

Your value of *T* is checked against Table 16.A1. The sample size is the actual number of scores ranked and so omits any data involving tied scores at Time 1 and Time 2. Your value of *T* must equal or be smaller than the listed value for your sample size in order to reject the null hypothesis in favour of the hypothesis at the 5 per cent level of significance. Our value of *T* is clearly smaller than the listed value of 6. Thus our findings are statistically significant.

Reporting your findings

- If your value of T is equal to or smaller than the listed value for your sample size, your Wilcoxon matched-pairs test is statistically significant at the 5 per cent level. In these circumstances we might write 'The participants' mental health scores before psychotherapy were compared with those after psychotherapy. There was an increase in the mean mental health score from 6.00 before psychotherapy to 9.60 after psychotherapy. The hypothesis that Gestalt psychotherapy is effective was supported ($T = 1$, $N = 10$, $p < 0.05$).'
- If your value of T is larger than the listed value for your sample size, your Wilcoxon matched-pairs test is *not* statistically significant at the 5 per cent level. In these circumstances we might write 'The participants' mental health scores before psychotherapy were compared with those after psychotherapy. There was a(n) _____ in the mean mental health score from _____ before psychotherapy to ____ after psychotherapy. This change was not statistically significant so the hypothesis that Gestalt psychotherapy is effective was rejected ($T = $ ____, $N = $ ____, n.s.).

BOX 16.2   WHEN TO USE THE WILCOXON MATCHED-PAIRS TEST

- The Wilcoxon matched-pairs test is a non-parametric test for comparing two related sets of scores.
- It is powerful – meaning that it is very likely to cause the acceptance of the hypothesis when the hypothesis is true.
- It is also computationally very straightforward and only involves calculating differences between pairs of scores, ranking and summing.
- It is especially useful when:

  - The difference scores show a very unsymmetrical distribution
  - There are outliers in the difference scores – that is a small number of difference scores are very different from the majority.
  - Or if you are just beginning to learn about statistics

- The related t-test (Chapter 19, pp. 238–40) is generally more powerful but the calculation of this is a little more difficult for beginners. It could be used instead of the Wilcoxon matched-pairs test if asymmetry or outliers are not a problem.

SUMMARY

- The related subjects design involves testing participants on at least two occasions.
- Without a control group it is not possible to determine causality with this design.
- The Wilcoxon matched-pairs test is a non-parametric test for determining any difference in the sum of ranked differences between the two occasions.

EXERCISE 16.1   CALCULATING THE WILCOXON MATCHED-PAIRS TEST

Analyse the data in Table 16.1 to test the hypothesis that children at six use more adjectives than children at five.

- What is the sum of the positive ranks?
- What is the sum of the negative ranks?
- What is the value of T?
- Is the level of significance one- or two-tailed?
- Is T statistically significant?

BOX 16.3   MATCHING

You may wonder why the Wilcoxon matched-pairs test is so called. Well it is obviously named after Mr Wilcoxon but why 'matched pairs'?

Mostly in psychology we use the Wilcoxon test in circumstances in which all of the participants serve in all of the conditions of the research. The reason for doing this is that the individual characteristics of the participants contribute less to the variation in the scores on the dependent variable.

The other way of doing something similar is to match your participants to be identical on variables you think might affect the scores on the dependent variable. For example, you might believe that a person's gender and their age might affect their scores.

The way to do this would be to find pairs of individuals who are alike on sex and age – i.e. matched on sex and age. Not all pairs will be alike but the two members of any one pair will be alike. So, for example, Pair 1 might consist of two young females, pair 2 of two elderly males, pair 3 of two elderly females and so forth.

The related t-test discussed in Chapter 19 can also be used on matched pairs of this sort.

Matching is quite difficult and time consuming. There is no point in matching on variables which are not related to the dependent variable.

ANSWERS TO THE EXERCISE

Answers to Exercise 16.1

The sum of the positive ranks is 21.

The sum of the negative ranks is 0.

The value of T is 0.

The level of significance is one-tailed because children at six were expected to use more adjectives than children at five.

T is statistically significant at less than the 0.05 level.

Table 16.A1 One- and two-tailed 0.05 probability values for the Wilcoxon matched-pairs test

Your value of T has to equal or be smaller than the listed value for your number of pairs of scores to accept the hypothesis and reject the null hypothesis.

Number of pairs of scores	One-tailed 0.05 level	Two-tailed 0.05 level
6	2	1
7	4	2
8	6	4
9	8	6
10	11	8
11	14	11
12	17	14
13	21	17
14	26	21
15	31	25
16	36	30
17	42	35
18	47	40
19	54	46
20	60	52
21	68	59
22	76	66
23	84	74
24	92	81
25	101	90

Note
The above table was calculated by the authors.

Part V

The essentials of designing experiments

17

Designing and running experiments

INTRODUCTION

This chapter is intended to provide a practical checklist for the designing and running of experiments. It consists of a number of checklists and similar materials that should help you with the practical business of experimental work in psychology. The design of experiments requires a number of different skills to be employed and it is very easy for any researcher to overlook important matters.

This chapter deliberately revises material dealt with, in part, in earlier chapters.

WHAT IS AN EXPERIMENT?

An *experiment* is an empirical study in which the researcher deliberately intervenes in the situation to change it in a crucial way. The range of such interventions is huge and could include the physical, social, psychological or any other aspect of the situation. Since the situation is altered or changed, intervention is called the *experimental manipulation*.

The researcher in an experiment is usually referred to as the *experimenter*. The word experimenter should only be used in relation to experiments as it implies a particular type of research.

The individuals who experience this manipulation are called the *experimental group*. Often it is stated that the experimental group is subjected to the experimental manipulation.

The *effect* of the changes in the situation is measured by the researcher.

In psychology, an experiment nearly always refers to a *controlled* experiment. This means that there is a comparison group or *control group* of people. The control group is not subjected to the experimental manipulation or intervention.

The control group provides a *baseline* against which to judge what has happened as a consequence of the effects of the experimental manipulation on the experimental group.

It is important that the experimental and control groups are identical except for any effects of the experimental manipulation. This means that the experimental and control groups should be similar prior to the experimental intervention. It is easy to confuse these pre-existing differences with the effect of the experimental manipulation.

In order to ensure that the experimental and control groups are alike except for the intervention or manipulation, participants are normally *randomly assigned* to the experimental and control conditions. Ideally, this should be done just prior to the experimental manipulation stage.

The simplest method of random assignment in an experiment is by tossing a coin. So in order to decide whether Natalie Preston is in the experimental or control condition, a coin is flipped. If it lands heads she is in the experimental condition, if it lands tails, she is in the control condition. This is repeated for each participant in the experiment. (There are other methods of randomisation – see Box 17.1 for details.)

The point of random assignment is to avoid systematic *bias* in the allocation process. In other words, the experimenter should not be able to influence which participants are

---

BOX 17.1 SOME WAYS OF RANDOMLY ASSIGNING PARTICIPANTS TO TWO CONDITIONS

First decide whether your procedure is to be blocked or unblocked. With blocked randomisation, the condition that is to be given to the first participant is decided at random. The remaining condition is then assigned to the second participant. After this the whole process is repeated afresh. One advantage of this procedure is that both conditions are run in close proximity to each other. With unblocked randomisation, the condition that is to be administered to each participant is determined anew for each participant. This procedure may result in the same condition being administered to three or more participants one after the other.

The simplest way of determining random assignment of participants to two conditions is to toss a coin, deciding beforehand which side of the coin is to denote which condition. With blocked randomisation the remaining condition is run second, after which the coin is tossed again to determine the order of the second block. With unblocked randomisation the coin is tossed to determine which condition is to be run on each occasion.

An alternative method is to write each condition on a slip of paper. With blocked randomisation, the two slips of papers are shuffled and the condition on the first slip selected is run first followed by the remaining condition. With unblocked randomisation the number of slips corresponds to the number of times that the two conditions are to be run and the slips are carefully shuffled. The order in which the conditions are run is determined by the final order of the shuffled slips.

Another way is to use the pre-assigned orders displayed in Table 17.A1 for unblocked randomisation and Table 17.A2 for blocked randomisation. The order in which you work through these tables (e.g. forwards, backwards, upwards, downwards) and the position you start from should ideally be decided at random.

allocated to the experimental condition. Without random assignment to the experimental or control conditions, it is possible that the experimenter inadvertently (or even deliberately) chooses the brightest people for the experimental group. This may in itself affect the outcome of the experiment. Similarly, with random allocation to the experimental and control groups, it is impossible for participants to influence which group they are placed in so that participants cannot influence whether they are in the experimental or control condition either.

Of course, random assignment does not guarantee that the experimental and control groups do not differ in some important respect. However, it does ensure that any differences between the two groups are purely chance matters. That is, that the process is free from *systematic biases*. With random allocation, the differences between the experimental and control groups are very unlikely to re-occur in a *replication* of the experiment. This is one reason why replications are important in research. However, experiments are not usually replicated for this purpose but to try to shed light on what explanations are responsible for the findings. If findings cannot be replicated, they do not need to be explained.

The consequence of strictly controlling the situation and randomly assigning the participants to the experimental or control conditions, is that any resulting differences between the experimental and control conditions are the result of the experimental manipulation. In other words, the experimenter can claim that the experimental manipulation was the *cause* of the differences.

As a consequence, experimenters can claim to test *causal explanations*.

ESSENTIAL FEATURES OF EXPERIMENTS

The main requirements of an experiment are the following. Make sure that you understand the concepts clearly as they are essential:

- There is an *experimental group* that is subjected to the experimental manipulation.
- There is a *control group* that is treated identically to the experimental group in all respects except for the experimental manipulation.
- Participants in the research are *randomly allocated* to the experimental and control conditions (perhaps by coin tossing – see Box 17.1).
- The variable that describes the difference in the treatments of the experimental and control groups is called the *independent variable*. So in a study of the effects of a drug on mood, the participants in the experimental condition will be given a drug. The control group will not be given this drug (although they might be given an inactive substance that appears to be the drug – a *placebo*). The independent variable in this case is whether the drug is given.
- The variable on which the *effects* of the independent variable are measured is called the *dependent variable*. In the drugs example, the researcher may wish to know how sleepy the drug makes people. Thus the dependent variable may be how sleepy the participants in the research feel three hours after being given the drug, for example.
- The analysis of a controlled experiment involves comparing the scores of the experimental group with those of the control group on the dependent variable. In

Table 17.1, for example, we can see that the experimental and control groups have apparently different mean (average) scores. The mean score on sleepiness for the experimental group is 10.42 whereas the mean score on sleepiness for the control group is 6.50. Quite clearly the experimental group may have been made sleepy by the drug.

Table 17.1 Data from drug experiment

Independent variable (amount of drug)	
Experimental group (drug)	Control group (no drug)
Participant 1 = 13	Participant 13 = 8
Participant 2 = 15	Participant 14 = 6
Participant 3 = 10	Participant 15 = 3
Participant 4 = 7	Participant 16 = 6
Participant 5 = 16	Participant 17 = 1
Participant 6 = 5	Participant 18 = 10
Participant 7 = 12	Participant 19 = 11
Participant 8 = 8	Participant 20 = 6
Participant 9 = 7	Participant 21 = 5
Participant 10 = 11	Participant 22 = 9
Participant 11 = 12	
Participant 12 = 9	
Mean score = 125/12 = 10.42	Mean score = 65/10 = 6.50

- In order to know whether we can generalise from our samples of data to the populations from which they came, it is necessary to carry out a test of statistical significance using a suitable statistical test. The calculation of the unrelated *t*-test is described in the next chapter. However, the Mann-Whitney *U*-test described in Chapter 15 would also be suitable.

PLANNING EXPERIMENTS: BASIC CONSIDERATIONS

Designing an experiment is not very difficult. However, designing a good one takes care, time and practice. It is probably true to say that there is no such thing as a perfect experiment – just ones that are as good as they can possibly be.

One of the basic difficulties is the number of different aspects that you need to think about when designing experiments. There are so many different considerations to bear in mind that it is easy to overlook important features.

Table 17.2 gives some advantages and disadvantages of controlled experiments, sample size is considered in Box 17.2, and Boxes 17.3 and 17.4 describe experimenter and participant bias, respectively.

Table 17.2 Some advantages and disadvantages of controlled experiments

Advantage	Disadvantage
The causal influence of variables can be assessed	Sometimes, experiments seem somewhat contrived and artificial which makes them seem irrelevant to real-life situations. Some refer to this as a lack of *ecological validity* in experiments
Because they are highly structured and pre-planned, the analysis of experiments tends to be relatively straightforward and to follow conventional steps	Experiments are quite exacting in terms of the rigour adopted by the researcher. Ideally all participants in the research should go through identical procedures with the exception of the experimental manipulation. Achieving standardisation is not easy and requires a lot of pre-planning
Experiments are often carried out in laboratories. The experimenter may find this convenient and an efficient use of time	Psychology laboratories are alien environments for many people and they may not behave naturally as a consequence. Furthermore, laboratories are usually in universities so students are a convenient source of participants. This has resulted in the criticism that psychological research has largely been done on students who may not be typical of people in general
Experiments are usually carried out using a small number of manipulations or variables	Real-life phenomena may involve a complex web of interrelated and interacting influences that are not readily separated from each other
	Standardising procedures can result in highly artificial situations. For example, some researchers have used tape recordings to give their instructions to their participants in a constant manner.

There are a great many different sorts of experimental designs. Many are very specialised in their use. The ones which are discussed in this book are:

- the unrelated subjects design; and
- the related subjects design.

BOX 17.2 SAMPLE SIZE

The question 'how big a sample do I need' sounds straightforward enough. After all, running an experiment or any other sort of study is very time consuming and it would be advantageous to avoid unnecessary labour. Unfortunately, there is no simple solution to the issue of adequate sample size. The answer is dependent on factors that you may not know in advance of running your study:

- The ideal sample size is affected by the strength of the effect of the independent variable on the dependent variable. The bigger this effect, the smaller the sample size will need to be. Quite clearly, this is not under your control although in general researchers might be best advised to study independent variables that are likely to have a big effect on the dependent variable.

- The ideal sample size is affected by the degree of standardisation that you can achieve in your experiment. The more variability and inconsistency in your procedures, the more uncontrolled error is introduced into the situation. Noisy, distracting environments in which it is difficult for the participants to understand your instructions and to think may well reduce the apparent effect of the independent variable on the dependent variable. The more uncontrolled error such as this, the larger the sample size has to be to achieve statistically significant findings. The solution is to standardise your procedures as much as possible.

- The reliability and validity of the dependent variable affects the ideal sample size. The more reliable and valid your measures the smaller your sample size needs to be. It should be obvious that poor measures are less likely to detect the effects of your independent variable. Spend time and effort in obtaining the best possible measure of your dependent variable.

- If you are replicating or adapting the procedures employed in a published study, this will give you some idea of an appropriate sample size.

- Although you might be told that the bigger the sample size the better, this is not strictly speaking correct. Statistically significant results with a small sample indicate a stronger effect of your independent variable on your dependent variable than a similar significance level with a larger sample size.

- However, if the effect is strong and the sample size is larger, the study will have greater credibility in the eyes of most psychologists. Very small sample sizes lead to the impression that a great deal rests on very few cases.

- Ideally then you should avoid using very small samples for anything other than pilot studies.

BOX 17.3 EXPERIMENTER BIAS

Various forms of experimenter bias have been distinguished. A useful little book on this subject is:

Barber, T. X. (1976) *Pitfalls in Human Research: Ten Pivotal Points*, Oxford: Pergamon Press.

Experimenter bias usually refers to the way in which characteristics or actions of the experimenter may unintentionally influence the data collected. For example, the age, sex, class or ethnicity of an interviewer may affect the kinds of answer given. One way of reducing this kind of bias is to ensure that the answers provided by the respondent cannot be seen by the interviewer. An alternative approach is to investigate the extent to which the answers given may be affected by characteristics of the interviewer. For example, we can see whether the answers given by men compared with women differ when interviewed by a man rather than a woman. However, it is most probably only worth doing this if we have good reason to believe that they may vary in some way.

More problematic is the experimenter expectancy effect where the experimenter may unknowingly behave in ways which may cause participants to act in ways that confirm the experimenter's hypothesis. For example, the experimenter may unintentionally show greater interest or approval when the participant behaves in the way desired by the experimenter. Various suggestions have been made as to how expectancy bias may be measured or reduced but most of these procedures are not really practicable for students to carry out and most researchers do not use them. One way of reducing expectancy bias is to minimise the contact between the experimenter and the participant so that the experimenter has less opportunity to influence the participant. One way of doing this is to deliver instructions to the participants through pre-recorded tapes played over loudspeakers. But obviously this creates a somewhat bizarre and unnatural situation.

RANDOM ALLOCATION TO EXPERIMENTAL AND CONTROL GROUPS

Tables 17.A1 and 17.A2 give randomised orders for experimental (e) and control groups (c). The tables have two different forms of randomisation:

- proper randomisation in which every case has an equal chance of selection at every stage (Table 17.A1); and
- blocked randomisation in which the cases are taken in pairs and the first of the pair is allocated at random to the experimental or control condition (Table 17.A2).

Proper randomisation can lead to runs in which, say, there are groups of two, three, four or more participants run in exactly the same condition. This cannot happen with the blocked randomisation for which the longest possible run is two. Blocked randomisation is likely to be the most practical in most circumstances.

BOX 17.4 PARTICIPANT BIAS AND DEMAND CHARACTERISTICS

Participants may also bias the results of a study by the attitudes that they hold about being a participant. Three main attitudes of co-operation, lack of co-operation and evaluation apprehension have been distinguished.

In general it is thought that participants have a co-operative attitude in which they want to behave as the experimenter wants them to behave. The experimenter and/or the experimental situation may give off cues, called *demand characteristics*, which demand that the participant behaves in a particular way. For example, it has been suggested that in Milgram's (1963, 1974) study there were cues that Milgram was unaware of which caused participants to obey.

A problem with the general notion of demand characteristics is that it is essentially untestable unless one suggests exactly what these characteristics are. Without doing this, little appears to be gained by generally proposing that the findings may be due to demand characteristics. In other words, normally the researcher claims that the experimental manipulation causes the experimental effect. With the demand characteristics explanation other features of the experimental manipulation are thought to determine the experimental effect.

One approach used to determine the potential influence of demand characteristics is telling participants they are expected to behave in a way which the experimenter really believes is opposite to the way participants are expected to behave in order to see whether these *counter-demand* instructions can affect the behaviour of participants (e.g. Cramer and Buckland 1995). If participants behave in the experimental condition in the way the experimenter expects and in the counter-demand condition in the way suggested they may behave, then this pattern of finding implies that their behaviour is susceptible to their expectations about how they should behave and is not the result of the experimental manipulation.

Some participants may act in an uncooperative fashion that may be reflected in behaviours such as not following the instructions, carrying out the task carelessly or trying to disconfirm what they believe to be the experimenter's hypothesis. Such behaviour may be minimised by establishing better rapport with the participants and by convincing them of the importance of the research.

Other participants may be apprehensive about taking part in studies because they feel that they are being personally evaluated. As a consequence, they may be keen to present themselves in a socially favourable or desirable light. One way of minimising this apprehension is to ensure that data are collected anonymously. If this is not feasible, stress that the research is concerned with looking at differences between groups of people and that it is not concerned with the information provided by a single particular individual.

The following book provides a more detailed account of this topic:

Adair, J. G. (1973) *The Human Subject: The Social Psychology of the Psychological Experiment*, Boston: Little, Brown.

- Decide whether you want proper randomisation or blocked randomisation.
- Select a way of going through the table – backwards, forwards, every alternate row forwards, or whatever you like.
- Then choose a 'random' starting point – closing your eyes and sticking your finger or pencil in the table is good enough.
- Finally, move through the table from your chosen starting point in the direction and manner that you predetermined. The simplest is to work through the table from your starting point moving along successive rows from left to right. C or c means that your next participant should receive the control manipulation, E or e means that the participant should be run in the experimental condition.

SUMMARY

- An experiment is basically a study in which the independent variable is manipulated by the researcher.
- Participants in the research are assigned to an experimental or control condition at random.
- Randomisation is a selection process by which each participant has an equal chance of being selected.
- Randomisation may be blocked to ensure equal numbers and to avoid runs of a particular condition.
- Compared with other forms of research, experiments can appear contrived and unrealistic. Researchers talk about the ecological validity of experiments.
- Planning experiments is quite complex in the sense that there are many different factors to consider. Worksheet 17.1 is provided to help you with this.
- Ideal sample size is a compromise between large numbers and practicalities. Without some idea from previous similar research about what sample size potentially can generate significant results, it is difficult to decide on an appropriate sample size. Many seemingly unrelated factors influence ideal sample size including the adequacy of your measures.

Worksheet 17.1 step-by-step guide to the design and analysis of a controlled experiment using just one experimental and one control group

The following steps should be followed as carefully as possible. They include ethical, methodological and statistical considerations. You may then use your answers to complete appropriate sections of your report.

Identifying your variables

Name your INDEPENDENT variable

_____

_____

(Remember that the independent variable is given a name which describes the experimental manipulation – that is the way in which the experimental and control group are treated differently. Thus, the independent variable might be 'drug treatment' or 'whether given Nodoze'.)

Name your DEPENDENT variable

_____

_____

(The dependent variable refers to the measurements you are taking. It is the variable that the experimental manipulation may affect. One usually collects SCORES on the dependent variable.)

Aim

The aim of the research is to investigate the influence of _____ (the

independent variable) on _____ (the _dependent_ variable).

(The aim is a statement of the topic being researched. This should be relatively easy to write for an experiment since the aims are always to study the effect of the independent variable on the dependent variable: 'The aim of the research was to investigate the influence of the drug "Nodoze" on drowsiness in young children'. If you vary the wording, DO NOT use phrases like 'The aim of the research was to _prove_ that "Nodoze" causes drowsiness'. This suggests that the researcher wants to prove something – the researcher is supposed to be a detached observer without any vested interest in the outcome of the research. Words such as show or demonstrate are also to be avoided for similar reasons.)

Hypotheses

The NULL HYPOTHESIS is that there is NO relationship between _____

(the *independent* variable) and _____ (the *dependent* variable).

The (*alternative*) HYPOTHESIS is that there *is* a relationship between

_____ (the *independent* variable) and _____ (the

dependent variable).

Participants/subjects

From what population will your participants be selected?

_____

(The population varies greatly from study to study. The population for your first studies may be other students in your class: 'Members of the 1st year psychology class served as participants'. The population for other studies may be different: 'Students at the local school served as participants'; 'Cat owners attending a veterinary surgery took part in the study'.)

What will you tell participants about the purpose of the research?

_____

_____

_____

_____

(This should be enough to give them a realistic idea of what the experiment entails but should avoid giving unnecessary detail so that they know or can guess what the hypothesis is.)

How will you contact participants?

_____

_____

_____

_____

(By putting up a poster? By approaching people directly? By obtaining the help of a teacher or lecturer? Through friends? By getting in touch with a key contact such as the head of the local nursery? Remember that the way in which you contact participants will have an effect on the sort of people who take part and will have an influence on how easy it is to obtain a reasonable number of recruits to your study.)

What additional information will you be collecting about the participants in your research? Sex, Age . . .

_____

_____

_____

_____

(Some basic demographic information such as sex and age of the participants is usually incorporated in your report. The report normally contains simple descriptive statistics such as the frequencies of each sex, and the mean and standard deviation of their ages, for example. Other information may be collected and reported according to the purposes of your research. Usually aspects such as the range of education level, types of occupation, and any other descriptive and potentially relevant information could be provided about your participants.)

Procedure

Write down the stages in the research step by step.

- _____
- _____
- _____
- _____
- _____
- _____
- _____
- _____
- _____
- _____

(Most of your research will have only a few steps.)

What verbal instructions will be given to ALL participants in the research at the start and during the course of the experiment?

_____

_____

_____

_____

_____

_____

_____

_____

How will the INDEPENDENT variable be manipulated? (See Box 18.1, p. 223.)

_____

_____

_____

_____

(Just write down how you are going to treat the experimental and control group differently.)

How will the verbal instructions differ between participants in the experimental group and participants in the control group?

_____

_____

_____

_____

_____

_____

_____

_____

(You may wish to write or type these two different sets of instructions on cards as a memory aid. One card for the experimental group, another for the control group.)

How will you _measure_ the scores on the DEPENDENT variable?

_____

_____

_____

(This has many possible answers depending on the nature of your experiment. But your answers might include things like: 'Reaction time will be measured in terms of the amount of time it takes the individual to press the button once a light is illuminated'; 'Creativity will be measured using the Howit–Cramer Test of Stupid Ideas'; 'Attitudes towards the police will be assessed using a specially-written five item "Police Attitudes Questionnaire"'; 'Group disunity will be measured in terms of the number of times hostile comments are made during a ten-minute observation period during which the group are discussing their likes and dislikes'; 'Television violence viewing will be measured in terms of the number of violent programmes watched each week'.)

How are participants to be allocated to the experimental and control groups?

_____

_____

(Just how are you going to randomise assignment to the experimental and control groups?)

Materials and apparatus

Will you need to build/make/reserve/obtain any equipment or questionnaires/tests for your experiment?

    Yes (If yes draw up a list of your requirements below.)   No

- _____

- _____

- _____

- _____

- _____

What is the procedure for obtaining the above?

_____

_____

(Who holds the equipment? A technician? Do you need authorisation? Do you need to complete a form?)

Data recording sheet

Design a data recording sheet on which you can record the data collected in your research. An example of this is given in Table 18.A2 (pp. 232–3).

Ethics

Complete the ethics checklist in Box 3.3 (pp. 29–30). Discuss your entries with your teacher or lecturer.

Practicalities

Most of the following issues will need to be taken into consideration although they are not normally reported when writing up experiments:

How long do you estimate that it will it take to run a participant through the experimental procedures?

_____

Will you need to book laboratories or rooms for your experiment? Yes   No
(If yes draw up a list of your requirements above. What dates and what times do you think you will need the facilities?)

- _____
- _____
- _____
- _____

How do you make laboratory and room bookings? Do you need the written approval of a member of staff?

_____

_____

_____

Table 17.A1 Random allocation of experimental and control conditions

Choose a random starting point (e.g. by closing your eyes and sticking in your finger).

ecec cecc eeee cecc eccc ecec eeee ecec ecee eeec cccc ecec ccec eccc eecc eece

ccee eece ccee ecce ccce ccee eeee cccc eeee eece eeee eece ccee ceee ceee ccee

eece eeec ccec ccce cece cece ecec eece ccee ecce eeee ceee ceee ecce eece cece

eeee eeee eeee cecc ccec eeee ecec ceec ccce ccce ecec cecc eccc ccce ecce ccec

ecee cecc cecc cccc eeee ccee cccc ecec ccec ecee ceec cece cecc ceec ccee ccce

ceec ecec eccc eecc ccec eeee eeec eece ccec eece eeec ccec cece cccc cecc eccc

eeec ecec ecce eccc ccec cecc ecec ecec cece ecee ecec ecce ceec cece ceee ecce

cecc cccc eeee eeee eeee ecee cccc eeee eecc ccee ccee ccce cccc cccc ccee cecc

ceec ccee ecee cecc ccec eece ceee ccee cccc ecce ccec ccce cecc ceec ecee ecee

ccec cece ccce eeec ccec eeec eecc eeec cece ceec ecce eeec ccec ceec eeec ceee

ceec ecec ccee cece ceec eece ecee ceee cece cccc ecee cece ecce cccc eece cece

ecce eeec ceec ecce ceec ccce ccee eecc ccce eeec ccec ccce eeec eeee ecce cecc

cccc eece ecee ccce cece ecce ecce ecce ccce cccc cecc eecc ceec ecce ccec eccc

cecc eecc eecc cecc ccec ecec eecc eeee cece ecee eeee eeec ecce eeee cccc ecec

cece eecc cccc ccec ecce cccc cccc cece eccc ceec eeee cece eecc cecc eeee ecce

ecec ccec eecc ceec eccc eeee eeec ccee eccc eecc ecce ccce ccee ccec ecee ecec

eece cecc eccc cecc ceec ecee eccc ccee ceec eccc ecee ecec ceec eece eeee eccc

ecec ccec eeee eeec cccc ceee cecc eeec cece ccee ccec ccee ceec eece ceee cecc

ccec ecec ecec eece ccee ecce eccc ecce ccee cece eece ceec cccc eeee cccc ecce

Table 17.A2 Blocked random allocation table

Choose a random starting point (e.g. by closing your eyes and sticking in a pencil). You should begin with the left hand member of each of the pairs of letters.

CE EC CE CE CE EC CE CE CE EC CE EC EC EC EC EC EC CE EC CE EC

CE EC EC EC EC EC CE CE EC EC CE CE CE CE CE CE CE CE EC EC EC

CE CE EC EC CE EC CE EC CE EC EC CE EC EC EC CE EC EC CE EC CE

CE EC CE CE CE CE CE EC CE CE CE CE CE CE EC EC CE CE EC CE EC

EC EC CE EC CE EC CE CE CE CE CE EC EC CE EC CE EC CE EC CE CE

EC EC CE CE EC CE EC EC EC EC CE EC EC EC EC EC EC EC EC EC CE

CE EC EC EC CE EC CE CE EC CE EC EC CE EC CE EC EC CE CE EC EC

CE EC CE CE CE EC CE EC EC EC CE EC EC EC EC EC CE EC CE CE EC

EC CE EC CE CE EC CE CE EC CE EC CE EC CE CE EC EC EC CE EC EC

CE CE CE CE EC EC EC EC CE CE EC EC CE EC EC CE EC CE CE EC EC

EC EC EC EC EC EC EC CE EC CE EC CE CE CE EC EC EC CE EC CE EC

EC EC CE CE EC EC EC CE CE CE EC CE CE CE EC CE EC CE EC CE CE

EC EC CE CE EC CE CE CE CE CE CE EC EC CE CE CE CE EC CE CE EC

CE CE CE CE CE CE EC CE EC CE EC CE CE EC CE CE EC EC CE CE EC

EC EC CE CE CE CE EC CE CE CE CE EC CE EC CE EC CE CE EC CE EC

CE EC EC EC CE CE CE CE CE EC CE EC EC CE CE CE CE EC EC EC CE

EC EC CE CE CE CE EC EC CE EC CE CE EC CE CE EC CE CE CE EC CE

CE CE EC CE CE EC CE CE EC EC CE EC CE EC CE EC EC CE EC EC CE

EC CE CE EC CE CE EC CE EC CE CE EC CE EC EC CE EC EC CE EC EC

EC EC EC CE EC EC CE EC EC CE CE CE CE EC EC EC EC CE CE EC EC

EC CE EC CE CE CE CE CE EC CE EC CE CE CE CE EC CE EC CE CE EC

CE EC EC CE EC EC EC CE CE CE CE CE EC CE EC EC CE EC CE EC CE

CE CE EC CE EC CE CE EC EC EC CE CE EC CE CE EC EC CE EC EC CE

EC CE EC CE EC CE EC CE CE CE CE CE EC CE EC CE EC EC CE EC CE

EC EC CE CE EC EC EC CE EC EC CE EC EC CE EC CE EC CE EC CE CE

CE EC CE EC CE CE CE EC CE CE EC CE EC EC CE CE EC CE CE CE CE

CE EC CE EC EC CE CE CE CE CE EC EC CE EC CE FE CE CE CE EC EC

CE EC EC EC CE CE CE CE EC CE EC EC EC CE CE CE CE CE CE EC CE

18

Comparing the scores of a randomly assigned experimental and control group

Unrelated *t*-test

INTRODUCTION

- This experimental design is also known as the unrelated subjects design.
- Unrelated designs of this sort are probably the commonest experimental designs.
- Its key feature is that participants in the research serve in *either* the experimental *or* the control condition but not in both.
- Being an experiment, it also involves *randomisation*. In the unrelated groups experiment, randomisation is used to decide whether a participant is in the experimental or control group.
- In this way, random assignment ensures that any differences between the experimental and control conditions are random except for the effects of the *experimental manipulation*.
- Figure 18.1 illustrates the unrelated groups design.

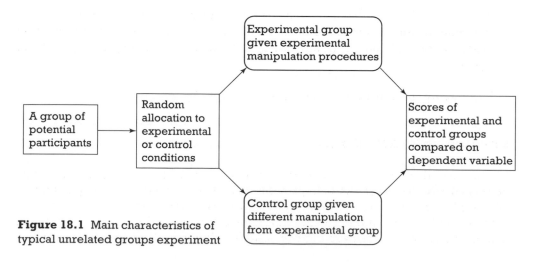

Figure 18.1 Main characteristics of typical unrelated groups experiment

WHEN TO USE THE UNRELATED DESIGN

This design usually has no particular disadvantages. This probably accounts for its enormous popularity. It is used to test practically any hypotheses other than those that predict change over time.

However, two points in particular need to be remembered:

- It does use more participants than some experimental designs. This is generally not a major problem except in the exceptional circumstances in which participants of a particular sort are scarce or hard to recruit.
- You do not know how well the random allocation has worked. It could be that the experimental and control group are different but this will not be known simply because there is no pre-test on the dependent variable prior to the experimental manipulation. Again it is uncertain whether this is a disadvantage in all circumstances.

An example of an unrelated experiment

A researcher wished to examine whether the sex of the author of a poem affected perceptions of the quality of their poetry. The hypothesis was that judgements about the quality of a poem are affected by the sex of its author. The null hypothesis is that judgements about poetry are unrelated to the sex of the author. At random, participants in the research were asked to rate a poem said to be by Paula Hetherington and the others rated *exactly* the same poem attributed to Paul Hetherington. Participants were allocated at random to each condition of the experiment. The ratings were on a 20-point scale ranging from 0 for the 'worst poem I have ever read' to 20 for the 'best poem I have ever read':

- The independent variable is the author's sex.
- The dependent variable is the rating of the quality of the poem.
- The experimental manipulation involves indicating the sex of the author through the use of a male or a female name.
- This is clearly an unrelated design since different people are involved in the experimental and control conditions. In this case unequal numbers appear in the experimental and control groups which mean that it could only be an unrelated design.

The data from this fictitious study appear in Table 18.1

STATISTICAL ANALYSIS

By the stage that you are carrying out controlled experiments you are likely to have developed your statistical knowledge somewhat. Consequently the analysis may be fairly sophisticated. Table 18.2 indicates the variety of appropriate statistics to apply to the unrelated groups experiment. All should be calculated and reported except where alternatives are given when you can decide which alternative best suits your needs.

Table 18.1 Data from the poetry experiment

Experimental group Female author	Control group Male author
13	8
15	6
10	3
7	6
16	1
5	10
12	11
8	6
7	5
11	9
12	
9	
Mean score = 125/12 = 10.42	Mean score = 65/10 = 6.50

It is vital to understand that descriptive statistics are not merely useful but that they are *essential* to any statistical analysis. Make sure that you use the methods described in Chapters 6 and 7 for summarising your results.

The means of the experimental and control groups are vital to understand the influence of the experimental manipulation. They tell you which group has the higher scores.

Other aspects of the descriptive statistics (e.g. the standard deviations or variances) are important in deciding what sort of inferential statistical test to apply.

As can be seen from Table 18.2, there are two main inferential statistics tests which could be used on these data. These are the Mann-Whitney test from Chapter 15 and the unrelated *t*-test which we shall learn how to calculate later in this chapter (see Worksheet 18.1).

How do you know which test to use? Once you have two groups of scores which come from unrelated groups of participants the choice is largely limited to these two tests.

How do you choose between the Mann-Whitney test and the unrelated *t*-test? This is a relatively subtle matter of judgement though our practical advice would be to use the unrelated *t*-test unless you have a very good reason not to. Figure 18.2 can be used to help you choose between the two.

The *t*-test essentially compares the difference between the means of the two groups with the variation that you would expect to get by chance from samples of that size. This chance variation is calculated from the variance of the scores in the two samples. In order for the difference between the means of the two groups to be statistically significant this difference has to be bigger than the variation expected by chance.

How much bigger this difference has to be depends on the combined size of the two samples. This information is presented in Table 18.A1. The smaller the combined size of the two samples, the bigger the value of *t* has to be to be statistically significant. For example, for a total sample of 8 participants *t* has to be 2.45 or bigger to be statistically significant at the two-tailed 0.05 level. While for a total sample of 20 it has to be 2.10 or bigger to be statistically significant at this same level.

At this point you should carry out Exercise 18.1.

EXERCISE 18.1   CALCULATING AN UNRELATED *T*-TEST

Analyse the data in Table 15.2 with an unrelated *t*-test to determine whether beaten children are more likely to show criminal behaviour than non-beaten children. Higher scores denote greater criminal behaviour.

What is the mean score for criminal behaviour in the beaten group?

What is the standard deviation for criminal behaviour in the beaten group?

What is the mean score for criminal behaviour in the non-beaten group?

What is the standard deviation for criminal behaviour in the non-beaten group?

What is the *t*-value?

What are the degrees of freedom?

Is the level of significance one- or two-tailed?

Are beaten children significantly more likely to show criminal behaviour than non-beaten children?

Table 18.2 Statistics for the controlled experiment

Statistical analysis	✔ ×	Pages
Calculate mean score for the experimental group		66–7
Calculate mean score of the control group		66–7
Calculate the standard deviation (or variance) for the experimental group		72–5
Calculate the standard deviation (or variance) for the control group		72–5
Draw histogram of scores for the experimental group		78–81
Draw histogram of scores for the control group		78–81
Test for statistical significance using Mann–Whitney *U*-test or unrelated *t*-test		181–2, 224–8

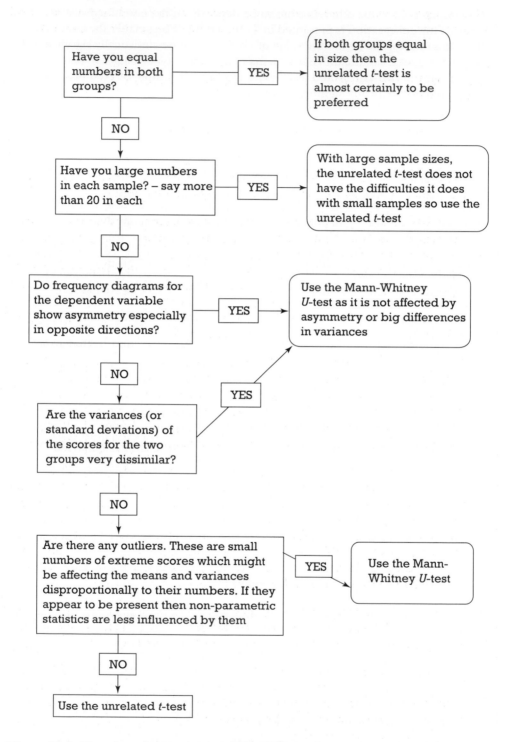

Figure 18.2 Choosing whether to use a Mann-Whitney *U*-test or an unrelated *t*-test

Box 18.1 gives ideas on manipulating independent variables and the Appendix Table 18.A2 provides a useful illustration for recording data in a controlled experiment.

BOX 18.1 IDEAS ON MANIPULATING INDEPENDENT VARIABLES

The main sources of experimental manipulations are as follows:

- The published literature may be scrutinised for similar research. You may well find that a particular way of manipulating the independent variable has general acceptance. You may wish to use this or a slight modification of it.

- Failing this, you may wish to develop your own procedure for manipulating the independent variable. The difficulty is that the participants in your research may not respond to the manipulation in the way you expected. In these circumstances you may wish to discuss how the participants in the experimental and control situations perceived the experiment. For example, you may have tried to anger the participants in the experimental condition but they report feelings of being depressed. In these circumstances it would be wrong to say that anger was the independent variable – it seems to be depression.

- Sometimes it may seem too complex to manipulate the situation directly. For example, the researcher might be interested in the effects of gender stereotyped advertisements on attitudes. Clearly it would be difficult to get different versions of the advertisements printed in magazines but it might be relatively easy to produce different versions using a word-processor and a photocopier. There are clearly disadvantages to this but it does help circumvent problems.

- Where this is possible it is always good practice to assess whether your manipulation has worked. For example, in testing the effect of the sex of the poet on the evaluation of poems, it would be worthwhile establishing whether our manipulation worked. This needs to be done subtly so that participants are not more likely to guess what the experiment is about. Consequently it may be preferable to obtain this information after participants have evaluated the poem. We could do this by asking participants what the sex of the poet was after we had collected their evaluation of the poem.

- If a few people failed to correctly recognise or recall the sex of the poet, we may wish to exclude them from the analysis of the data. If many of them failed to do this, we would have to make the manipulation more effective.

- Of course, when manipulating sex with only one name any effect may be due to the effect of that name and not the sex represented by that name. Consequently, we could include more examples of female and male names. Alternatively we could describe the authors as 'Ms' or 'Mr'.

Worksheet 18.1 for the unrelated t-test

Step 1: Enter your scores for the experimental group in Column 1.
Step 2: Enter your scores for the control group in Column 3.
Step3: Square each score in Column 1 and enter the squared value in Column 2. Then square each score in Column 3 and enter the squared value in Column 4.

Column 1	Column 2	Column 3	Column 4
Experimental group scores X_e	Square of previous column X_e^2	Control group scores X_c	Square of previous column X_c^2
13	169	8	64
15	225	6	36
10	100	3	9
7	49	6	36
16	256	1	1
5	25	10	100
12	144	11	121
8	64	6	36
7	49	5	25
11	121	9	81
12	144		
9	81		
$\sum X_e = 125$	$\sum X_e^2 = 1427$	$\sum X_c = 65$	$\sum X_c^2 = 509$
Mean $= \bar{X}_e$ $= \sum X_e / N_e$ $= 125/12 = 10.417$		Mean $= \bar{X}_e$ $= \sum X_c / N_e$ $= 65/10 = 6.5$	

Sample size for $X_e = N_e = 12$ Sample size for $X_c = N_c = 10$
Degrees of freedom $= N_e + N_c - 2 = 12 + 10 - 2 = 20$

Key

X_e = scores in the experimental group

X_e^2 = squares of the scores in the experimental group

X_c = scores in the control group

X_c^2 = squares of the scores in the control group

$\sum X_e$ = sum of all of the scores for the experimental group (Column 1)

$\sum X_e^2$ = sum of all of the squared scores for the experimental group (Column 2)

$\sum X_c$ = sum of all the scores for the control group (Column 3)

$\sum X_c^2$ = sum of all of the squared scores for the control group (Column 4)

N_e = sample size of experimental group

N_c = sample size of control group

$\overline{X}_e$ = mean (average) score in the experimental group

$\overline{X}_c$ = mean (average) score in the control group

The value of *t* can be calculated from the following equation substituting values from above.

$$t = \cfrac{\overline{X}_e - \overline{X}_c}{\sqrt{\left(\cfrac{\left[\sum X_e^2 - \cfrac{\left(\sum X_e\right)^2}{N_e}\right] + \left[\sum X_c^2 - \cfrac{\left(\sum X_c\right)^2}{N_c}\right]}{N_e + N_c - 2}\right)\left(\cfrac{1}{N_e} + \cfrac{1}{N_c}\right)}}$$

Some readers may find this a little difficult at first. So as an alternative do each of the following step-by-step calculations:

1 Calculate *D*

$$D = \overline{X}_e - \overline{X}_c$$
$$= \quad 10.417 - 6.500$$
$$= \quad 3.917$$

(*D* is the difference between the means of the experimental and control groups.)

2 Calculate E

$$E = \sum X_e^2 - \frac{\left(\sum E_e\right)^2}{N_e}$$

$$= 1427 - \frac{125^2}{12}$$

$$= 1427 - \frac{15625}{12}$$

$$= 1427 - 1302.083$$

$$= 124.917$$

(E is the sum of squares for the experimental group.)

3 Calculate C

$$C = \sum X_c^2 - \frac{\left(\sum E_c\right)^2}{N_c}$$

$$= 509 - \frac{65^2}{10}$$

$$= 509 - \frac{4225}{10}$$

$$= 509 - 422.5$$

$$= 86.5$$

(This is the sum of squares for the control group.)

4 Calculate F

$$F = N_e + N_c - 2$$
$$= 12 + 10 - 2$$
$$= 20$$

(This is the degrees of freedom.)

5 Calculate W

$$W = \frac{1}{N_e} + \frac{1}{N_c}$$

$$= \frac{1}{12} + \frac{1}{10}$$

$$= 0.0833 + 0.1000$$

$$= 0.183$$

(This is a weighting factor making adjustments more precise when you have unequal sample sizes.)

6 Calculate H

$$H = \left(\frac{E + C}{F}\right) \times W$$

$$= \left(\frac{124.917 + 86.500}{20}\right) \times 0.183$$

$$= \left(\frac{211.417}{20}\right) \times 0.183$$

$$= 10.571 \times 0.183$$

$$= 1.93$$

7 Calculate G

$$G = \sqrt{H}$$

$$= \sqrt{1.934}$$

$$= 1.391$$

8   Calculate t

$$t = \frac{D}{G}$$

$$= \frac{3.917}{1.391}$$

$$= 2.81$$

Step 4: The bigger the value of t the greater is the difference between our sample means expressed relative to the standard error of the differences between sample means. We use Table 18.A1 to check the statistical significance of our value of t (2.81) by checking against the row for 20 degrees of freedom (i.e. $N_e + N_c - 2 = 20$ degrees of freedom). This table tells us that our value of t is in the extreme 5 per cent of the distribution because it is larger than 2.09 at the two-tailed level. Consequently the null hypothesis that there is no difference between the experimental and control group is rejected. Our study showed that poems thought to be composed by women were rated as being of higher quality than those thought to be written by men.

Reporting your findings

- If your value of t is *larger* than or equal to the listed value (remember that we are ignoring negative signs): Your t value is statistically significant at the 5 per cent level. In these circumstances we might write 'The mean score for the experimental group on ratings of quality (female author) was 10.42, whereas that for the control group (male author) was 6.50. The difference was statistically significant ($t = 2.81$, *d.f.* = 2, *p* < 0.05). Thus the hypothesis that perceptions of the quality of poetry are related to the attributed sex of the author was accepted.'
- If your value of t is *smaller* than the listed value (remember that we are ignoring negative signs): Your t value is not statistically significant at the 5 per cent level. In these circumstances we might write 'The mean score for the experimental group on ratings of quality (female author) was ____ whereas that for the control group (male author) was ____. The difference was not statistically significant ($t = $ ____, *d.f.* = ____, *n.s.*). Thus the hypothesis that perceptions of the quality of poetry are related to the attributed sex of the author was rejected.'

For notes on more complex experiments see Box 18.2.

SUMMARY

- An unrelated subjects design is one containing at least two groups.
- In a true experiment participants are randomly assigned to the two groups, which differ according to the manipulation of the independent variable.
- A parametric test for determining whether the difference between the means of the two groups is statistically significant is the unrelated t-test.
- This test can also be used to test for difference in means of any two groups such as women and men.

BOX 18.2 MORE COMPLEX EXPERIMENTS

Not all research has to follow the simple model described in this chapter. More advanced experimental designs require much more statistical understanding and are not covered in this workbook. You can, for example:

- Have more than one experimental group and more than one control group.
- Have more than one independent variable.
- Compare the experimental and control group before the experimental manipulation in order to see that they do not differ initially on the dependent variable.

If you are planning any of the above consult a more advanced statistics textbook (e.g. Cramer 1998; Howitt and Cramer 2000).

If you want to use more than one dependent variable this is no problem. You simply analyse scores on each dependent variable taking each dependent variable separately. It is like pretending you had done several different experiments with a different dependent variable each time.

ANSWERS TO EXERCISE

Answers to Exercise 18.1

The mean score for criminal behaviour in the beaten group is 6.83.

The standard deviation for criminal behaviour in the beaten group is 1.60.

The mean score for criminal behaviour in the non-beaten group is 2.86.

The standard deviation for criminal behaviour in the beaten group is 1.57.

The *t*-value is 4.50.

The degrees of freedom are 11.

The level of significance is one-tailed because beaten children were expected to be more likely to show criminal behaviour than non-beaten children.

Beaten children are significantly more likely to show criminal behaviour than non-beaten children.

Table 18.A1 One- and two-tailed 0.05 probability values for the unrelated t-test

- Your t-value (ignoring sign) should be equal to or greater than the listed values in the second or third columns to be statistically significant at the stipulated level.
- The degrees of freedom for the unrelated t-test is the total number of scores in the two groups – 2.
- If your required number of degrees of freedom is missing from the table, take the next smaller listed value.

Degrees of freedom	One-tailed 0.05 level	Two-tailed 0.05 level
1	6.31	12.71
2	2.92	4.30
3	2.35	3.18
4	2.13	2.78
5	2.02	2.57
6	1.94	2.45
7	1.90	2.37
8	1.86	2.31
9	1.83	2.26
10	1.81	2.23
11	1.80	2.20
12	1.78	2.18
13	1.77	2.16
14	1.76	2.15
15	1.75	2.13
16	1.75	2.12
17	1.74	2.11
18	1.73	2.10
19	1.73	2.09
20	1.73	2.09
21	1.72	2.08
22	1.72	2.07
23	1.71	2.07
24	1.71	2.06
25	1.71	2.06
26	1.71	2.06

Table 18.A1 continued

Degrees of freedom	One-tailed 0.05 level	Two-tailed 0.05 level
27	1.70	2.05
28	1.70	2.05
29	1.70	2.05
30	1.70	2.04
35	1.69	2.03
40	1.68	2.02
45	1.68	2.01
50	1.68	2.01
60	1.67	2.00
70	1.67	1.99
80	1.66	1.99
90	1.66	1.99
100	1.66	1.98
∞	1.65	1.96

Note
The above table was calculated by the authors.

Table 18.A2 Illustration of a data recording sheet for a controlled experiment

Case number	Experimental or control	Score if in experimental condition	Score if in control condition	Sex	Age	Date	Time began	Notes
1	E	22		M	19	20 Jan	10.00	
2	C		17	M	18	20 Jan	10.30	
3	E	19		F	22	20 Jan	11.00	
4	E	24		M	39	20 Jan	12.00	
5	C		13	F	23	21 Jan	10.00	Guessed hypothesis
6	E	27		F	18	21 Jan	10.30	
7	E	–		M	19	21 Jan	11.00	Withdrew from study
8	C		10	F	23	21 Jan	11.30	
9	C		15	F	20	21 Jan	12.00	
10	C		–	M	20	24 Jan	10.00	Apparatus failed to function
11	E	15		M	38	24 Jan	11.30	
12	E	21		M	18	24 Jan	12.00	
13	C		14	F	21	25 Jan	11.30	
14	E	24		F	18	26 Jan	10.30	
15	C		7	M	17	26 Jan	11.30	
16	C		20	F	22	26 Jan	12.00	

Table 18.A2 continued

Case number	Experimental or control	Score if in experimental condition	Score if in control condition	Sex	Age	Date	Time began	Notes
17	E	19		F	21	27 Jan	10.00	
18	C		15	M	19	27 Jan	10.30	Had spoken with other participants
19	E	23		F	18	27 Jan	11.00	
20	C		8	F	19	27 Jan	11.30	
21	E	17		M	25	27 Jan	12.00	
22	C		16	F	19	28 Jan	11.30	
23								
24								
25								

19

Comparing the scores of a counterbalanced related subjects experiment

Related *t*-test

INTRODUCTION

The key feature of the related subjects experiment is that participants in the research serve in *both* the experimental and control conditions.

Being an experiment, it also involves *randomisation*. In the case of a related design, randomisation is used to decide whether the participant goes through the experimental or the control conditions first.

Random assignment to order in this way helps the researcher untangle the effects of the experimental manipulation from the effects of time discussed in Chapter 16 (p. 193).

The following is the test–retest design:

Control condition ➡ Experimental condition

With this design it is impossible to know whether differences between the experimental and control conditions are merely due to, for instance, the participants becoming tired following the control condition, thus affecting their performance in the experimental condition.

The solution to this is to employ *counterbalancing*. This merely involves studying half of the participants in the control condition first followed by the experimental condition *and* the other half of participants in your experiment in the experimental condition first followed by the control condition.

Order 1: Control condition ➡ Experimental condition
Order 2: Experimental condition ➡ Control condition

In this way, the effects of tiredness would apply to the experimental and control conditions equally – half of the participants in each case would be affected.

To be fully effective, counterbalancing should involve *equal* numbers of participants in the two different orders of experimental and control conditions. That is, exactly half of the participants should receive the experimental treatment first and the other half of the participants should receive the control treatment first.

As we have said, randomisation in this type of experiment involves random allocation to one or other of the two *orders*. (Obviously, since all participants are in both the experimental and control conditions, it is not possible to randomly allocate to the experimental or control groups.) It is clearly important to use a randomisation procedure which ensures that equal numbers of participants are in each order.

Randomisation is used to avoid the risks of biasing the outcomes by choosing a particular sort of participant to run through the experimental condition first.

Generally speaking, all of the requirements of the unrelated experiment described in Chapter 17 apply to the related experiment. So ethical, procedural and most other considerations apply to this sort of research also. The only differences of any note are:

a   Random allocation to order rather than to different conditions (see Table 19.A2).
b   That the test of statistical significance used will be one suitable for related scores. We will be using the related *t*-test in this chapter but the Wilcoxon matched-pairs test is also appropriate (Chapter 16, pp. 194–6).

WHEN TO USE THE RELATED DESIGN

In theory, if not in practice, the counterbalanced related subjects design could be used to study any of the research questions tackled by an unrelated subjects design provided that the manipulation does not produce irreversible effects.

Furthermore, there would appear to be very good reasons for choosing the counterbalanced related subjects experiment over the unrelated subjects design. The related subjects design is more efficient since it can be carried out with rather fewer participants than the unrelated design but achieve the same level of statistical significance.

Unfortunately, since the participants serve as their own control they are aware of both the experimental and control conditions. This may make it easier for them to guess the purposes of the experiment, for example, and respond according to their expectations. Sometimes this awareness of both conditions would lead to a rather silly set of circumstances. (See Table 19.4 for advantages and disadvantages of the related subjects design.)

For that reason, it is essential to think carefully about how it would feel to be a participant in the related experiment before employing the design. If it is likely to appear rather 'silly' or too obvious to the participant then err towards the unrelated experiment.

AN EXAMPLE OF A COUNTERBALANCED RELATED EXPERIMENT

A researcher believes that people's subjective assessments of weight are affected by the volume of the object. A set of five shapes of varying weights from 5 grams to 50 grams was made. A set of identical shapes with identical weights was also made but this second set was three times the volume of the first set. Thus the two sets varied in terms of volume. Participants in the research were asked to judge the weights of the larger volume shapes and also the weights of the smaller volume shapes. The average of the weight given to the five shapes formed the estimated weight. Half the participants judged the larger volume weights first, the other half the smaller volume weights first. All participants judged both sets of weights.

This division by experimental versus control group and first and second treatment means that there are 2 × 2 or 4 different sets of scores collected. This can be seen in Table 19.1.

Table 19.1 The weights experiment showing counterbalanced orders

Person	Experimental group first (grams)		Control group second (grams)
1	35	⇒	29
2	50	⇒	53
3	33	⇒	25
4	42	⇒	46
5	40	⇒	38
6	45	⇒	42

Person	Control condition first (grams)		Experimental condition second (grams)
7	48	⇒	57
8	42	⇒	49
9	41	⇒	42
10	22	⇒	30
11	45	⇒	52
12	25	⇒	33

The counterbalanced related experiment needs all of the planning associated with an unrelated experiment. This means that all of the steps in Worksheet 17.1 need to be followed.

The basic difference in the analysis of the data is that it is usual to compare *all* of the experimental condition scores with *all* of the control condition scores using a related test such as the related *t*-test or the Wilcoxon matched-pairs test. This entails a slight rearrangement of the data. This is shown in Table 19.2.

Table 19.2 The weights experiment rearranged into experimental and control condition columns

Person	Experimental condition score irrespective of order	Control condition score irrespective of order
1	35	29
2	50	53
3	33	25
4	52	46
5	40	38
6	45	42
7	57	48
8	49	42
9	42	41
10	30	22
11	52	46
12	33	25
	Mean = 43.17	Mean = 38.00

Analysing a counterbalanced related samples design

The first task is to rearrange the data into two columns – one column for the experimental condition scores and the other column for the control condition scores. Data from each participant should be side by side. This is shown in Table 19.2.

The first six rows of data in the second column are for people who went through the experimental condition first, while the second six rows of data in this column are for people who went through the experimental condition second.

Now that the data have been rearranged, the design looks much the same as any of the two groups designs we have studied so far. We could, if we wished, use the Wilcoxon matched-pairs test (Chapter 16, pp. 194–6) to test whether there is a statistically significant difference between the judgements of weights in the experimental versus the control condition. However, if its assumptions are met (see Box 19.1), then the related *t*-test will generally be a slightly better choice.

There is quite a substantial difference between the means of the experimental and control conditions in Table 19.2. The difference is 43.17 – 38.00 = 5.17. That is the judgements of weights are higher when the weight has a bigger volume.

The related *t*-test is based on the assumption that the two sets of scores are correlated with each other. If this is the case, then the amount of error is substantially reduced. If the scores are not correlated then the related *t*-test becomes inferior to the unrelated *t*-test which assumes no correlation between the scores.

Table 19.3 shows the stages involved in this statistical analysis.

Worksheet 19.1 for the related t-test

Step1: Very carefully enter *all* the scores for the experimental condition in Column 2. It does not matter whether the experimental condition was first or second.

Step 2: Enter the corresponding score for the control condition in Column 3. That is to say, the person's scores in the experimental and control conditions are entered side by side in Column 2 and Column 3.

Column 1	Column 2	Column 3	Column 4	Column 5
Person	Experimental condition X_1	Control condition X_2	Difference $D = X_1 - X_2$	Squared difference D^2
1	35	29	+6	36
2	50	53	−3	9
3	33	25	+8	64
4	52	46	+6	36
5	40	38	+2	4
6	45	42	+3	9
7	57	48	+9	81
8	49	42	+7	49
9	42	41	+1	1
10	30	22	+8	64
11	52	45	+7	49
12	33	25	+8	64
13				
14				
15				
16				
17				
18				
19				
20				
21				
22				
23				
24				
25				

26				
27				
28				
29				
30				
Sums	$\sum X_1 = 518$	$\sum X_2 = 456$	$\sum D = 62$	$\sum D^2 = 466$
Means	$\bar{X}_1 = 43.17$	$\bar{X}_2 = 38.00$	$\bar{D} = 5.17$	

N = number of difference scores = 12

Step 3: Row by row, subtract the score in Column 3 from the score in Column 2. Enter this value in Column 4 – remember to include the negative signs of the difference.

Step 4: Row by row, square the difference in Column 4 and enter this squared difference into the adjacent box in Column 5. Sum each column separately from Column 2 to Column 5.

Step 5: Enter each of the sums in the Sums row near the bottom of the table. Calculate the means of the following columns separately: Column 2, Column 3, and Column 4. Enter the means in the final row of the above table. This merely involves dividing the sum of the column by the number of difference scores.

Step 6: To calculate *t* you can substitute the values from the calculation worksheet in the following formula in order to obtain the standard error of sample means:

$$\text{standard error of sample means} \quad (\text{se}) = \frac{\sqrt{\dfrac{\sum D^2 - \dfrac{\left(\sum D\right)^2}{N}}{N-1}}}{\sqrt{N}}$$

If you are comfortable with the above formula, then by all means calculate the standard error using the formula. The value of *t* may be calculated by substituting $\bar{D}$ and the standard error (se) in the following formula:

$$t = \frac{\bar{D}}{\text{se}} = \frac{5.17}{1.05} = 4.92$$

Otherwise, you can follow the calculations in Step 7. Ideally, use the above formulae then check your accuracy using the calculations in Step 7.

Step 7: *Alternatively*, follow these step by step instructions

☺ $A = \sum D \times \sum D = 62 \times 62 = 3844$

☺ $B = \dfrac{A}{N} = \dfrac{3844}{12} = 320.33$

☺ $C = \bar{D}^2 - B = 466 - 320.33 = 145.67$

☺ $E = N - 1 = 12 - 1 = 11$

☺ $F = \dfrac{C}{E} = \dfrac{145.67}{11} = 13.24$

☺ $G = \sqrt{F} = \sqrt{13.24} = 3.64$

☺ $H = \sqrt{N} = \sqrt{12} = 3.46$

☺ $I = G/N = 3.64/3.46 = 1.05$

☺ $t = \dfrac{\bar{D}}{I} = \dfrac{5.17}{1.05} = 4.92$ (This may be a positive or negative number.)

Whichever method you use, the value of t is the same at 4.92. t is the test statistic and basically indicates how unusual the difference between your two samples is *if* the null hypothesis is true. This value is an unusually high value of t.

Assessing statistical significance

- Write your calculated value of t here 4.92 (ignore the sign).
- Write your value of N (the number of PAIRS of scores) here 12
- The degrees of freedom is $N - 1 = 12 - 1 = 11$
- Turn to Table 19.A1. Find the *row* for 11 degrees of freedom. The final column gives you the minimum value of t to be significant at the 5 per cent level. This minimum value of significance (the critical value) is 2.20. Quite clearly our value of 4.92 is far larger than this and so is statistically significant at the 5 per cent level.

Reporting your findings

- If your value of t is larger than or equal to the listed value (remember that we are ignoring negative signs): Your t-value is statistically significant at the 5 per cent level (2-tailed test). In these circumstances we can say 'The difference between the experimental and control condition is 5.17 which is significant at the 5 per cent level ($t = 4.92$, *d.f.* = 11, $p < 0.05$). Thus we can reject the null hypothesis that the volume of an object has no influence on its perceived weight. We accept the hypothesis that the volume of a weight is related to its perceived weight.'
- If your value of t is smaller than the listed value (ignoring sign): Your t value is not statistically significant at the 5 per cent level (2-tailed test). In these circumstances we can say 'The difference between the experimental and control condition is ____ which is not statistically significant at the 5 per cent level ($t = $ ____ , *d.f.* = ____ , not significant). Thus we can accept the null hypothesis that the volume of an object has no influence on its perceived weight. We reject the hypothesis that the volume of a weight is related to its perceived weight.'

After reading carefully through Worksheet 19.1 carry out Exercise 19.1.

EXERCISE 19.1   CALCULATING A RELATED T-TEST

Analyse the data in Table 16.1 with a related *t*-test to determine whether children at six use more adjectives than the same children at five.

What is the mean score for the number of adjectives used by the children at six?

What is the standard deviation for the number of adjectives used by the children at six?

What is the mean score for the number of adjectives used by the children at five?

What is the standard deviation for the number of adjectives used by the children at five?

What is the *t*-value?

What are the degrees of freedom?

Is the level of significance one- or two-tailed?

Are children at six significantly more likely to use adjectives than the same children at five?

Table 19.3 Statistical analysis of counterbalanced related experiment

Statistical analysis	✔ ×	Pages
The mean of the experimental group		66–7
The mean of the control group		66–7
The standard deviation (or variance) of the experimental group		72–5
The standard deviation (or variance) of the control group		72–5
The difference between the means of the experimental and control groups		
A histogram of the difference scores – these should ideally be symmetrical and normally distributed if a related *t*-test is to be used.		78–81
The related *t*-test (or the Wilcoxon matched-pairs test)		238–40 (or 194–6)
The correlation between the scores in the experimental and control conditions – if there is no correlation then the unrelated *t*-test would be better		113–15
The counterbalanced design needs more complex statistics for a full analysis, see Box 19.2.		

BOX 19.1   WHAT IS THE RELATED *T*-TEST?

The related *t*-test is used in the following circumstances:

- When you have scores which are related. That is each individual has been measured at two different points in time on the same variable.
- When you wish to know if the mean (average) scores in the two separate sets of scores are different from each other.
- When you feel that the assumptions of parametric significance testing are met. This essentially means when your (difference) scores follow a symmetrical, bell-shaped histogram or frequency curve. If not, use a non-parametric significance test such as the Wilcoxon matched-pairs test (Worksheet 16.1)

You do *not* use the related *t*-test when you wish to compare the means of samples of scores obtained from *two* different groups of people. In these circumstances you use the unrelated *t*-test (Worksheet 18.1). The only exception to this is when you use matching (p. 197).

The related *t*-test involves transforming your two sets of scores into a single set of *difference* scores. Difference scores are an individual's score in the experimental condition minus the same individual's score in the control condition.

It is an easy matter to work out the standard error of samples of difference score means by calculating the standard deviation of the difference scores using the usual standard deviation formula and then dividing this by $\sqrt{N}$ (i.e. the square root of the sample size).

Remember that the standard error is simply the 'average' amount by which the means of samples differ from the population mean (or mean of sample means).

We then simply calculate the value of *t* which is the number of standard errors by which our particular sample mean differs from the population mean (in other words the mean of sample means). This number of standard errors is then checked against the table of the *t*-distribution for our particular sample size (or more usually the number of degrees of freedom).

SUMMARY

- In the related subjects experiment *all* participants serve in the experimental and control conditions.
- Half of participants serve in the experimental condition first and the other half serve in the control condition first. This controls for order effects which otherwise could be confused for effects of the experimental treatment.
- It can be used instead of the unrelated groups experiment (Chapter 18) although care should be taken to avoid doing so if serving in both the experimental and control conditions may be a silly experience or reveals the hypothesis too obviously.

BOX 19.2 IDEAL ANALYSIS OF COUNTERBALANCED RELATED SUBJECTS EXPERIMENT

The ideal analysis of this research design is rather more advanced than this book demands. Consequently, the simplest analysis has been presented.

A simpler analysis would be to test the significance of the experimental versus the control conditions for the experimental condition first, and then the significance of the experimental versus the control conditions for the control condition first. If *both* are significant and show a trend in the same direction (e.g. the experimental condition is significantly higher than the control condition in both comparisons), then the order effect cannot explain the experimental versus control differences. If one is significant and the other is *not* significant or the trends are in opposite directions, then there is an *order effect* which cannot be dealt with using the simple statistics employed in this book.

The mixed-design Analysis of Variance of ANOVA (e.g. Cramer 1998; Howitt and Cramer 2000) would be a better analysis. Experimental versus control would be the *related* variable whereas order (first versus second) would be the unrelated variable. The interaction of the two needs to be significant to convince us that the experimental condition was having an effect which is not an order effect. This is a rather complex statistical analysis which needs a higher level of statistical sophistication.

- The statistical analysis is by the related *t*-test so long as the distribution of difference scores is roughly symmetrical and bell shaped. If not, the Wilcoxon matched-pair test is probably better. The scores in the two conditions should correlate otherwise an unrelated *t*-test might be more appropriate.

ANSWERS TO EXERCISE

Answers to Exercise 19.1

The mean score for the number of adjectives used by the children at six is 17.50.

The standard deviation for the number of adjectives used by the children at six is 3.27.

The mean score for the number of adjectives used by the children at five is 8.33.

The standard deviation for the number of adjectives used by the children at five is 4.32.

The *t*-value is 15.25.

The degrees of freedom are 5.

The level of significance is one-tailed because children at six were expected to use more adjectives than the same children at five.

Children at six are significantly more likely to use adjectives than the same children at five.

Table 19.4 Advantages and disadvantages of the counterbalanced related subjects design

Advantages	Disadvantages
Requires fewer participants and so saves time and effort recruiting participants	Care must be taken to ensure that equal numbers of participants are run in the two different orders
You have baseline measurements of how individuals perform in the control condition to compare with their performance in the experimental condition	Because they are aware of both conditions of the research design, it is easier for the participants to guess the hypothesis and respond accordingly
You can assess the effect of order	Because participants are aware of both the experimental and control conditions, sometimes it is difficult to find ways of creating the two conditions which do not seem silly
	The statistical analysis using the related t-test assumes that individuals' scores in the two conditions are correlated. If they are not then this design produces less significant results than the equivalent unrelated design
	The ideal statistical analysis is more complex because of potential time or test–retest effects. Consequently, this design warrants much more advanced statistical treatment than unrelated experiments do
	Extending the design to cover more than one experimental and control group is an exacting task. With three conditions (A, B, and C), *six* different orders of running through the three conditions have to be included: ABC, ACB, BCA, BAC, CAB, and CBA. With four conditions the number of orders increases dramatically. Sometimes only a selection of orders is used but then the experiment no longer assesses all the order effects

Table 19.A1 One- and two-tailed 0.05 probability values for the related *t*-test

Your *t*-value (ignoring sign) should be equal to or greater than the listed values in the second or third columns to be statistically significant at the stipulated level.

The degrees of freedom for the related *t*-test is the number of *pairs* of scores − 1.

If your required number of degrees of freedom is missing from the table, take the next smaller listed value.

Degrees of freedom	One-tailed 0.05 level	Two-tailed 0.05 level	Degrees of freedom	One-tailed 0.05 level	Two-tailed 0.05 level
1	6.31	12.71	21	1.72	2.08
2	2.92	4.30	22	1.72	2.07
3	2.35	3.18	23	1.71	2.07
4	2.13	2.78	24	1.71	2.06
5	2.02	2.57	25	1.71	2.06
6	1.94	2.45	26	1.71	2.06
7	1.90	2.37	27	1.70	2.05
8	1.86	2.31	28	1.70	2.05
9	1.83	2.26	29	1.70	2.05
10	1.81	2.23	30	1.70	2.04
11	1.80	2.20	35	1.69	2.03
12	1.78	2.18	40	1.68	2.02
13	1.77	2.16	45	1.68	2.01
14	1.76	2.15	50	1.68	2.01
15	1.75	2.13	60	1.67	2.00
16	1.75	2.12	70	1.67	1.99
17	1.74	2.11	80	1.66	1.99
18	1.73	2.10	90	1.66	1.99
19	1.73	2.09	100	1.66	1.98
20	1.73	2.09	∞	1.65	1.96

Note
The above table was calculated by the authors.

Table 19.A2 Random allocation of orders

The following table gives randomised orders for experimental (e) and control groups (c). The table has two different forms of randomisation:

* proper randomisation in which every case has an equal chance of selection at every stage; and
* blocked randomisation in which the cases are taken in pairs and the first of the pair is allocated at random to the experimental first or control first condition.

Proper randomisation can lead to runs in which, say, there are groups of two, three, four or more participants run in exactly the same condition first. This cannot happen with blocked randomisation for which the longest possible run is two. Blocked randomisation is likely to be the most practical in most circumstances. Remember that you need to have equal numbers of cases in the experimental first and control first conditions. If you choose proper randomisation then once you have reached your group size for one condition, the rest of the experiment will have the other condition run until the group sizes are the same.

* Decide whether you want proper randomisation or blocked randomisation.
* Select a way of going through the table – backwards, forwards, every alternate row forwards, or whatever you like.
* Then choose a random starting point – closing your eyes and sticking your finger in the table is good enough.
* Finally, follow your chosen order through. C or c means that your participant should be run in the control condition first followed by the experimental condition, E or e means that the participant should be run in the experimental condition first followed by the control condition.

Randomised order

Choose a random starting point

cccc	ecec	cecc	cccc	ccce	ceec	cccc	eeee	cece	eecc	ecec	ccee	eeee	eece	ceec	eeee
eeee	ecec	ceee	ecce	cccc	ecec	ccee	ecee	cccc	ceec	ceee	cece	eece	ccee	ecce	ceee
cccc	ccce	eecc	ceee	ccee	ceec	ceec	ecce	eeec	eecc	ccee	eeec	ccce	eece	eeec	cccc
cccc	ceec	ecee	ecce	eeee	ccec	cecc	eeec	ecec	ceec	ceec	ceec	eeec	eeee	ecee	ccee
ecce	ceec	eece	ceee	eeec	ecee	ccee	ccee	ecee	eece	cece	ccee	ecee	cccc	eece	cece
cece	ccec	eecc	ceec	ceee	ceec	eecc	ecec	ccec	ecce	eeee	cccc	eeee	ceec	ecec	cece
ecee	cccc	ecee	ceee	cece	cccc	cece	cecc	ccce	eeee	cece	eece	ceee	ccee	ccec	cecc
eecc	ccec	eeec	eecc	eece	cecc	cece	ecce	ccec	ecee	ceee	ecee	ecce	cecc	ceee	eecc
ecce	ceee	cecc	cece	ecce	ccec	cccc	ceee	eecc	cece	eece	cccc	ccce	eeee	eccc	ecee
ccce	ecec	eecc	eece	eecc	ecce	ccec	cccc	eecc	ceec	eeec	eecc	cccc	eeee	cccc	ccec
cccc	ccec	eecc	eccc	eecc	eecc	ceec	ccec	ccce	eece	eeec	eece	cecc	ecce	ecec	ecee
ecce	eecc	eeec	eeec	ecce	cece	ceee	ccee	eece	cccc	ccce	ccec	eece	ccec	ccce	eece
ecec	eeee	ecee	ceee	ceee	ccce	cece	ceec	ceee	eece	ccee	cece	cece	ecec	cecc	cece
ceec	ecec	ecec	cece	ccec	eecc	ceec	cccc	eccc	eccc	ceec	ccec	ecec	cccc	cccc	cccc
cccc	ecee	eece	cccc	cece	ecce	eeec	eeec	cece	ecee	ceee	eeec	ceec	eece	cecc	cecc
ecee	ecee	eeee	cccc	eecc	eeee	cece	ecce	ecec	eccc	ceec	ccee	ecee	eeee	cccc	cccc
cccc	cecc	eeee	cccc	ccee	eecc	eecc	eeec	eeee	eeee	eecc	ecee	ceec	ecce	eecc	cecc
ecee	eece	ccec	eccc	eecc	eeee	ceec	eece	eeec	ecee	ecce	cecc	cecc	eece	eece	ecec
eeec	ccce	eece	ccce	ccee	ccce	ecec	ecce	ceec	ccce	eece	ecce	ccce	eccc	ccce	ecce
cece	eecc	ecec	ecce	ccec	cecc	eccc	ecec	eeee	cecc	ecec	ceec	eeee	ccec	ecec	ecee

Blocked randomised order

Choose a random starting point, starting with the left hand letter of the chosen pair

CE CE EC EC EC CE CE EC CE EC CE EC CE CE CE EC CE CE EC CE EC

EC CE CE EC CE CE CE CE CE EC CE EC EC CE EC CE EC EC CE CE CE

EC CE CE CE EC CE CE CE CE CE EC EC CE EC CE CE CE EC CE EC EC

CE CE CE CE EC EC CE EC CE CE EC CE CE EC CE CE CE EC CE CE CE

EC CE CE EC CE CE EC EC EC EC CE CE CE EC CE CE EC EC EC EC EC

EC CE CE EC CE EC CE CE CE EC EC CE CE CE EC CE EC EC CE EC CE

EC CE EC EC CE CE CE EC CE CE EC EC EC EC CE CE CE CE EC EC CE

EC EC EC CE EC CE CE EC CE CE EC EC EC CE EC CE CE CE CE CE EC

CE CE EC EC EC EC CE EC EC EC CE EC CE CE CE EC CE CE CE EC EC

CE EC CE CE CE EC CE EC CE EC EC EC EC EC CE CE EC CE EC EC EC

CE CE CE EC CE EC EC EC EC EC CE EC CE CE EC EC CE EC CE EC CE

EC EC CE EC CE EC CE EC CE CE EC CE CE EC CE CE CE EC EC EC EC

CE CE CE CE CE CE CE CE EC EC EC CE CE EC EC CE EC CE EC CE CE

EC CE CE CE CE EC EC EC CE CE CE CE CE EC CE EC EC CE CE CE EC

CE EC CE EC EC EC CE CE CE CE CE EC CE CE CE EC CE EC CE CE EC

CE EC EC CE CE CE CE CE EC EC EC CE EC CE CE EC EC CE EC CE EC

CE CE CE EC CE EC CE EC EC EC CE CE CE EC CE EC CE EC EC EC EC

EC EC CE CE CE CE EC EC EC EC EC CE EC CE CE CE CE CE CE EC CE

EC CE EC EC CE CE EC CE EC EC EC EC CE EC EC EC EC EC EC EC EC

CE EC EC CE EC CE CE EC EC EC CE CE CE CE EC CE EC EC EC CE CE

CE CE CE EC EC CE EC EC CE EC EC EC CE CE EC CE EC CE EC EC EC

CE EC EC CE EC CE CE CE CE CE EC EC EC EC CE EC CE CE EC EC CE

EC EC EC CE EC CE CE CE CE EC EC CE EC CE CE EC CE CE EC CE EC

CE CE EC CE EC EC CE EC EC CE EC EC EC EC EC CE CE EC CE CE CE

CE CE EC EC EC CE CE CE EC CE CE CE CE CE CE EC CE EC CE EC EC

CE EC EC CE EC CE CE EC EC EC EC CE CE CE EC CE CE CE CE EC EC

CE EC CE CE EC EC CE CE EC EC CE EC CE EC CE EC EC CE CE CE CE

EC CE EC CE CE CE CE EC CE EC CE CE EC CE CE EC EC CE CE CE CE

EC CE CE EC CE CE CE CE CE CE EC CE EC CE EC CE EC CE EC CE CE

20

Comparing three or more groups on a numerical score

Many studies in psychology measure scores (e.g. scores on a depression scale or the number of words correctly recalled) from more than two conditions of the independent variable. There are many different possible designs using three or more groups but mostly they are too advanced for this book.

Furthermore, the research designs that were discussed earlier can be extended in other ways. Instead of having just one independent variable, it is possible to have several independent variables.

We will briefly discuss a variety of designs available and show you how to analyse the commonest and simplest of these – where you have more than two conditions of the independent variable.

FACTORS AND LEVELS OF THE INDEPENDENT VARIABLE

The independent variable is the variable whose effects we are studying (Chapter 17, p. 203). The dependent variable is the variable we think might be affected by the independent variable.

In more advanced research designs, the term *factor* is often used instead of independent variable.

The groups within a factor are referred to as *levels*. So, for example, the factor of sex would have two levels consisting of females and males while the factor of marital status might comprise the four levels: (1) never married; (2) married; (3) divorced/separated; and (4) widowed. In this context the term, dependent variable, is still generally applied to the variable on which the groups are compared.

A factor is called *unrelated* if the scores on the dependent variable all come from different individuals. An example of an unrelated factor would be where different individuals received each of the treatments. For instance, one group of individuals may be tested after not having drunk alcohol and a different group of individuals after having drunk a specified amount of alcohol. Another example of an unrelated factor would be comparing women and men.

A factor is called *related* if the scores are expected to correlate with each other. Most usually, the term is used to describe circumstances in which the participants in the research are measured in all of the conditions. We might expect the scores in the different conditions to correlate simply because they come from the same individuals. This is much the same as for the related designs discussed in Chapters 16 and 19.

FIVE FACTORIAL DESIGNS

We will use this new terminology to introduce examples of five factorial designs involving more than two groups of individuals.

One unrelated factor (with more than two levels)

An example of such a design is the relationship between the dependent variable of depression and the unrelated factor of employment status which might have the four categories: (1) employed full-time; (2) employed part-time; (3) unemployed and looking for work; and (4) one category for all other groups.

Another example is the relationship between the dependent variable of working efficiently and the unrelated factor of working with classical, popular or no music playing.

In both these examples the groups or levels making up the unrelated factor would consist of different individuals.

Although, in general, for these advanced designs you need to consult a statistics textbook, for this design we have included a worksheet (Worksheet 20.1). Taken in junction with the section on unplanned comparisons below (pp. 253–5), this will allow you to extend the unrelated research designs given in Chapters 15 and 18 to cover more than two groups.

One related factor (with more than two levels)

An example of this design is the relationship between the dependent variable of anxiety and the related factor of being tested one week before taking part in a competition, one hour before the competition and one hour after it was over.

Another example is the relationship between the dependent variable of working efficiently and the related factor of working with classical, popular or no music playing.

In both these examples the groups or levels comprising the related factor would consist of the same individuals.

Two unrelated factors

An example of this design is the relationship between the dependent variable of depression and the two unrelated factors of employment status and gender.

Another example is the relationship between the dependent variable of working efficiently and the two unrelated factors of the presence of classical, popular or no music and being tested in either the morning or afternoon.

In both these examples the groups or levels making up the two unrelated factors would comprise different individuals.

Worksheet 20.1 for the unrelated one-way analysis of variance

Step 1: *Data table*: Enter your data under the columns headed X and do indicated calculations. Delete any superfluous columns.

Group 1		Group 2		Group 3		Group 4	
X_1	X_1^2	X_2	X_2^2	X_3	X_3^2	X_4	X_4^2
7	49	4	16	5	25		
8	64	2	4	2	4		
9	81	1	1	6	36		
12	144	5	25	4	16		
9	81			5	25		
12	144						
$Total_1 =$ 57	$SS_1 =$ 563	$Total_2 =$ 12	$SS_2 =$ 46	$Total_3 =$ 22	$SS_3 =$ 106	$Total_4 =$	$SS_4 =$
$N_1 = 6$		$N_2 = 4$		$N_3 = 5$		$N_4 =$	

SS_1, SS_2 etc. are the sums of squares. That is the sum of the squared scores for Group 1, Group 2, etc.

N_1, N_2, etc. are the numbers of scores in Group 1, Group 2, etc.

In the above table, we would delete the final two columns as we have only three groups in this case.

Step 2: Calculate the sum of squares for all of the scores in the above table. The sum of squares is merely the top part of the variance formula in Worksheet 7.2 expressed slightly differently. Obviously the calculation needs slight adjustment according to the number of groups you have.

The total number of scores is $N_1 + N_2 + N_3 + N_4 = 6 + 4 + 5 = 15$.

Total sum of squares:

$$\frac{(SS_1 + SS_2 + SS_3 + SS_4 - (\text{Total}_1 + \text{Total}_2 + \text{Total}_3 + \text{Total}_4)^2}{\text{Total number of scores}}$$

$$= (563 + 46 + 106) - \frac{(57 + 12 + 22)^2}{15}$$

$$= 715 - \frac{91^2}{15}$$

$$= 715 - \frac{8281}{15}$$

$$= 715 - 552.067$$

$$= 162.933$$

Enter this value in the analysis of variance summary table (Table 20.1) in the total row in the column for sum of squares.

Step 3: Calculate the sum of squares for the groups as follows:

Sum of squares for groups = sum of squares between groups =

$$\frac{(\text{Total}_1)^2}{N_1} + \frac{(\text{Total}_2)^2}{N_2} + \frac{(\text{Total}_3)^2}{N_3} + \frac{(\text{Total}_4)^2}{N_4} - \frac{(\text{Total}_1)^2 + (\text{Total}_2)^2 + (\text{Total}_3)^2 + (\text{Total}_4)^2}{\text{Total number of scores}}$$

$$= \frac{57^2}{6} + \frac{12^2}{4} + \frac{22^2}{5} - 552.067$$

$$= \frac{3249}{6} + \frac{144}{4} + \frac{484}{5} - 552.067$$

$$= 541.500 + 36.000 + 96.800 - 552.067 = 674.300 - 552.067$$

$$= 122.233$$

Notice that the last part of the formula has already been calculated in Step 2 so this value was from Step 2.

Enter this value in the analysis of variance summary table (Table 20.1) in the row for between groups under sum of squares.

Table 20.1 The analysis of variance summary table

Source of variation	Sum of squares	Degrees of freedom	Mean square	F-ratio	Significance level
Between groups	122.233	2	61.117	18.02	0.05
Error	40.700	12	3.392		
Total	162.933	14			

Step 4: The error mean square is calculated as follows:

| The error sum of squares | = | the total sum of squares from Step 2 | − | the total sum of squares for groups from Step 3 |

Enter this value in the analysis of variance summary table in the row for error under the column for mean square (Table 20.1).

Step 5: The degrees of freedom need to be entered in Table 20.1. They are easily calculated as follows:

The total degrees of freedom = the total number of scores − 1 = $15 - 1 = 14$
The between groups degrees of freedom = the number of groups − 1 = $3 - 1 = 2$
The error degrees of freedom = the total degrees of freedom − the between groups degrees of freedom = $14 - 2 = 12$

Step 6: The mean squares in Table 20.1 are calculated by dividing the sums of squares by the corresponding degrees of freedom.

$$\text{The mean square for the groups} = \frac{\text{sum of squares between groups}}{\text{degrees of freedom between groups}}$$

$$= \frac{122.233}{2} = 61.117$$

$$\text{The mean square for error} = \frac{\text{sum of squares error}}{\text{degrees of freedom error}} = \frac{40.700}{12} = 3.392$$

Step 7: The F-ratio is calculated by dividing the between groups mean square by the error mean square:

$$F\text{-ratio} = \frac{\text{between groups mean square}}{\text{error mean square}}$$

$$= \frac{61.117}{3.392}$$

$$= 18.02$$

Step 8: The significance of the F-ratio is obtained from Table 20.A1. You need to find the column for the Between groups degrees of freedom and the row for the Error degrees of freedom. Your F-ratio needs to be equal to or larger than the tabulated value to be statistically significant at the 5 per cent level with a two-tailed test.

Indicate a statistically significant F-ratio in the final column of the analysis of variance summary table (Table 20.1).

Reporting your findings

If you obtained statistical significance, this means that overall the means of the different groups of participants differed from each other. That is, the group affects the scores on the dependent variable. This could be reported as 'The means of the various groups differed from each other ($F_{2,12}$ = 18.02, $p < 0.05$).' However, finding a significant F-ratio does not mean that all of the means are significantly different from each other. In order to know this it is necessary to compare the means using several t-tests using Table 20.A2 to adjust for the number of t-tests carried out. Had the F-ratio not been significant, it would usually be regarded as the end of the analysis and further analysis inappropriate.

Two related factors

An example of this design is the relationship between the dependent variable of mood and the two related factors of time of day (morning versus afternoon) and the time of week (Monday, Wednesday and Friday).

Another example is the relationship between the dependent variable of working efficiently and the two related factors of the presence of classical, popular or no music and the intake of non-decaffeinated and decaffeinated coffee.

In both these examples the groups or levels making up these two related factors would consist of the same individuals.

One unrelated factor and one related factor

An example of this design is the relationship between the dependent variable of anxiety, the unrelated factor of team versus individual competition and the related factor of one week before the competition, one hour before the competition and one hour after the competition was over.

Another example is the relationship between the dependent variable of weight loss, the unrelated factor of either being on a particular diet or not and the related factor of being tested on the day the diet began and two weeks later.

In these examples the groups or levels making up the unrelated factor would consist of different individuals while the groups or levels making up the related factor would consist of the same individuals.

This design is called a mixed design because it includes both a related and an unrelated independent variable.

PLANNED AND UNPLANNED COMPARISONS

There are statistical tests that are used to determine whether the factors are statistically significant. Parametric tests are most widely used for this purpose. These tests are called *analysis of variance* (or ANOVA for short) and *multivariate analysis of variance* (or MANOVA).

The way to calculate these tests varies somewhat according to the design of the study. Worksheet 20.1 shows how to carry out the simplest of these tests which is a one-way unrelated ANOVA. Other variants of these tests can be found elsewhere (e.g. Cramer 1998; Howitt and Cramer 2000).

These tests only suggest whether groups in a factor are likely to differ significantly. They do not show which groups actually differ.

Tests for determining whether the means of two groups differ significantly have already been described in this book. For an unrelated factor they are the unrelated t-test (Chapter 18) while for a related factor they are the related t-test (Chapter 19).

Some statisticians have argued that t-tests should be used regardless of whether the analysis or multivariate analysis of variance have found a factor to be statistically significant.

Non-parametric tests can also be used when appropriate such as the Mann-Whitney U for unrelated factors (Chapter 15) and the Wilcoxon for related factors (Chapter 16).

The only difference in applying these tests from that previously described is that the probability level of the test has to be adjusted for the number of comparisons made when differences for these comparisons have not been predicted.

When we have predicted the direction of the difference between two groups we use the one-tailed probability level and we do not have to adjust for the number of comparisons made.

These comparisons or tests are called *planned* or *a priori*.

An *unplanned* or *post hoc* comparison or test is made when we have no strong grounds for expecting a difference between two groups but we wish to determine whether the difference between two groups is statistically significant.

When we do this we use the two-tailed level which we have to adjust by dividing this probability by the number of comparisons we wish to make.

If we make only two unplanned comparisons, we divide the two-tailed 0.05 level by 2 so that the appropriate probability value in conventional tables is that for the 0.025 level of significance. However, if our comparison is significant using the 0.025 level we nevertheless report it as being significant at the 0.05 level.

If we make three unplanned comparisons we divide the two-tailed 0.05 level by 3 so that the appropriate significance level in conventional tables for the three comparisons becomes 0.0167 (0.05/3 = 0.0167).

The effect of dividing the two-tailed 0.05 by the number of comparisons is to reduce the probability that a particular difference will be significant.

With only one unplanned comparison the probability level is 0.05 (or 5 times out of 100) while with three unplanned comparisons it is reduced to 0.0167 (or about 1.7 times out of 100). Notice that the three unplanned comparisons actually add up to a combined probability level of 0.05.

The reason for making these adjustments is to control the probability level for the number of comparisons we make. If, for example, we make 100 independent comparisons we would expect 5 of them by chance to be statistically significant at the 0.05 level. Consequently, we need to adjust the probability level, which in this case would become 0.0005 (0.05/100 = 0.0005).

We will illustrate the use of planned and unplanned comparisons with the data in Table 20.2 which show the mean depression score for four groups varying in marital status. Higher scores indicate greater depression.

Suppose that we had predicted that married people would be less depressed than the divorced/separated and the widowed because separation and bereavement are known to be distressing events but we had not predicted what the nature of any differences would be between the other groups.

To compare the depression scores of the married group with that of the divorced/ separated and the widowed group we would use the one-tailed 0.05 level.

If we were interested in determining whether any of the other groups differed significantly we would use the two-tailed 0.05 level adjusted for the number of comparisons.

There are four such comparisons:

1 Single vs Married;
2 Single vs Divorced/separated;
3 Single vs Widowed; and
4 Divorced/separated vs Widowed.

Consequently, for these four comparisons we would have to adjust the two-tailed 0.05 by dividing it by 4 which would reduce it to 0.0125.

Table 20.2 Mean depression scores for four marital groups

Single	Married	Divorced/separated	Widowed
12	10	16	14

The practical difficulty for students is that most tables of significance do not give the necessary probability levels to make these adjustments. So, for example, you will find it hard to find significance tables giving the 0.0167 level of significance. Because of this, we have provided the 5 per cent significance values for up to 10 unplanned comparisons in Table 20.A2.

N refers to the number of participants in the two groups being compared which will generally vary for the comparisons if they consist of differing numbers of participants.

Remember that for the unrelated t-test N refers to the total number of participants in the two groups while for the related t-test it refers to the number of pairs of individuals.

When writing up the results of unplanned comparisons we need to indicate that the two-tailed 0.05 level has been adjusted for the particular number of comparisons made.

When the results are statistically significant we can do this using the following general format and adding the missing details: '($t =$ ___, $d.f. =$ ___, two-tailed $p < 0.05$ adjusted for ___ comparisons).'

When the results are not statistically significant, the following general format can be used: '($t =$ ___, $d.f. =$ ___, two-tailed p n.s. adjusted for ___ comparisons).'

Remember that the degrees of freedom for the (pooled variances) unrelated t-test is the number of participants in the two groups minus 2 while for the related t-test it is the number of pairs of cases minus 1.

EXERCISE 20.1 MAKING MORE THAN ONE COMPARISON ON ONE OR TWO FACTORS

Two groups of people wishing to learn to relax were randomly assigned to two treatments. One was called 'relaxation training' while the other was a 'discussion–control' treatment in which they discussed the kind of things that made them tense. The two groups were tested before the treatment began ('pre-test'), immediately after the treatment was over ('post-test') and three months later ('follow-up'). One way change was measured was in terms of a relaxation scale where lower scores indicated greater relaxation. The means for this scale for the six groups are shown in Table 20.3.

Table 20.3 Means for mixed-design study of relaxation therapy

	Pre	Post	Follow-up
Relaxation	21	15	17
Control	20	18	19

a What kind of factor are the two treatments?
b How many levels does this factor have?
c What kind of factor are the three testing periods?
d How many levels does this factor have?
e Does there appear to be an interaction?
f What test would you use to compare the mean relaxation scores between the two treatments at pre-test.
g What would be the probability level for this test?
h What test would you use to compare the mean relaxation scores between the two treatments at post-test and follow-up?
i What would be the probability level for this test.
j What test would you use to see if the mean relaxation scores for the control group varied between pre-test, post-test and follow-up?
k What would the probability level be for this test

The answers to these questions are at the end of this chapter.

INTERACTIONS BETWEEN TWO FACTORS

One of the advantages of having more than one factor in a study is that it is possible to determine whether that factor *interacts* with another factor. Although it is possible to look at interactions between three or more factors, we will restrict ourselves to interactions between two factors as these are the easiest to interpret. Also, it is very unlikely that you will be required to examine interactions between three or more factors. Interactions between two factors are often referred to as *two-way* interactions.

An interaction occurs when the relative value of the dependent variable (e.g. working efficiently) for the levels of one factor (e.g. working with music being played or not) is not the same for all the levels of the other factor (e.g. working in the morning or the afternoon). We will illustrate one possible kind of interaction between the factor of working with music being played or not and the factor of working in the morning or afternoon. It does not matter whether either of these factors are unrelated or related.

Let us suppose that working efficiently was measured by an index where higher scores meant greater efficiency. The average or mean of this index for the participants in the music group was 89 when tested in the morning and 81 when tested in the afternoon. The mean of this index for the participants in the no-music group was 83 in the morning and 87 in the afternoon.

Table 20.4 Mean scores of the work efficiency index for four groups

	am	pm
Music	89	81
No-music	83	87

These data are presented in Table 20.4 for easy reference. It would appear that whether the music group performed better than the no-music group depended on whether it was tested in the morning or afternoon. In other words, the relative value of this work efficiency index for the music and no-music groups was not the same in the morning as in the afternoon.

These data can be said to represent an interaction if:

- the difference in the index between the music and no-music groups in either the morning or afternoon was significantly different; or
- the difference in the index between the music and no-music group was statistically significant in both the morning and the afternoon but the direction of these differences was reversed.

Note that, in the case of this interaction, if we had simply compared the mean of the music group across the morning and afternoon [(89 + 81)/2 = 170/2 = 85] with the mean of the no-music group across the morning and afternoon [(83 + 87)/2 = 170/2 = 85] there would have been no difference between the two groups. In other words, the difference between these two conditions was hidden by their interaction with time of day.

GRAPHICALLY DISPLAYING AN INTERACTION

An interaction is generally much easier to appreciate when it is portrayed in the form of a graph. We will draw such a graph for these data. This graph is shown in Figure 20.1.

The vertical axis of the graph (called the *ordinate* axis or *y*-axis) represents the mean work efficiency index of the four groups of participants. Higher readings on the vertical axis indicate greater average efficiency.

The horizontal axis (called the *abscissa* or *x*-axis) represents the time of testing. Two points on this line have been marked, the first indicating testing in the morning and the second testing in the afternoon.

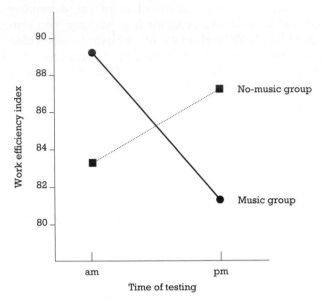

Figure 20.1 One possible interaction between working with music or no music and working in the morning or afternoon

The two groups or levels of the other factor are represented by two lines on the graph. The continuous line represents the music group and the dashed line represents the no-music group.

The dashed line for the no-music group starts at the point on the graph representing 83 on the vertical axis and the mark labelled 'am' on the horizontal axis. It ends at the point representing 87 on the vertical axis and the mark labelled 'pm' on the horizontal axis.

The continuous line for the music group begins at the point on the graph indicated by 89 on the vertical axis and the mark labelled 'am' on the horizontal axis. It finishes at the point indicated by 81 on the vertical axis and the mark labelled 'pm' on the horizontal axis.

Note that it normally does not matter which factor is represented by the horizontal axis and which factor is represented by the lines on the graph.

An interaction between two factors is suggested when the two lines on the graph are not parallel as in this case.

Other examples of possible interactions are shown in Figure 20.2.

In Figure 20.2(a) the music group performs less efficiently in the afternoon than in the morning while the no-music group works as efficiently in the afternoon as in the morning.

In Figure 20.2(b) the music group performs as poorly in the afternoon as in the morning and less well than the no-music group in the afternoon.

While in Figure 20.2(c) the no-music and music groups perform about equally efficiently in the afternoon while the no-music group performs more efficiently in the morning and less efficiently in the afternoon.

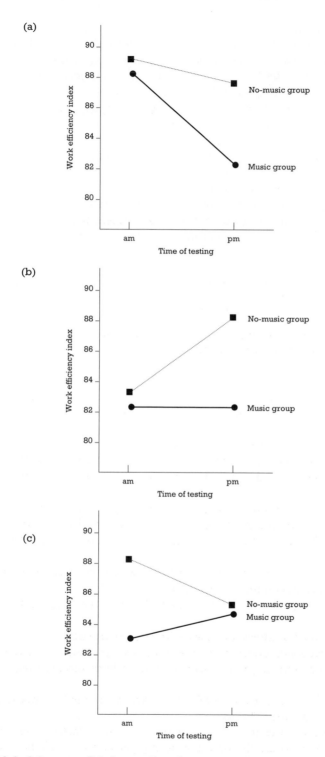

Figure 20.2 Other possible interactions between treatment and time of testing

In the case of these interactions where the lines representing the other factor do not cross, an interaction occurs if the difference in the dependent variable (e.g. work efficiency index) between two of the levels of one factor (e.g. music and no-music groups) for one level of the other factor (e.g. morning) was significantly bigger than the difference for another level of this other factor (e.g. afternoon).

A non-interaction between two factors is suggested when the lines representing the other factor appear parallel or almost parallel. Examples of non-interactions are displayed in Figure 20.3.

In Figure 20.3(a) the no-music group performs more efficiently than the music group in both the morning and the afternoon and there is no difference in performance between the morning and afternoon groups.

In Figure 20.3(b) the music and no-music groups work better in the morning than in the afternoon and the no-music group performs better than the music group.

Finally, in Figure 20.3(c) the music and no-music groups perform more efficiently in the afternoon than in the morning and the music group works better than the no-music group.

In other words, in all three of these examples the relative value of this work efficiency index for the music and no-music groups was the same in both the morning and the afternoon. Of course, whether these differences are statistically significant needs to be determined with the appropriate test.

We suggest you now try Exercise 20.1.

SUMMARY

- The score variable used to compare two or more groups is known as the dependent variable.
- The variables used to form the groups are called factors or independent variables.
- When differences between groups have been predicted, the one-tailed 0.05 significance level is used which does not have to be adjusted for the number of comparisons made.
- When differences between groups have not been predicted, the two-tailed significance level must be divided by the number of comparisons being made to give the proper significance level.
- One advantage of having two or more independent variables is that it is possible to look for interactions between these variables.
- An interaction is when the relative value of the dependent variable for one of the factors does not remain the same for the other factors.
- It is more readily understood when the mean values for the dependent variable are displayed for the independent variables in the form of a graph.
- An interaction is suggested when the lines representing one of the factors appear not to be parallel.
- Statistical tests need to be used to determine whether the groups making up the interaction are significantly different.

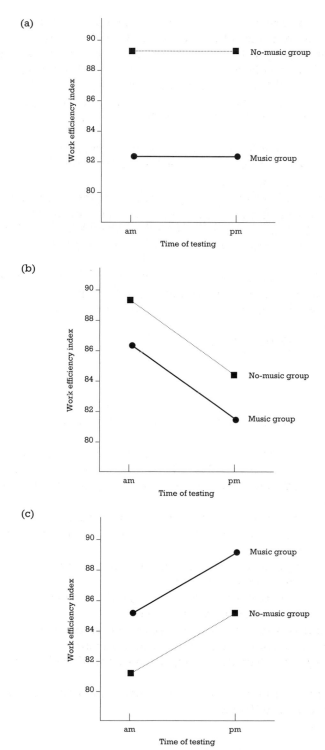

Figure 20.3 Possible non-interactions between treatment and time of testing

ANSWERS TO EXERCISE

Answers to Exercise 20.1

a The two treatments are an unrelated factor.
b This factor has two levels.
c The three testing periods make up a related factor.
d This factor has three levels.
e There appears to be an interaction because the relative values of the mean relaxation scores between the two treatments do not seem to be the same at the three testing periods.
f The difference in the mean relaxation scores between the two treatments at pre-test would be tested with an unrelated t-test.
g The probability level for this test would be the two-tailed 0.05 level. Because the participants had been randomly assigned to the two conditions, the mean relaxation scores would not be expected to differ between the two treatments.
h The difference in the mean relaxation scores between the two treatments at post-test and follow-up would also be tested with an unrelated t-test.
i The probability level for this test would be the one-tailed 0.05 test because relaxation training would be expected to result in greater relaxation at both periods.
j Differences in the mean relaxation scores for the control group between pre-test, post-test and follow-up would be tested with a related t-test.
k The probability level for this test would be the two-tailed 0.05 level because we would not expect the mean relaxation scores to vary much between the three periods. If we made all three comparisons (pre vs post; pre vs follow-up; and post vs follow-up) we would adjust this level for the three comparisons.

Table 20.A1 5 per cent Significant values of the F-ratio for ANOVA (two-tailed test)

Your value has to be equal to or larger than the tabled value to be significant at the 5 per cent level for a two-tailed test (i.e. to accept the hypothesis).

		Degrees of freedom for between-treatments mean square (or variance estimate)				
		1	2	3	4	5
	5	6.61	5.79	5.41	5.19	5.05
	6	5.99	5.14	4.76	4.53	4.39
	7	5.59	4.74	4.35	4.12	3.97
	8	5.32	4.46	4.07	3.84	3.69
	9	5.12	4.26	3.86	3.63	3.48
	10	4.96	4.10	3.71	3.48	3.33
	11	4.84	3.98	3.59	3.36	3.20
	12	4.75	3.89	3.49	3.26	3.11
	13	4.67	3.81	3.41	3.18	3.03
	14	4.60	3.74	3.34	3.11	2.96
	15	4.54	3.68	3.29	3.06	2.90
	16	4.49	3.63	3.24	3.01	2.85
Degrees of freedom for error	17	4.45	3.59	3.20	2.96	2.81
or within-cells mean square	18	4.41	3.55	3.16	2.93	2.77
(or variance estimate)	19	4.38	3.52	3.13	2.90	2.74
	20	4.35	3.49	3.10	2.87	2.71
	21	4.35	3.47	3.07	2.84	2.68
	22	4.30	3.44	3.05	2.82	2.66
	23	4.28	3.42	3.03	2.80	2.64
	24	4.26	3.40	3.01	2.78	2.62
	25	4.24	3.39	2.99	2.76	2.60
	26	4.23	3.37	2.98	2.74	2.59
	27	4.21	3.35	2.96	2.73	2.57
	28	4.20	3.34	2.95	2.71	2.56
	29	4.18	3.33	2.93	2.70	2.55
	30	4.17	3.32	2.92	2.69	2.53
	35	4.12	3.27	2.87	2.64	2.49

Table 20.A1 continued

		Degrees of freedom for between-treatments mean square (or variance estimate)				
		1	2	3	4	5
	40	4.08	3.23	2.84	2.61	2.45
	45	4.06	3.20	2.81	2.58	2.42
	50	4.03	3.18	2.79	2.56	2.40
	60	4.00	3.15	2.76	2.53	2.37
	70	3.98	3.13	2.74	2.50	2.35
	80	3.96	3.11	2.72	2.49	2.33
	90	3.95	3.10	2.71	2.47	2.32
	100	3.94	3.09	2.70	2.46	2.31
	∞	3.84	3.00	2.60	2.37	2.21

Note
The above table was calculated by the authors.

Table 20.A2 Two-tailed 0.05 critical values for 1 to 10 unplanned comparisons

	Number of comparison									
d.f.	1	2	3	4	5	6	7	8	9	10
5	2.57	3.16	3.53	3.81	4.03	4.22	4.38	4.53	4.66	4.77
6	2.45	2.97	3.29	3.52	3.71	3.86	4.00	4.12	4.22	4.32
7	2.37	2.84	3.13	3.34	3.50	3.64	3.75	3.86	3.95	4.03
8	2.31	2.75	3.02	3.21	3.36	3.48	3.58	3.68	3.76	3.83
9	2.26	2.69	2.93	3.11	3.25	3.36	3.46	3.55	3.62	3.69
10	2.23	2.63	2.87	3.04	3.17	3.28	3.37	3.45	3.52	3.58
11	2.20	2.59	2.82	2.98	3.11	3.21	3.30	3.37	3.44	3.50
12	2.18	2.56	2.78	2.93	3.06	3.15	3.24	3.31	3.37	3.43
13	2.16	2.53	2.75	2.90	3.01	3.11	3.19	3.26	3.32	3.37
14	2.15	2.51	2.72	2.86	2.98	3.07	3.15	3.21	3.27	3.33
15	2.13	2.49	2.69	2.84	2.95	3.04	3.11	3.18	3.24	3.29
16	2.12	2.47	2.67	2.81	2.92	3.01	3.08	3.15	3.20	3.25
17	2.11	2.46	2.66	2.79	2.90	2.98	3.06	3.12	3.17	3.22
18	2.10	2.44	2.64	2.77	2.88	2.96	3.03	3.10	3.15	3.20
19	2.09	2.43	2.63	2.76	2.86	2.94	3.01	3.07	3.13	3.17
20	2.09	2.42	2.61	2.74	2.85	2.93	3.00	3.06	3.11	3.15
21	2.08	2.41	2.60	2.73	2.83	2.91	2.98	3.04	3.09	3.14
22	2.07	2.41	2.59	2.72	2.82	2.90	2.97	3.02	3.07	3.12
23	2.07	2.40	2.58	2.71	2.81	2.89	2.95	3.01	3.06	3.10
24	2.06	2.39	2.57	2.70	2.80	2.88	2.94	3.00	3.05	3.09
25	2.06	2.38	2.57	2.69	2.79	2.87	2.93	2.99	3.04	3.08
26	2.06	2.38	2.56	2.68	2.78	2.86	2.92	2.98	3.02	3.07
27	2.05	2.37	2.55	2.68	2.77	2.85	2.91	2.97	3.01	3.06
28	2.05	2.37	2.55	2.67	2.76	2.84	2.90	2.96	3.01	3.05
29	2.05	2.36	2.54	2.66	2.76	2.83	2.89	2.95	3.00	3.04
30	2.04	2.36	2.54	2.66	2.75	2.83	2.89	2.94	2.99	3.03
35	2.03	2.34	2.52	2.63	2.72	2.80	2.86	2.91	2.96	3.00
40	2.02	2.33	2.50	2.62	2.70	2.78	2.84	2.89	2.93	2.97
45	2.01	2.32	2.49	2.60	2.69	2.76	2.82	2.87	2.91	2.95

Table 20.A2 continued

d.f.	Number of comparison									
	1	2	3	4	5	6	7	8	9	10
50	2.01	2.31	2.48	2.59	2.68	2.75	2.81	2.86	2.90	2.94
60	2.00	2.30	2.46	2.58	2.66	2.73	2.79	2.83	2.88	2.92
70	1.99	2.29	2.45	2.56	2.65	2.72	2.77	2.82	2.86	2.90
80	1.99	2.28	2.44	2.56	2.64	2.71	2.76	2.81	2.85	2.89
90	1.99	2.28	2.44	2.55	2.63	2.70	2.75	2.80	2.84	2.88
100	1.98	2.28	2.44	2.54	2.63	2.69	2.75	2.79	2.83	2.87
∞	1.96	2.24	2.39	2.50	2.58	2.64	2.69	2.73	2.77	2.81

Note
The above table was calculated by the authors.

Part VI

The report

21

Writing a research report

INTRODUCTION

Research reports in psychology are quite complex pieces to write. The skills have to be built up gradually. While no one can tell you exactly how to write a research report since they need to be tailored to a particular study, there are many routine features that can be quickly checked.

The following is based on the American Psychological Association's guidelines for writing psychological reports for publishing in a psychology journal.

American Psychological Association (1994) *Publication Manual of the American Psychological Association* (4th edn). Washington, DC: American Psychological Association.

This is the skeleton of a psychological report. The broad structure can be modified and not all reports will necessarily feature all of the components given in the guidelines. Experiments fit this structure best of all.

All of the components are important and weaknesses in any are likely to be seen as overall rather than specific weaknesses. For this reason, you ought to spend time considering each component in turn especially once a draft of the report has been written-up.

Figure 21.1 gives the conventional structure of a psychological report. It should be modified if your research does not fit that structure. However, the closer you keep to the structure the easier it is for the reader to know what to expect where.

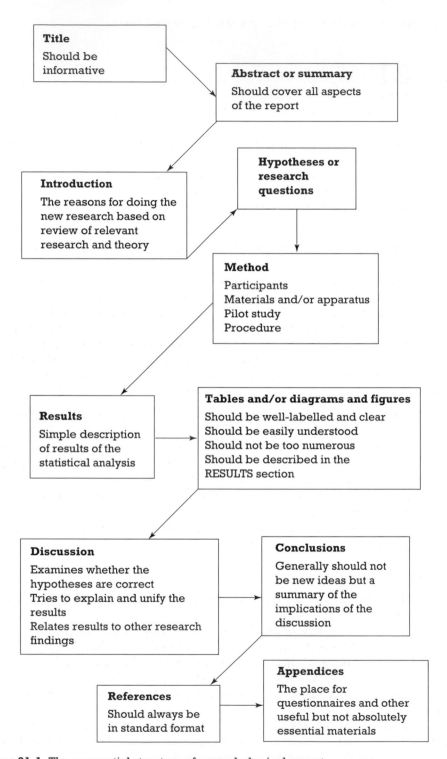

Figure 21.1 The sequential structure of a psychological report

GENERAL PRINCIPLES OF REPORT WRITING

Style

A report should communicate effectively and quickly to its readers. Having a fairly standard structure helps achieve this.

All components of the report from the title onwards have a role to play in effective communication.

Research reports are written in an impersonal style since the quality of the writing is judged by the quality of the evidence provided.

Opinions unsubstantiated by research or theory are not normally included.

The data obtained should be as open to scrutiny as possible.

Reports are written in the past tense.

Remember:

- Never use long sentences if at all possible. Generally keep sentences to ten words or fewer.
- Never write in the first person if it is at all possible – that is avoid 'I' and 'We'. One of the reasons for this is that it encourages a more active style of writing which is shorter and more direct. For example, instead of 'We distributed two hundred questionnaires to participants for them to be completed . . .' it is better to write 'Two hundred questionnaires were distributed to participants for completion . . .'. Similarly, one does not write 'our study' or 'my study' but 'the present study'.
- It is best to avoid abbreviations as far as possible. Their use can make your writings more difficult to absorb quickly as they may not be familiar to the reader.

No one can tell you exactly how to write a report as research varies enormously. It is important, however, to obtain reports from psychology journals on which to model your writing. Obviously some of these will be better than others. There is nothing wrong with using such reports as models for your own writing. They are especially useful for checking how to write your references/citations.

The arguments contained in the report should be logically presented as well as being presented in a coherent order.

The whole numbers one, two, three ... up to nine are written in words. Numbers 10, 11, 12 and higher are written as numbers.

The title

Titles must be informative. They are the first opportunity to tell your reader what your report is about.

Since most research in psychology is about the relationship between two or more variables, these variables should normally be mentioned in the title.

Remember the need for effective communication so make sure that the terms used in the title are likely to be ones that readers will generally understand. Rephrase the title if the concepts and terms used are insufficiently clear for the potential readers of the report.

Titles should not be merely clever or catchy. Although you will see such titles sometimes in the research literature, they are generally avoided as it is normally more important to inform readers rather than amuse them.

Titles may be quite long and contain subtitles. Length obviously allows more information to be transmitted.

Generally speaking, titles should *not* include phrases such as 'An investigation of . . .' or 'A study into . . .' as these are redundant and contain no worthwhile information.

Titles can be used to indicate whether the study is an experiment or not.

For an experiment, the title includes such phrases as 'The effect of the independent variable(s) [e.g. alcohol] on the dependent variable(s) [e.g. motor co-ordination]' or 'The dependent variable [e.g. Motor co-ordination] as a function of the independent variable(s) [e.g. alcohol]'. These phrases indicate that causal relationships between variables have been investigated.

For non-experiments, the title simply lists the main variables of interest such as 'Alcohol consumption and road-rage in elderly drivers'.

The abstract or summary

The abstract may vary in length from about 100 to 200 words depending on the purpose of the report. A published journal article is usually limited to 5,000 words so abstracts for these should be no more than 120 words.

The abstract is a brief summary of *all* the important components of the report.

The abstract should, therefore, cover the introduction, method, findings and conclusions. It is *not* simply a description of the empirical research.

The abstract, after the title, is likely to be the part of the report read by the greatest number of people. The abstract tells potential readers what the report is about and helps them to decide whether to read the rest of the report.

It is not easy to summarise a variety of ideas and to know how much detail to give. Abstracts may need a lot of polishing because of this.

The purpose of the abstract, generally, is to allow the reader to decide whether or not the research should be studied further. It helps comprehension of your report by giving the reader a good idea of what to expect in the report.

Although the abstract is normally placed at the beginning of the report, it is the last section to be completed.

The introduction

The introduction justifies the research you are describing in your report.

This is done largely by describing the pertinent previous research and theory and then explaining how your research develops from what has gone before.

You find relevant published research using the following methods:

* a search of the indexes of your institutional library;
* a search of the psychological abstracts; and
* A search of the Social Sciences Citation Index.

In many cases these are available using computers.

You may also find it useful to look through past copies of journals held in your library that are likely to contain that research as well as trying to find recent journal or book reviews on that topic.

Sometimes, the practical or social implications of the research will be offered as part of the reason for doing it.

The introduction is rarely or never a literal account of the reading and planning which led to the research. It is much more orderly than that. It is not a chronological account of your thinking either.

The introduction is an intellectual justification for your research.

Figure 21.2 will give you some idea of the features of the introduction.

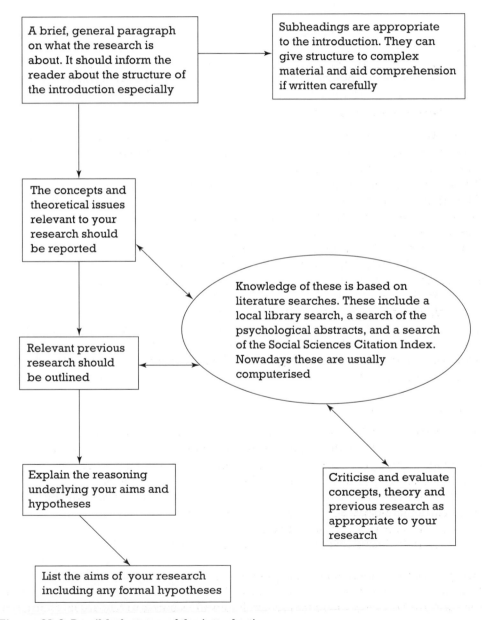

Figure 21.2 Possible features of the introduction

Method

This can have the following components:

* design;
* pilot study;
* participants;
* apparatus or materials or measures or questionnaires;
* procedure; and
* ethics.

Design

Where an experimental design is used it is usual to have a brief section summarising its main features such as whether it was a between- or within-subjects design and what the independent and dependent variables were.

Pilot study

Not all reports will have such a section. However, if the development of the research included a pilot study then it may be informative to the reader to report how the pilot study influenced the final study.

* Generally a paragraph or so will be sufficient.
* Often the pilot study is reported in passing in other parts of the report (e.g. the introduction or the materials sections). In these circumstances a separate section is not necessary.
* Generally speaking, broad statements such as 'a questionnaire was modified on the basis of the pilot study', are all that is required.

Participants

Describe the important characteristics of the participants used in the study. This will include their gender, mean age, age range or variance/standard deviation, their broad social characteristics such as first-year psychology students, first-time mothers attending a pre-natal clinic, manual workers in a bacon factory, etc. Sometimes this will include how they were contacted as this often makes the nature of the participants clearer.

Apparatus or materials or measures or questionnaires

It is not usual to include all of these subheadings but merely the ones most appropriate to your particular research:

* Describe the apparatus you used, naming it if it is commercially available, together with any modifications made.
* Briefly describe its functions and any evidence of its reliability and validity that is available.
* The same is true of questionnaires. Many questionnaires are standard or established measures and need only be reported in brief and references given to publications

about them. Their reliability and validity should be mentioned as well as the number of items and the answer format. Modifications to the wording should be mentioned. It is useful to include examples of one or two of the items to give the reader an idea of the kind of questions used.

• If you have constructed your own questionnaire, you should discuss at greater length its characteristics, structure and any evidence of its reliability and/or validity that you have. Sometimes it may be more appropriate to give these details in the *Results* section.

• In student reports, it is useful to include copies or photographs of the materials or apparatus. This would not be the case in published reports except where the materials are novel.

Procedure

This is a description of how your research was carried out.

• The length of this section will depend on how complex the procedure was.
• The level of detail given has to be balanced against the length. Student reports should not be too lengthy as this probably implies too much detail is being given. The length of a report will usually be recommended to students by their teachers.
• Normally the procedure is given in the correct time-sequence as experienced by the participants.
• Sometimes pilot research is mentioned in this section.
• It may be advantageous to add subheadings within this section as with other sections.

Ethics

This is usually an optional section but is often worthwhile including.

• It can incorporate brief statements of any special provision made to deal with ethical issues.
• Mention any permissions obtained from Ethics Committees.
• Only discuss in great detail obvious important ethical problems. However, to reiterate from Chapter 3, no student work should stray into ethically contentious areas.

Results

As far as possible, the results are a straightforward description of your statistical analyses and findings.

Never simply give your tables and diagrams *without* a commentary. All tables and diagrams are subject to interpretation and it is important that the reader knows how you are interpreting their contents.

Give descriptive statistics, especially the mean scores of groups and the variance of the scores, using tables, bar charts, pie-diagrams and histograms to the extent that they add clarity.

Remember to report the statistical significance of your findings using the methods we used throughout the book (e.g. $t = 3.27$, $d.f. = 21$, $p < 0.05$).

It is *not* appropriate to describe the statistics employed in more detail than this. It should be assumed that the reader has some training in and knowledge of psychological research methods and the statistical analysis of data.

Tables and diagrams

Tables and diagrams are very important in writing reports. However, it is important to make sure that they communicate effectively and that they are clear and accurate. Remember that some readers will look at the tables and diagrams before reading the text so they need to be readily understood. Here are a few suggestions:

- Always number your tables as Table 1, Table 2, etc. and call your diagrams Figure 1, Figure 2, etc., so that they can be referred to in the text.
- Always give your tables and figures clear and informative titles such as 'Means and standard deviations of the dependent variable [e.g. motor co-ordination] for the independent variable [e.g. three treatments]'. There is no need to say what the sample is unless there is the possibility of confusion (e.g. because you have several different samples or because you are reporting data based on a sub-sample).
- Ensure that all parts of the tables and figures are clearly labelled. This includes axes of scattergrams, columns of tables, and so forth.
- Remember that if a table or figure is not clear to you then it is unlikely to be clear to anyone else.
- Avoid multiple similar tables that refer to different variables. These often can be combined into a single table.
- Keep the number of tables and figures to a minimum. We would recommend a limit of four or five for most reports. The reason for this is to avoid breaking up the text too much and to encourage you to plan your tables and figures carefully.
- It is a common error in student work to give a long series of small tables and figures followed by short explanations. This is extremely difficult to follow and looks amateurish.

Discussion

What to include in the discussion will vary somewhat according to circumstances and the findings of the research.

Figure 21.3 describes some of the important aspects to include.

Conclusions

- These should summarise the main outcomes of your discussion.
- Try not to add new material at this stage.
- Sometimes a numbered list will be sufficient.

Reference list

This should normally only include the works you cite in your report. It is not a bibliography of your reading – if it is then head it *Bibliography and references* rather than *References*.

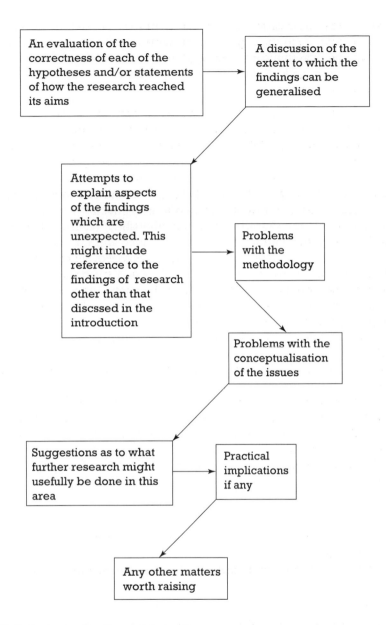

Figure 21.3 Features of a discussion section

The references should be in standard format. Although this is a complex matter as there are a vast array of types of sources, the main ones are as follows:

Books

Howitt, D. and Cramer, D. (2000) *An introduction to statistics in psychology* (2nd ed.), London: Pearson Education Ltd.

This contains enough information for anyone interested to track down the book. It consists of (a) the authors in the order they appear on the book cover, (b) the date of publication of the book as you consulted it, (c) the title underlined (or italicised), (d) the place of publication, and (d) the name of the publisher.

Journal articles

Howitt, D. (1995) Pornography and the paedophile: Is it criminogenic? *British Journal of Medical Psychology* 68(3): 15–27.

Again this contains sufficient information for obtaining the original. Notice that it is the journal title which is underlined (or italicised) – not the title of the article. Also notice how capitals are used in the title. The order is (a) the authors in the order they appear in the article, (b) the year the article was published, (c) the title of the article using capitals just as you would in an ordinary sentence and no underlining, (d) the title (underlined) of the journal in which the article appeared, (e) the volume number of the journal, i.e. 68 here, which is sometimes accompanied by the part or issue number of the journal in brackets, (3), and finally the page numbers of the article.

Articles or chapters in books

Cramer, D. and Howitt, D. (1998) Romantic love and the psychology of sexual behaviour: Open and closed secrets. In V.C. de Munck (ed.) *Romantic love and sexual behavior: Perspectives from the social sciences* (pp. 113–132), Westport, CT: Praeger.

The order is (a) the authors of the book article or chapter as they appear in the book, (b) the date of publication of the book, (c) the title of the article or chapter using capitals as in an ordinary sentence, (d) the editor(s) of the book (notice that their initials come first), (e) the title of the book as for a book title, (f) the pages in the book where the article is to be found, (g) the place of publication of the book and (h) the publisher of the book. (CT in the above reference is the US abbreviation for the State of Connecticut.)

The references should be listed strictly in alphabetical order.

You may notice that there may be slight differences between the style currently recommended by the American Psychological Association (APA) and styles used previously by the APA or by other journals. You need not worry about these differences as they are very minor. Just stick to the format shown above.

Appendices

These are useful for providing information which is too bulky or lengthy to be included in the main body of the report.

Appendices can be confusing if they are not carefully numbered and titled. They should be presented as clearly and be as carefully structured as the rest of the report.

For a student project, incorporate your data table as far as is reasonably practicable.

SUMMARY

- Reports in psychology generally follow a standard structure which includes a title, abstract or summary, introduction, methods, results, discussion and conclusions.
- This structure helps organise the material so the reader knows exactly where to find what.
- Sometimes the structure has to be modified especially when the study is not an experiment.
- It is important to learn the stylistic conventions of report writing, initially by comparing your report with examples in psychology texts and journals if possible.
- This chapter includes numerous guidelines which, if used intelligently, should help you write a good report and avoid the more obvious mistakes.

REFERENCES

Adair, J. G. (1973). *The human subject: The social psychology of the psychological experiment*, Boston: Little, Brown.

American Psychological Association (1992) Ethical principles of psychologists and code of conduct, *American Psychologist* 47: 1597–1611.

American Psychological Association (1994) *Publication manual of the American Psychological Association* (4th edn), Washington, DC: American Psychological Association.

Barber, T. X. (1976) *Pitfalls in human research: Ten pivotal points*. Oxford: Pergamon Press.

Baumrind, D. (1964) Some thoughts on ethics of research: After reading Milgram's 'Behavioral Study of Obedience', *American Psychologist* 19: 421–423.

British Psychological Society (1993) Ethical principles for conducting research with human participants, *The Psychologist* 6(1): 33–35.

Bryman, A. and Cramer, D. (1999) *Quantitative data analysis with SPSS Release 8 for Windows: A guide for social scientists*, London: Routledge.

Cramer, D. (1998) *Fundamental statistics for social research: Step-by-step calculations and computer techniques using SPSS for Windows*, London: Routledge.

Cramer, D. and Buckland, N. (1995) Effect of rational and irrational statements and demand characteristics on task anxiety, *Journal of Psychology* 129(3): 269–275.

Howitt, D. and Cramer, D. (2000) *An introduction to statistics in psychology* (2nd ed.), Hemel Hempstead: Prentice-Hall/Harvest Wheatsheaf.

Howitt, D. and Cramer, D. (1999) *A guide to computing statistics with SPSS Release 8 for Windows*, Hemel Hempstead: Pearson Education Ltd.

Howitt, D. and Owusu-Bempah, J. (1990) The pragmatics of institutional racism: Beyond words, *Human Relations* 43: 885–899.

Milgram, S. (1963) Behavioral study of obedience, *Journal of Abnormal and Social Psychology* 67: 371–378.

Milgram, S. (1964) Issues in the study of obedience: A reply to Baumrind, *American Psychologist* 19: 848–852.

Milgram, S. (1974) *Obedience to authority*, New York: Harper & Row.

INDEX

acquiescence or yea-saying response set 44
Adair, J. G. 208, 280
American Psychological Association 22, 21,
    269, 278, 280
analysis of variance 157, 164
    mixed design 243
    multivariate analysis of variance 253
    one-way unrelated 157, 250–253
attrition 193
axes
    horizontal, abscissa or x axis 102, 257
    vertical, ordinate or y axis 102, 257

Barber, T. X. 207, 280
bar charts 55–56, 60
baseline 201
Baumrind, D. 22, 280
British Psychological Society 22, 280
Bryman, A. 156, 280
Buckland, N. 208, 280

categories 49–52, 53–61
causal explanations or relationships 12,
    15–17, 193, 203
'ceiling' effects 184
chi-square 51–52, 97, 123, 142–150, 157,
    164
    calculating expected frequencies 144–145
    minimum expected frequencies 143
    and phi 149–150
conditions 13

confidence interval or margin of error 92–97
consent form, example of 29
consent of participants 23
consultation 24–25
contingency table 119, 122, 126, 128,
    144–145, 147–148
correlation 97, 110, 241
    and chi 149–150
    Pearson's (product moment) correlation
        110–116, 117, 120, 122, 126, 130–131,
        133–134, 157
    phi 110, 117, 119–123, 126, 157
    point-biserial correlation 122–123, 157
    Spearman's (rank order) correlation
        110–111, 116, 118, 134, 156–157
    statistical significance 125–134
    verbal descriptions of strength 111
counter-balancing order of conditions
    234–236
    advantages and disadvantages 244
counter-demand instructions 208
covariance 115
Cramer, D. 153, 156, 208, 229, 243, 253,
    277, 278, 280

data collection sheet, example of 186–187,
    232–233
debriefing 24–25
degrees of freedom 95, 131
    chi-square 148
    correlation 131

one-way unrelated analysis of variance 263
  related *t*-test 240
  unrelated *t*-test 228
demand characteristics 208
dichotomous variable 55, 117, 119–120
distribution of scores 68–69, 76–82
  normal curve or distribution 77–78
  skewed 68–69
  symmetrical 68

ecological validity 17, 206
eta coefficient 123
ethics 21–31, 275
  consent forms 29
  consent of participants 23–24
  consultation 24–25
  physiological research 28
  protection of participants 24
  'rules' 26–27
experimenter bias 207
experimenter expectancy effect 207
experiments 11–14, 19, 201–209
  advantages and disadvantages 19, 205

factor, in analysis of variance 248
factorial designs 249, 253
'floor' effects 184
frequencies or frequency counts 50, 56

histograms 55–56, 60, 63, 77–81, 170, 181,
  221, 241
Howitt, D. 23, 153, 156, 229, 243, 253, 277,
  278, 280
hypothesis 5–7, 128, 131–132, 162–163,
  166–174, 179, 192
  hypothesis or alternative hypothesis 5, 128,
    162–163, 166–171, 173–174, 179, 192
  directional 5–7, 131–132
  non-directional 5–7, 131–132
  null 7, 128, 162–163, 166–174, 179, 192

interactions 256–261
interquartile range 56
interviews 14–15, 37
  advantages 15

levels 13, 248
limits 78

manipulation, of the independent variable
  12–13, 201–203, 218, 223

Mann-Whitney *U*-test 51, 164, 181–183,
  204, 220–222, 254
marginal totals 144
matching 197
maximum value 56, 63
mean, arithmetic 56, 63–64, 66–68, 77, 82,
  92, 97, 156, 181, 221, 271
median 56, 63–68
measurement
  category 49–52
  interval or equal interval 50, 52
  nominal, *see* category
  numerical scores 49, 52
  ordinal 50–52
  ratio 51–52
  types of 51–52
measures 32–45
  objective measures 36
  reliability 34–36
  standard measures 32–33
  structured measures 37
  subjective measures 36
  validity 34–36
  unstructured measures 37
Milgram, S. 22–23, 208, 280
minimum value 56, 63
mode 56, 63–68
multivariate analysis of variance 253

non-parametric tests 51–52, 172, 183
normal curve or distribution 77–78
numerical scores 49–52, 53–56, 63–83

observation 11, 17–19, 37
  advantages and disadvantages 19
operational definition 165
outliers 107–108, 123, 156–157, 222
Owusu-Bempah, J. 23, 280

parametric tests 51–52, 172, 181
participant or subject bias 208
percentages 56–57
pie charts or diagrams 55–56, 59–60
pilot study 155–156, 274
planned or a priori comparisons
  254–255
polygon 63, 77, 81–82
pre-test-post-test design 191, 193
proportions 56, 58
protection of participants 24
Psychological Abstracts 272

questionnaires, self-completion 14–15, 37–45
   advantages 15
   multiple-choice 15, 39

random assignment, randomisation 12–14,
      202–203, 207, 218, 234
   blocked randomisation 202, 207, 217, 247
   unblocked randomisation 202, 207, 216,
      246
random number table 136–139
random samples 85, 87, 88–91, 97, 127
random sampling with replacement 169–170
range 56, 63, 70, 97
relationships between variables 101–108
   curvilinear or non-linear relationship
      105–106
   negative or inverse relationship 105
   perfect linear relationships 102–103
   positive or direct relationships 101–102
reliability 34–36, 184
   inter-item reliability 34
   inter-judge/rater reliability 35
   test-retest reliability 34
research ideas 7–8
research report 269–279
   abstract or summary 272
   appendices 278
   discussion 276–277
   introduction 272–273
   method 274–275
   references 276–278
   results 275–276
   style 271
   title 271–272
research steps 7, 9, 155, 210–215
   experiment 210–215
   survey/non-experiment 155
response rates 91
response sets 44–45
rounding decimals 58

sample size 206
sampling 85–93
   cluster sampling 86–87, 89, 91
   convenience sampling 86–88
   quota sampling 86–87, 91
   random sampling 85, 87, 88–91, 97,
      169–170
   response rates 91
   sampling frame 85, 88–91
   simple random sampling 86–89

stratified random sampling 86–87, 89
snowball sampling 86–88
types of 86–89, 91
scale, self-completion 38–45
   advantages 39–40
   response formats 40–41
   response sets 44–45
   scoring 41–43
   writing items 42
scattergram or scatterplot 101–108, 123,
      156–157
significance tables
   chi-square, 2-tailed 0.05 critical values 152
   F-ratio, 2-tailed 0.05 critical values
      263–264
   Mann-Whitney U-test, 2-tailed 0.05 critical
      values 188–189
   Pearson's correlation, 1- and 2-tailed 0.05
      critical values 140
   related t-test, 1- and 2-tailed 0.05 critical
      values 245
   Spearman's correlation, 1- and 2-tailed
      0.05 critical values 141
   unplanned comparisons, 2-tailed 0.05
      critical values 265–266
   unrelated t-test, 1- and 2-tailed 0.05 critical
      values 230–231
skewness 68–69, 78, 156–157
Social Sciences Citation Index 272
spontaneous remission 193
spurious relationship 16
standard deviation 56, 63, 70–71, 74–75,
      76–77, 82, 97, 156, 221, 241
   population standard deviation 71, 76
   standard deviation estimate 63, 76, 95
standard error 92, 96–97, 172
statistic 164
statistical significance 125–134, 148–149
   chi-square 148–149
   correlation coefficient 125–134
   degrees of freedom 131
   differences between means 161–174
   directional or 1-tailed level 131–133,
      163–164
   non-directional or 2-tailed level 131–132,
      163–164
statistics
   descriptive statistics for category variables
      61
   descriptive statistics for numerical scores
      63

inferential statistics 97, 161, 174
surveys/non-experiments 11, 14–17, 19,
    84–85, 153–157
  advantages and disadvantages 19

t-test 51, 164, 172
  related t-test 192, 196, 235–243, 254
  unrelated t-test 181, 204, 220–222,
    224–228, 241, 254
tables
  frequency 63–64
  means 63, 82
ties or tied scores 116
Type I and Type II errors 163

unplanned or post hoc comparisons 254–255

validity 34–36, 184
  construct 35
  convergent 35
  discriminant 35
  face 35
variable 4, 12, 16

category 49
confounding 16
continuous 34
dependent variable 12–13, 177–178, 180,
    184, 191, 203
dichotomous 55, 118–120
discrete 34
independent variable 12–13, 178, 180,
    191, 203
measuring 32–45
numerical 49
variance 56, 63, 70–71, 72–73, 76, 92, 111,
    115, 172, 181, 221, 241
  population variance 70, 76
  sample or estimated population variance
    or variance estimate 70, 76, 92,
    172
  shared variance or covariance 111, 115

Wilcoxon matched pairs test 164, 194–196,
    235–237, 241–243, 254

z or standard scores 77, 172